Praise for *Why We L*

"Fascinating . . . [Fisher's] passion keeps the book, which has detailed descriptions of brain function, readable."—*Pittsburgh Post-Gazette*

"The most comprehensive and comprehensible account I have ever read of the brain chemistry of attachment. Read it and learn some of the most important lessons anyone can achieve: how and why we—and other living things—love."

—David P. Barash, professor of psychology, University of Washington, and author of *The Survival Game* and *The Myth of Monogamy*

"Fascinating."—*The Dallas Morning News*

"A fascinating tour of the science and art of love . . . From sage poets to brain scans, *Why We Love* provides the most gripping and scientifically sound book yet written about this most bafflingly complex human experience."

—David M. Buss, author of *The Evolution of Desire: Strategies of Human Mating*

"A standout."—*The Hartford Courant*

"Helen Fisher's book will entice you, charm away your resistance to its thesis, seduce you into accepting it. It is poetic, sexy, beguiling, and, all at the same time, scientific."

—Richard Dawkins, author of *The Selfish Gene*

"Entertainingly balancing poetic plaudits with scientific sanctions, Fisher presents both the chemistry behind love's rashest behavior and the understanding necessary to weather the emotional upheavals associated with falling in love."—*Booklist*

"Very readable and enlightening . . . Fisher joins a growing chain of very fine writers, including Antonio Damasio, whose book about consciousness, *The Feeling of What Happens* she cites here, and Bill Buford's current bestseller, *A Short History of Nearly Everything*, books that explain ourselves, our nature and behavior, to the general reader."—*Pittsburgh Tribune-Review*

"Intriguing . . . Well written as a reference tome that provides insight."—*Midwest Book Review*

Also by Helen Fisher

*The First Sex*

*Anatomy of Love*

*The Sex Contract*

# Why We Love

# Why We Love

## *The Nature and Chemistry of Romantic Love*

Helen Fisher, Ph.D.

ST. MARTIN'S GRIFFIN
NEW YORK

*For Lorna, Ray, Audrey,*
*and the rest of my family*



www.stmartins.com

Designed by Victoria Hartman
Illustration by Laura Hartman Maestro

The Library of Congress has cataloged the Henry Holt edition as follows:

Fisher, Helen E.
Why we love : the nature and chemistry of romantic love / Helen Fisher.—1st ed.
p. cm.
Includes bibliographical references and index.
ISBN 978-0-8050-7796-4
1. Love. 2. Love—Physiological aspects. 3. Human evolution. 4. Sex. 5. Sex differences. I. Title.

BF575.L8F53 2004
152.4'1—dc22

2003065277

Originally published by Henry Holt and Company

D 30 29 28 27 26 25 24 23

(Hark close and still what I now whisper to you,
    I love you, O you entirely possess me,
O that you and I escape from the rest, and go utterly off,
    free and lawless,
Two hawks in the air, two fishes swimming in the sea
    not more lawless than we;)
That furious storm through me careering.
    I passionately trembling;
The oath of the inseparableness of two together,
    of the woman that loves me, and whom I love
    more than my life, that oath swearing,
    O I willingly stake all for you,

Walt Whitman
"From Pent-up Aching Rivers"

# *Contents*

# Contents

# *To the Reader*

"What is love?" Shakespeare mused. The great bard was not the first to ask. I suspect our ancestors pondered this question a million years ago as they sat around their campfires or lay and watched the stars.

In this book I have tried to answer this seemingly unanswerable question. Several things motivated me. I have loved and won and loved and lost; I have certainly experienced the joy and agony of romantic love. Moreover, I am convinced that this passion is a foundation stone of human social life, that just about every human being who has ever lived has felt the ecstasy and the despair of romantic love. Perhaps most important, a clearer understanding of this whirlwind may help people find and sustain this glorious passion.

So in 1996 I began a multipart investigation to unravel that mystery of mysteries, the experience of "being in love." Why we love. Why we choose the people that we choose. How men and women vary in their romantic feelings. Love at first sight. Love and lust. Love and marriage. Animal love. How love evolved. Love and hate. The brain in love. These became major themes of this book. I also hoped to gain some insight into how we might control this unpredictable and often dangerous fire in the heart.

Romantic love, I believe, is one of three primordial brain networks that evolved to direct mating and reproduction. *Lust,* the craving for sexual gratification, emerged to motivate our ancestors to seek sexual union with almost any partner. *Romantic love,* the elation and obsession of "being in love," enabled them to focus their courtship attentions on a single individual at a time, thereby conserving precious mating time and energy. And male-female *attachment,* the feeling of calm, peace, and security one often has for a long-term mate, evolved to motivate our ancestors to love this partner long enough to rear their young together.

In short, romantic love is deeply embedded in the architecture and chemistry of the human brain.

But what actually produces this thing called love?

To investigate this, I decided to make use of the newest technology for brain scanning, known as functional magnetic resonance imaging (fMRI), to try to record the brain activity of men and women who had just fallen madly in love.

For this important part of my investigation, I was fortunate to be joined by two exceptionally gifted colleagues, Dr. Lucy L. Brown, a neuroscientist at the Albert Einstein College of Medicine, and Dr. Arthur Aron, a research psychologist at the State University of New York at Stony Brook. Debra Mashek, then a doctoral candidate in psychology at SUNY Stony Brook, Greg Strong, another SUNY psychology graduate student, and Dr. Haifang Li, a radiologist at SUNY Stony Brook, all talented individuals, also played crucial roles. Over a period of six years, we scanned the brains of more than forty men and women who were wildly in love, collecting some one hundred forty-four pictures of brain activity from each. Half of our participants were men and women whose love was reciprocated; the rest had recently been rejected by someone they adored. We wanted to record the range of feelings associated with "being in love."

The results were startling. We found gender differences that may help explain why men respond so passionately to visual stimuli and why women can remember details of the relationship. We discovered ways in which the brain in love changes over time. We established some of the brain regions that become active when you feel romantic ecstasy, information that suggests new ways to sustain romance in long-term partnerships. I came to believe that animals feel a form of romantic attraction for one another. Our findings shed new light on stalking behavior and other crimes of passion. And I now understand more about why we feel so depressed and angry when we are rejected, and even some ways to stimulate the brain to soothe the anguish.

Most important, our results changed my thinking about the very essence of romantic love. I came to see this passion as a fundamental human drive. Like the craving for food and water and the maternal instinct, it is a physiological *need,* a profound urge, an instinct to court and win a particular mating partner.

This drive to fall in love has produced some of humankind's most compelling operas, plays, and novels, our most touching poems and haunting melodies, the world's finest sculptures and paintings, and our most colorful festivals, myths, and legends. Romantic love has adorned the world and brought many of us tremendous joy. But when love is scorned, it can cause excruciating sorrow. Stalking, homicide, suicide, profound depression from romantic rejection, and high divorce and adultery rates are prevalent in societies around the world. It's time to seriously consider Shakespeare's question: "What is love?"

I hope this book will be as useful to you as writing it has been to me, in our mutual and eternal dance with this monumental force: the instinct to fall in love.

# Why We Love

# I

# "What Wild Ecstasy": *Being in Love*

The world, for me, and all the world can hold
Is circled by your arms; for me there lies,
Within the lights and shadows of your eyes,
The only beauty that is never old.

James Weldon Johnson
"Beauty That Is Never Old"

"Fires run through my body—the pain of loving you. Pain runs through my body with the fires of my love for you. Sickness wanders my body with my love for you. Pain like a boil about to burst with my love for you. Consumed by fire with my love for you. I remember what you said to me. I am thinking of your love for me. I am torn by your love for me. Pain and more pain. Where are you going with my love? I'm told you will go from here. I am told you will leave me here. My body is numb with grief. Remember what I've said, my love. Goodbye, my love, goodbye."[1] So spoke an anonymous Kwakiutl Indian of southern Alaska in this wrenching poem, transcribed from the native tongue in 1896.

How many men and women have loved each other in all the seasons that preceded you and me? How many of their dreams have been fulfilled; how many of their passions wasted? Often as I walk or sit and contemplate, I wonder at all the heartrending love affairs this planet has absorbed. Fortunately, men and women around the world have left us a great deal of evidence of their romantic lives.

From Uruk, in ancient Sumer, come poems on cuneiform tablets that hail the passion of Inanna, Queen of Sumeria, for Dumuzi, a shepherd boy. "My beloved, the delight of my eyes," Inanna cried to him over four thousand years ago.[2]

Vedic and other Indian texts, the earliest dating between 1000 and 700 B.C., tell of Shiva, the mythic Lord of the Universe, who was infatuated with Sati, a young Indian girl. The god mused that "he saw Sati and himself on a mountain pinnacle / enlaced in love."[3]

For some, happiness would never come. Such was Qays, the son of a tribal chieftain in ancient Arabia. An Arabic legend, dating to the seventh century A.D., has it that Qays was a beautiful, brilliant boy—until he met Layla, meaning "night" for her jet black hair.[4] So intoxicated was Qays that one day he sprang from his school chair to race through the streets shouting out her name. Henceforth he was known as Majnun, or madman. Soon Majnun began to drift with the desert sand, living in caves with the animals, singing verses to his beloved, while Layla, cloistered in her father's tent, slipped out at night to toss love notes to the wind. Sympathetic passersby would bring these appeals to the wild-haired, almost-naked poet boy. Their mutual passion would eventually lead to war between their tribes—and death to the lovers. Only this legend remains.

Meilan also lived by dying. In the twelfth century A.D. Chinese fable "The Jade Goddess," Meilan was the pampered fifteen-year-old daughter of a high official in Kaifeng—until she fell in love with Chang Po, a vivacious lad with long tapered fingers and a gift for carving jade. "Since the heaven and earth were created, you were made for me and I was made for you and I will not let you go," Chang Po declared to Meilan one morning in her family's garden.[5] These lovers were of different classes in China's rigid, hierarchical social order, however. Desperate, they eloped—then were soon discovered. He escaped. She was buried alive in her father's garden. But the tale of Meilan still haunts the souls of many Chinese.

Romeo and Juliet, Paris and Helen, Orpheus and Eurydice, Abelard and Eloise, Troilus and Cressida, Tristan and Iseult: thousands of romantic poems, songs, and stories come across the centuries from ancestral Europe, as well as the Middle East, Japan, China, India, and every other society that has left written records.

Even where people have no written documents, they have left evidence of this passion. In fact, in a survey of 166 varied cultures, anthropologists found evidence of romantic love in 147, almost 90 percent of them.[6] In the remaining 19 societies, scientists had simply failed to examine this aspect of people's lives. But from Siberia to the Australian Outback to the Amazon, people sing love songs, compose love poems, and recount myths and legends of romantic love. Many perform love magic—carrying amulets and charms or serving condiments or concoctions to stimulate romantic ardor. Many elope. And many suffer deeply from unrequited love. Some kill their lovers. Some kill themselves. Many sink into a sorrow so profound that they can hardly eat or sleep.

From reading the poems, songs, and stories of people around the world, I came to believe that the capacity for romantic love is woven firmly into the fabric of the human brain. Romantic love is a universal human experience.

What is this volatile, often uncontrollable feeling that hijacks the mind, bringing bliss one moment, despair the next?[7]

## *The Love Survey*

"O tell me the truth about love," exclaimed poet W. H. Auden. To understand what this profound human experience actually entails, I canvassed the psychological literature on romantic love, culling those traits, symptoms, or conditions that were mentioned repeatedly. Not surprising, this potent feeling is a complex of many specific traits.[8]

Then, to satisfy myself that these characteristics of romantic passion are universal, I used them as the basis for a questionnaire I designed on romantic love. And with the assistance of Michelle Cristiani, then a graduate student at Rutgers University, as well as Dr. Mariko Hasagawa and Dr. Toshikazu Hasagawa at the University of Tokyo, I distributed this survey among men and women at and around Rutgers University in New Jersey and the University of Tokyo.

The poll began: "This questionnaire is about 'being in love,' the feelings of being infatuated, being passionate, or being strongly romantically attracted to someone.

"If you are not currently 'in love' with someone, but felt very passionately about someone in the past, please answer the questions *with that person in mind.*" Participants were then asked several demographic questions, covering age, financial background, religion, ethnicity, sexual orientation, and marital status. I also asked questions about their love affairs. Among them: "How long have you been in love?" "About what percent of an average day does this person come into your thoughts?" And "Do you sometimes feel as if your feelings are out of your control?"

Then came the body of the questionnaire (see the Appendix). It contained fifty-four statements, such as: "I have more energy when I am with _____." "My heart races when I hear _____'s voice on the phone." And "When I'm in class/at work my mind wanders to _____." I designed all these questions to reflect the characteristics most commonly associated with romantic love. Subjects were required to indicate to what extent they agreed with each query on a seven-point scale from "strongly disagree" to "strongly agree." A total of 437 Americans and 402 Japanese filled out the questionnaire. Then statisticians MacGregor Suzuki and Tony Oliva assembled all these data and did a statistical analysis.

The results were astonishing. Age, gender, sexual orientation, religious affiliation, ethnic group: none of these human variables made much difference in the responses.

For example, people of different age groups answered with no significant statistical differences on 82 percent of the statements. People over age forty-five reported being just as passionate about their loved one as those under age twenty-five. Heterosexuals and homosexuals gave similar responses on 86 percent of the questions. On 87 percent of the queries, American men and women responded virtually alike: there were few gender differences. American "whites" and "others" responded similarly on 82 percent of the questions: race played almost no role in romantic zeal. Catholics and Protestants showed no significant variance on 89 percent of the statements: church affiliation was not a factor. And where these groups did show "statistically significant" differences in their responses, one group was usually just a little more passionate than the other.

The greatest differences were between the Americans and the Japanese. On most of the forty-three questions where they showed statistically significant variations, one nationality simply expressed somewhat greater romantic passion. And the twelve questions showing dramatic differences all appeared to have rather obvious cultural explanations. For example, only 24 percent of Americans agreed with the statement, "When I am talking to _____, I am often afraid that I will say the wrong thing," whereas a whopping 65 percent of Japanese agreed with this declaration. I suspect this particular variation occurred because young Japanese often have fewer and more formal relations with the opposite sex than Americans do. So, all things considered, within these two very different societies, men and women were much alike in their feelings of romantic passion.

Romantic love. Obsessive love. Passionate love. Infatuation. Call it what you will, men and women of every era and every culture have been "bewitched, bothered, and bewildered" by this irresistible power. Being in love *is* universal to humanity; it is part of human nature.[9]

Moreover, this magic visits each of us in much the same way.

### *"Special Meaning"*

One of the first things that happens when you fall in love is that you experience a dramatic shift in consciousness: your "love object" takes on what psychologists call "special meaning." Your beloved becomes novel, unique, and all-important. As one smitten man phrased it, "My whole world had been transformed. It had a new center, and that center was Marilyn."[10] Shakespeare's Romeo expressed this feeling more succinctly, saying of his adored one, "Juliet is the sun."

Before the relationship grows into romantic love, you may feel attracted to several different individuals, addressing your attention to one, then another. But eventually you begin to concentrate your passion on just one. Emily Dickinson called this private world "the realm of you."

This phenomenon is related to the human inability to feel romantic passion for more than one person at a time. In my survey, 79 percent of men and 87 percent of women said they would not go out on a romantic date with someone else when their beloved was unavailable (Appendix, #19).

### *Focussed Attention*

The love-possessed person focusses almost all of his or her attention on the beloved, often to the detriment of everything and everyone around them, including work, family, and friends. Ortega y Gasset, the Spanish philosopher, called this "an abnormal state of attention which occurs in a normal man." This focussed attention is a central aspect of romantic love.

Infatuated men and women also concentrate on all of the events, songs, letters, and other little things they have come to associate with the beloved. The time he stopped in the park to show her a spring bud; the evening she tossed lemons to him as he made the drinks: to the love-possessed, these casual instants breathe. Seventy-three percent of the men and 85 percent of the women in my survey remembered trivial things that their beloved said and did (Appendix, #46). And 83 percent of men and 90 percent of women replayed these precious episodes in their mind's eye as they mused about their dearest (Appendix, #52).

Billions of other lovers have probably felt a surge of tenderness when thinking of moments spent with a sweetheart. A touching Asian example of this comes from a ninth-century Chinese poem, "The Bamboo Mat," by Yuan Chen. Chen agonized, "I cannot bear to put away / the bamboo sleeping mat: / that night I brought you home, / I watched you roll it out."[11] For Chen, an everyday object had acquired iconic power.

The twelfth-century tale *Lancelot,* by Chrétien de Troyes, illustrates this same aspect of romantic passion. In this epic, Lancelot finds Queen Guinevere's comb lying in the road after she and her entourage have passed. Several of her golden hairs are tangled in its teeth. As de Troyes wrote, "He began to adore the hairs; a hundred thousand times he touched them to his eyes, his mouth, his forehead, and his cheeks."[12]

## *Aggrandizing the Beloved*

The infatuated person also begins to magnify, even aggrandize tiny aspects of the adored one. If pressed, almost all lovers can list the things they do not like about their amor. But they cast these perceptions aside or persuade themselves that these defects are unique and charming. "So lovers manage in their passion's cause / To love their ladies even for their flaws," mused Molière. Quite so. Some even adore their beloved for their faults.

And lovers dote on the positive qualities of their sweethearts, flagrantly disregarding reality.[13] It's life through rose-colored glasses, what psychologists call the "pink-lens effect." Virginia Woolf described this myopic view vividly, saying, "But love . . . it's only an illusion. A story one makes up in one's mind about another person. And one knows all the time it isn't true. Of course one knows; why one's always taking care not to destroy the illusion."

Our sample of Americans and Japanese certainly illustrates this pink-lens effect. Some 65 percent of men and 55 percent of women in the survey agreed with the statement: "______ has some faults but they don't really bother me"(Appendix, #3). And 64 percent of men and 61 percent of women agreed with the statement, "I love everything about ______"(Appendix, #10).

How we delude ourselves when we love. Chaucer was right: "Love is blynd."

## *"Intrusive Thinking"*

One of the primary symptoms of romantic love is obsessive meditation about the beloved. It is known to psychologists as "intrusive thinking." You simply can't get your beloved out of your head.

Examples of intrusive thinking abound in world literature. The fourth-century Chinese poet, Tzu Yeh, wrote, "How can I not think of you—."[14] An anonymous eighth-century Japanese poet moaned, "My longing has no time when it ceases." Giraut de Borneil, a troubadour of twelfth-century France, sang out, "Through too much loving . . . So terribly do my thoughts torment me."[15] And a Maori native of New Zealand expressed his suffering with these words: "I lie awake the livelong night, / For love to prey on me in secret."

Perhaps the most striking example of intrusive thinking, however, comes from Wolfram von Eschenbach's medieval masterpiece, *Parzifal.* In this story, Parzifal was cantering along on his steed when he saw three drops of blood in the winter snow, shed by a wild duck that had been wounded by a falcon. It reminded him of the crimson and alabaster complexion of his wife, Condwiramurs. Transfixed, Parzifal sat in contemplation, frozen in his stirrups. "And thus he mused, lost in thought, until his senses / deserted him. Mighty love held him in thrall."[16]

Unfortunately, Parzifal was holding his lance erect—a chivalric signal of challenge. Soon two knights who were camped in a nearby meadow with King Arthur took notice and galloped out to joust with him. Not until one of Parzifal's followers draped a yellow scarf over the drops of blood did he shake off his love trance, lower his weapon, and stave off a deadly battle.

Mighty is love. Not surprisingly, 79 percent of the men and 78 percent of the women in my survey reported that when they were in class or at work their mind returned continually to their beloved (Appendix, #24). And 47 percent of men and 50 percent of women agreed that "no matter where it starts, my mind always seems to end up thinking about______" (Appendix, #36). Other surveys report similar findings. Informants report they think about their "love object" over 85 percent of their waking hours.[17]

How apt of Milton in *Paradise Lost* to have Eve say to Adam, "With thee conversing, I forget all time."

## *Emotional Fire*

Of the 839 American and Japanese people in my survey of romantic love, 80 percent of men and 79 percent of women agreed with the statement, "When I feel certain that _____ is passionate about me, I feel lighter than air"(Appendix, #32).

No single aspect of "being in love" is so familiar to the stricken lover as the torrent of intense emotions that pour through the mind. Some become painfully shy or awkward when in the presence of the beloved. Some turn pale. Some flush. Some tremble. Some stammer. Some sweat. Some get weak knees, feel dizzy, or have "butterflies in the stomach." Others report quickened breathing. And many report feelings of fire in the heart.

Catullus, the Roman poet, was certainly swept away. Writing to his beloved, he said, "You make me crazy. / Seeing you, My Lesbia, takes my breath away. / My tongue freezes, my body / is filled with flames."[18] Ono No Komachi, a ninth-century female Japanese poet, wrote, "I lie awake, hot / the growing fires of passion / bursting, blazing in my heart."[19] The woman in the Song of Songs, the Hebrew love lyrics composed between 900 and 300 B.C., bemoaned, "I am faint with love."[20] And American poet Walt Whitman described this emotional whirlwind perfectly, saying, "That furious storm through me careering—I passionately trembling."[21]

Lovers ride a kite of exhilaration so swift that many find it difficult to eat or sleep.

## *Intense Energy*

Loss of appetite and sleeplessness are directly related to another of love's overwhelming sensations: tremendous energy. As a young man on the South Pacific island of Mangaia told an anthropologist, when he thought of his beloved, he "felt like jumping in the sky!"[22] Sixty-four percent of the men and 68 percent of the women in our survey also reported that their hearts raced when they heard their beloved's voice on the phone (Appendix, #9). And 77 percent of men and

76 percent of women reported that they had a surge of energy when they were with their beloved (Appendix, #17).

Bards, minstrels, poets, playwrights, novelists: men and women have sung for centuries of this energizing chemistry, as well as the awkward stammering and nervousness, the pounding heart and breathlessness that can accompany romantic love. But of all who have discussed this psychic and physical pandemonium, none has been as graphic as Andreas Capellanus, or Andreas the Chaplain, a learned Frenchman of the 1180s who traveled in high courtly circles and wrote *On the Art of Honorable Loving,* a literary classic of the times.

It was during his century that the tradition of courtly love emerged in France. This conventionalized code prescribed the conduct of the lover toward the beloved. The lover was frequently a troubadour—a highly educated poet, musician, and singer, often of knightly rank. His beloved was, in many cases, a woman wed to the lord of a distinguished European household. These troubadours composed, then sang highly romantic verse to worship and flatter the lady of the house.

Yet these "romances" were expected to be chaste—and rigidly observant of complex codes of chivalrous conduct. So in his book, Capellanus codified the rules of courtly love. Unknowingly, he also listed many of the primary traits of romantic love, among them the lover's inner turbulence. As he aptly expressed it, "On suddenly catching sight of his beloved, the heart of the lover begins to palpitate." "Every lover regularly turns pale in the presence of his beloved."[23] And "A man tormented by the thought of love eats and sleeps very little."[24]

This sophisticated churchman also spoke of the "intrusive thinking" that lovers experience, declaring, "Everything a lover does ends in the thought of his beloved." And "A true lover is continually and without interruption obsessed by the image of his beloved." He also clearly recognized that the lover focusses all of his or her attention on a single person when they love, saying, "No one can love two people at the same time."[25]

Fundamental aspects of romantic love have not changed nearly a thousand years later.

### *Mood Swings: From Ecstasy to Despair*

"He drifts on blue water / under the clear moon, / picking white lilies on South Lake. / Every lotus blossom / speaks of love / until his heart will break."[26] For the eighth-century Chinese poet Li Po, romance was painful.

Feelings of love soar and dive. If the beloved showers the lover with attention, if he or she calls regularly, writes affectionate e-mails, or joins the lover for an afternoon or evening of food and frolic, then glows the world. But if the adored one seems indifferent, shows up late or not at all, fails to respond to e-mails, phone calls, or letters, or sends some other negative signal, the lover begins to feel despair. Listless, depressed, such wooers mope until they can account for the loved one's actions, relieve their trampled hearts, and renew the chase.

Romantic passion can produce a variety of dizzying mood changes ranging from exhilaration when one's love is returned to anxiety, despair, or even rage when one's romantic ardor is ignored or rejected. As the Swiss writer Henri Frédéric Amiel put it, "The more a man loves, the more he suffers." The Tamil peoples of South India even have a name for this malaise. They call this state of romantic suffering *mayakkam*, meaning intoxication, dizziness, and delusion.

It came as no surprise to me that 72 percent of the men and 77 percent of the women in my survey did not agree with the statement, "______'s behavior has no effect on my emotional well-being" (Appendix, #41). And 68 percent of men and 56 percent of women supported the statement, "My emotional state depends on how _____ feels about me"(Appendix, #37).

## *Yearning for Emotional Union*

"Come to me in my dreams, and then / By day I shall be well again. / For so the night will more than pay / the hopeless longing of the day."[27] Lovers crave emotional union with a beloved, as poet Matthew Arnold knew.[28] Without this connection to a sweetheart, they feel acutely incomplete or hollow, as if an essential part of them is missing.

This overwhelming need for emotional union so characteristic of the lover is memorably expressed in *The Symposium,* Plato's account of a dinner party held in Athens in 416 B.C. On this festive evening some of the greatest minds of classical Greece convened to dine in the home of Agathon. As they reclined on their couches, one guest proposed that they amuse themselves with a topic of sportive discussion: each would take his turn describing and praising the god of love.

All agreed. The flute-girl was dismissed. Then one by one, they took their turns eulogizing the god of love. Some regarded this supernatural figure as the most "ancient," the most "honored," or the most "undiscriminating" of all the gods. Others maintained that the god of love was "young," "sensitive," "powerful," or "good." Not Socrates. He began his homage by recounting his dialogue with Diotima, a wise woman from Mantinea. Speaking of the god of love, she told Socrates, "He always lives in a state of need."[29]

"A state of need." Perhaps no single phrase in all of literature so clearly captures the essence of passionate romantic love: Need. In my survey, 86 percent of men and 84 percent of women agreed with the statement, "I deeply hope _____ is as attracted to me as I am to him/her" (Appendix, #30).

This craving to merge with the beloved pervades world literature.

The sixth-century A.D. Roman poet Paulus Silentiarius wrote, "And there lay the lovers, lip-locked / delirious, infinitely thirsting, / each wanting to go completely inside the other."[30] Yvor Winters, the twentieth-century American poet, wrote, "May our heirs seal us in a single urn, / A single spirit never to return."[31] And Milton expressed this perfectly in *Paradise Lost* when Adam says to Eve, "We are one, / One flesh; to lose thee were to lose myself."

Philosopher Robert Solomon believes this intense desire is the primary reason the lover says, "I love you." This is not statement of fact but a request for confirmation. The lover yearns to hear those potent words, "I love you, too."[32] So deep is this need for emotional union with the beloved that psychologists believe the lover's sense of self becomes blurred. As Freud said, "At its height, the state of being in love threatens to obliterate the boundaries between ego and object."

Novelist Joyce Carol Oates vividly caught this feeling of blissful fusion, writing, "If they turn suddenly toward us we draw back / the skin shudders wetly, finely / will we be torn into two people?"

## *Looking for Clues*

When lovers don't know whether their love is cherished and returned, however, they become hypersensitive to the cues that the adored one sends. As Robert Graves wrote, "Listening for a knock, waiting for a sign." In my survey, 79 percent of men and 83 percent of women reported that when they were strongly attracted to someone, they dissected their beloved's actions, looking for clues about his or her feelings toward them (Appendix, #21). And 62 percent of men and 51 percent of women said that they sometimes searched for alternative meanings to their beloved's words and gestures (Appendix, #28).

## *Changing Priorities*

Many infatuated people also change their clothing styles, their mannerisms, their habits, sometimes even their values to win the beloved. A new interest in golf, tango lessons, antique collecting, a new hair style, Mozart instead of Country Western music, even moving to a new city or starting a new career: love-struck men and women adopt all manner of novel interests, beliefs, and lifestyles in order to please their dearest ones.

The twelfth-century champion of courtly love, Andreas Capellanus, summed up this impulse, penning the words, "Love can deny nothing to love."[33] While a love-besotted American man put it bluntly, "Anything that she liked, I liked."[34] He was one of many. Seventy-nine percent of American men and 70 percent of American women in our survey agreed with the statement, "I like to keep my schedule open so that if _____ is free, we can see each other"(Appendix, #47).

Lovers rearrange their lives to accommodate a beloved.

## *Emotional Dependence*

Lovers also become dependent on the relationship, very dependent. As Shakespeare's Antony declared to Cleopatra, "My heart was to thy rudder tied by the strings." An ancient Egyptian hieroglyphic poem described the same dependency, saying, "My heart would be a slave / should she enfold me."[35] The twelfth-century troubadour Arnaut Daniel wrote, "I am hers from head to foot."[36] But Keats was the most impassioned, writing, "Still, still to hear her tender-taken breath, / And so live ever—or else swoon to death."

Because lovers are so dependent on a beloved, they suffer terrible "separation anxiety" when they are out of touch. An anonymous

Japanese poem, written in the tenth century, aches with this despair. "Early morning glows / in the faint shimmer / of first light. Choked with sadness, / I help you into your clothes."[37]

Lovers are puppets dangling from the heartstrings of another.

### *Empathy*

As a result, lovers often feel tremendous empathy for the beloved. In my survey, 64 percent of men and 76 percent of women agreed with the statement, "I feel happy when _____ is happy and sad when he/she is sad"(Appendix, #11).

Poet e. e. cummings wrote charmingly of this, saying, "she laughed his joy she cried his grief." Many lovers are even willing to sacrifice themselves for their sweetheart. Perhaps Adam's sacrifice for Eve is the most dramatic offering of any in Western literature. As Milton described it, upon discovering that Eve has eaten the forbidden apple, Adam chooses to eat the apple himself—which he knows will lead to his expulsion with her from the Garden of Eden and death. Adam says, "for with thee / Certain my resolution is to die."[38]

### *Adversity Heightens Passion*

Adversity often feeds the flame. I call this curious phenomenon "frustration-attraction" but it is better known as the "Romeo and Juliet effect." Social or physical barriers kindle romantic passion.[39] They enable one to discard the facts and focus on the terrific qualities of the other. Even arguments or temporary breakups can be stimulating.

One of the funniest literary examples of how adversity heightens romance is Chekhov's one-act play, *The Bear*.[40]

In this drama, an ill-tempered landowner, Grigory Stepanovich Smirnov, appears at the home of a young widow to collect money owed him by her dead husband. The woman refuses to pay a single kopek.

She is in mourning, she explains, and curtly shouts at him, "I am in no mood to concern myself with monetary matters." This sends Smirnov into a tirade against all women—calling them hypocrites, phonies, gossips, scandalmongers, haters, slanderers, liars, petty, fussy, ruthless, and illogical. "Brrrr!" he sputters, "I'm shaking with fury." His rage triggers her anger and they begin to shout insults at each other. Soon he calls for a duel. Itching to put a hole in his head, the widow retrieves her dead husband's pistols and they take their positions.

But as their rancor builds, so does mutual respect—and attraction. Suddenly Smirnov exclaims, "Now this is what a woman is! This I understand! A real woman! This is not a whiner, this is not a wimp, this is a fireball, a rocket, this is gunpowder! A shame to have to kill her, though!" A moment later he declares undying love and asks her to be his wife. As her servants rush into the drawing room to defend their mistress with axes, rakes, and pitchforks, they stumble on the lovers—swept up in a mad embrace.

This odd relationship between adversity and romantic ardor is seen in all the star-crossed lovers of the world's great legends. Fueled by difficulties of one kind or another, they just love all the harder.

The most familiar Western story of this kind, of course, is Shakespeare's tragic tale *Romeo and Juliet*. These young lovers of sixteenth-century Verona are caught in a bitter feud between two powerful families, the Montagues and the Capulets. Romeo is a Montague, Juliet a Capulet. Yet Romeo falls in love with Juliet the moment he sees her at a family party, exclaiming, "O, she doth teach the torches to burn bright! / Did my heart love till now? forswear it, sight! / For I ne'er saw true beauty till this night."[41] Juliet, too, succumbs to Cupid's arrow. As Romeo departs the banquet, she asks her nurse, "Go ask his name. If he be married, / My grave is like to be my wedding bed."[42] The play unfolds with a series of obstacles and confusions that only intensify their passion.

Sixty-five percent of the men and 73 percent of the women in my survey agreed with the statement, "I never give up loving _____, even when things are going poorly" (Appendix, #26). And 75 percent of men and 77 percent of women agreed with the statement, "When the relationship with _____ has a setback, I just try harder to get things going right" (Appendix, #6).

One of my unexpected survey results is almost certainly attributable to the role of adversity in love. Homosexual respondents, both gay men and lesbians, reported more emotional turmoil than did heterosexuals. These individuals were more bedeviled by insomnia, loss of appetite, and the yearning for emotional union with a beloved. I think this psychic distress occurs, at least in part, because of the social barriers that many homosexual lovers must surmount.

Those who answered my questionnaire while thinking about a former lover also seemed more emotionally fragile. They, too, had a harder time eating and sleeping. They were more shy and awkward around their former sweetheart. They suffered more "intrusive thinking" and more mood swings. And they more often reported having a racing heart when thinking about their old flame. I suspect that many of these respondents had been rejected by their beloved—and this adversity heightened their romantic zeal.

Like rowboats on a troubled sea, both men and women ride the swells of anguish and exhilaration that are romantic love. And barriers intensify these emotions. If your beloved is married to someone else, if he or she lives across an ocean, if you speak different languages, come from different ethnic groups, or just come from different parts of town, this obstacle can heighten romantic passion. Dickens said of this, "Love often attains its most luxuriant growth in separation and under circumstances of the utmost difficulty." Alas, 'tis true.

## *Hope*

"Say that I might live in hope," King Pyrrhus pleads with Andromache in Racine's drama of love and death. Why do lovers continue to hope, even when the dice of life come up relentlessly against them? Most still hope the relationship will spring back to life—even years after it has ended bitterly. Hope is another predominant trait of romantic love.

A charming sixteenth-century poem by Michael Drayton expresses this optimism. It begins, "Since there's no help, come, let us kiss and part! / Nay, I have done, you get no more of me; / And I am glad, yea, glad with all my heart, / That thus so cleanly I myself can free. / Shake hands for ever, cancel all our vows; / And when we meet at any time again, / Be it not seen in either of our brows, / That we one jot of former love retain." With these words Drayton declares, with apparent confidence, that the affair is finally and easily finished. Yet at the very end of the poem, he suddenly changes his tune. Overcome by hope, he argues that "Love" can be still be saved: "Now, if thou wouldst, when all have given him over, / From death to life thou might'st him yet recover."[43]

I think this tendency to hope became implanted in the human brain eons ago so our ancient forebears would doggedly pursue potential mates until the last flicker of possibility had expired.

## *A Sexual Connection*

"I would rather die a hundred times than be without your sweet love-making. I love you. I love you desperately. I love you as I love my own soul."[44] So declared Psyche to her husband, Eros, in *The Golden Ass,* the second-century novel by Apuleius. "Burning with desire," the tale continues, "she leaned over and kissed him impulsively, impetuously, with kiss after kiss after kiss, fearful he would waken before she had finished."[45]

Poetry from around the world attests to the lover's intense craving for sexual union with the beloved, another basic characteristic of romantic love.

In the Song of Solomon, the woman calls out, "O north wind, awake. / South wind, rise up. / Blow on my garden / and let my spices flow. / Let my love enter his garden / and eat his sweet fruit."[46] Inanna, queen of ancient Sumeria, was enraptured by Dumuzi's sexuality, saying, "O Dumuzi! Your fullness is my delight!"[47] But the sweetest to my ear is the anonymous old English poem that wails, "Western wind, when wilt thou blow? / The small rain down can rain,— / Christ, if my love were in my arms / And I in my bed again!"

Freud, as well as many scholars and laymen, maintained that sexual desire is a central component of romantic love.[48] Hardly a new idea. Those who study the Kama Sutra, the love manual of fifth-century India, know that the word "love" comes from the Sanskrit, "Lubh," meaning "to desire."

It certainly makes sense that feelings of romantic love are intertwined with sexual craving. After all, if romantic passion evolved among our forebears in order to motivate them to focus their mating energy on a "special" individual *at least until insemination had been completed* (as I will maintain in subsequent chapters), then romantic passion must be linked with sexual desire.

The results of my survey support this proposition. A substantial 73 percent of the men and 65 percent of the women daydreamed about having sex with their beloved (Appendix, #34).

## *Sexual Exclusivity*

Lovers also crave sexual exclusivity. They do not wish to have their "sacred" relationship sullied by outsiders. When someone hops in bed with "just a friend," they often don't much care if this bed partner is also coupling with another. But once a man or woman falls in love and begins to yearn for emotional union with a sweetheart, they profoundly want this mate to remain sexually faithful—to them.

Many of the world's love stories reflect this sexual possessiveness, as well as the lover's desire to maintain his or her sexual fidelity. For example, while estranged from Iseult the Fair, Tristan wed another woman with a similar name, Iseult of the Fair Hands—largely because this woman bore much of his beloved's appellation. But Tristan could not bring himself to consummate the marriage. When, in the Arabian legend, Layla was betrothed to someone other than her beloved Majnun, she, too, avoided the wedding bed. And some 80 percent of the men and 88 percent of the women in my survey agreed with the statement, "Being sexually faithful is important when you are in love" (Appendix, #42).

Of all the properties of romantic love, this longing for sexual exclusivity is the most interesting to me. It probably evolved for two essential reasons: to protect ancestral men from being cuckolded and raising another's child; and to protect ancestral women from losing to a rival a potential husband and father to her children. This craving for sexual exclusivity enabled our forebears to protect their precious DNA as they expended almost all their time and energy courting someone they adored.

But along with a drive to ensure sexual fidelity during courtship came a less appealing trait of romantic love, Shakespeare's "green ey'd monster," jealousy.

## *Jealousy: The "Nurse of Love"*

In his book on the rules of courtly love, Capellanus wrote, "He who does not feel jealousy is not capable of loving." He called jealousy the "nurse of love" because he believed it nourished romantic fire.[49]

This insightful cleric, as usual, had it right. In every society where anthropologists have studied romantic passion, they report that both sexes get jealous, very jealous.[50] As the I Ching, the Chinese book of wisdom written over three thousand years ago, warned, "A close bond is possible only between two persons; a group of three engenders jealousy."[51]

### *Emotional Union Trumps Sexual Union*

But even the desire for sexual intercourse and the craving for sexual fidelity are less important to the lover than the longing for emotional union with the beloved. The love-stricken man or woman wants the beloved to call and say, "I adore you," to bring flowers or some other token gift, to invite them to a ball game or the theater, to laugh and hug and shower them with attention. The lover aches to have his or her love returned. This yearning for emotional togetherness far surpasses the desire for mere sexual release.

Seventy-five percent of the men and 83 percent of the women in my survey agreed with the statement, "Knowing that _____ is 'in love' with me is more important to me than having sex with him/her" (Appendix, #50).

### *Involuntary, Uncontrollable Love*

"Behold a deity stronger than I, who, coming, will rule me from that time forward. Love quite governed my soul."[52] Dante wrote these words in the thirteenth century to describe the moment he first saw Beatrice. He knew the dominating force of romantic love. Indeed, at the core of this obsession is its power: romantic love is often unplanned, involuntary, and seemingly uncontrollable.

How many lovers have felt this magnetic pull?

Billions, probably.

"The Jade Goddess," the twelfth-century Chinese romance, says of Chang Po and Meilan, "The more they tried to stop the love that had been awakened, the more they felt themselves in its power."[53] And in twelfth-century France, Chrétien de Troyes wrote of Guinevere in *Lancelot,* "In spite of herself she was forced to love."[54]

But insights into the irresistible nature of romantic attraction have not been confined to the literary imagination. An American business executive in his fifties wrote of an office colleague, "I am advancing toward the thesis that this attraction for Emily is a kind of biological, instinct-like action. That it is not under voluntary or logical control. It directs me. I try desperately to argue with it, to limit its influence, to channel it, to deny it, to enjoy it, and, yes, damn it, to make her respond! Even though I know that Emily and I have absolutely no chance of making a life together, the thought of her is an obsession."[55]

Even the sober-sided American Founding Father, George Washington, knew the pull of romantic love. In 1795 he wrote a letter to his step-granddaughter advising her to beware lest love become "an involuntary passion."[56]

Contemporary men and women also feel the helplessness that accompanies this experience. Sixty percent of the men and 70 percent of the women in my survey agreed with the statement, "Falling in love was not really a choice; it just struck me" (Appendix, #49).

## *A Transient State*

But as love arrives unbidden, it can also steal away. As Violetta, in Verdi's tragic opera *La Traviata,* sings, "Let's live for pleasure alone, since love, like flowers, swiftly fades."

Plato knew this aspect of the god of love, saying, "By nature he is neither immortal nor mortal. Sometimes on a single day he shoots into life . . . then dies, and then . . . comes back to life again."[57] Love is fickle, volatile, inconstant; it can expire, then rekindle, then fade away again.

How long does love's magic last?

No one knows. A team of neuroscientists recently concluded that romantic love normally lasts between twelve and eighteen months.[58] As you will see in chapter three, our study of the brain suggests love can last at least seventeen months. But I would bet that love's duration varies dramatically, depending on the cast of characters involved. Most people have felt a passing infatuation that lasted only days or weeks. And as you know, when there is a barrier to the relationship, this flame can burn for many years. Adversity stimulates romantic ardor.[59]

But this fire in the heart does tend to diminish as partners settle into the daily joys of togetherness, often replaced by another elegant circuit in the brain: attachment—the feelings of serenity and union with one's beloved.

## *Love's Many Forms*

Of course, romantic love can take a variety of forms. You can wake up alone in the middle of the night with feelings of abandonment and despair. Then you get a call or e-mail from your lover in the morning and your hopes begin to soar. Then you meet your sweetheart for dinner and talk and laugh and your ecstasy turns to sensations of security and peace. After supper you climb into bed to read together and soon you are overcome by lust. Then in the morning your beloved dashes off, forgetting to say good-bye, even breaks a forthcoming date or calls you by another's name—and you plunge into despondency again.

"What mad pursuit? What struggle to escape? / What pipes and timbrels / What wild ecstasy?" John Keats clearly knew that romantic love is a tumult of wildly different motivations and emotions that mix to form myriad states of mind. Compassion, ecstasy, desire, fear, suspicion, jealousy, doubt, awkwardness, embarrassment: at any moment this kaleidoscope of feelings can shift, then shift again.

"Passions are liken'd best to floods and streams," wrote Sir Walter Raleigh.[60] We swim these tides. But psychologists generally distinguish between two basic types of romantic love: reciprocated love—associated with fulfillment and ecstasy; and unrequited love—associated with emptiness, anxiety, and sorrow.[61] Almost all of us know both the agony and elation of romantic love.

We are not alone. In his book *The Expression of the Emotions in Man and Animals,* Charles Darwin hypothesized that human beings share many of their feelings with "lower" animals.[62] Indeed, many furred and feathered beings who share this planet seem to feel some version of romantic passion.

# 2

# Animal Magnetism:
## *Love among the Animals*

Unweary still, lover by lover,
They paddle in the cold
Companionable streams or climb the air;
Their hearts have not grown old;
Passion or conquest, wander where they will,
Attend upon them still.

William Butler Yeats
"The Wild Swans at Coole"

As February blizzards cloak the meadows of Hokkaido, Japan, in winter white, a male red fox begins to fixate on a vixen, gazing at her intently, following obsessively. Pausing as she rests, he leaps to lick and nibble at her face, then frolics at her side as she lopes along. A skunky fragrance emanates from his urine in the snow. It is mating time. And as this musky odor wafts through the brittle cold, the couple court and copulate over and over for about two weeks. Then they scent-mark their territory in the woods and fields and excavate several dens where they will rear their young.

Do foxes love?

Excessive energy, focussed attention on a partner, dogged pursuit, and all the tender licks and nibbles that foxes bestow on one another are certainly reminiscent of human romantic love. And foxes are but one of many species that show aspects of romance.

At the beginning of the breeding season or a mating bout, many choose specific partners, then center their attention on this "special" individual, often to the exclusion of all around them. Devotedly, they follow "him" or "her." They stroke, kiss, nip, nuzzle, pat, tap, lick, tug, or playfully chase this chosen one. Some sing. Some whinny. Some squeak, croak, or bark. Some dance. Some strut. Some preen. Some chase. Most play. On the grasslands of Africa's Serengeti, in the jungles of Amazonia, on the tundras of the Arctic, creatures great and small show excessive energy as they woo. Adversity heightens their pursuit—just as barriers intensify romantic passion in people. And many become possessive—jealously guarding this mate from other suitors until their breeding time has passed.

These courtship traits are similar to some characteristics of romantic passion in humans. So I think animals love. Most creatures probably feel this magnetism for only seconds; others appear to be infatuated for hours, days, or weeks. But animals feel some sort of attraction to "special" others. Many even fall in love at first sight. From this "animal attraction" I believe human romantic love would eventually emerge.

## *Animal Attraction*

"It was evidently a case of love at first sight, for she swam about the new-comer caressingly . . . with overtures of affection."[1] Charles Darwin was describing a female mallard duck who had become infatuated with a male pintail duck—a duck of a different species. We all make mistakes.

Darwin believed that animals feel attraction to one another. A male blackbird, a female thrush, a black grouse, a pheasant, these and many other birds, he reported, "fell in love with one another."[2] In fact, Darwin maintained that all the higher animals share "similar passions, affections and emotions, even the more complex ones, such as jealousy, suspicion, emulation, gratitude and magnanimity." They "even have a sense of humour; wonder and curiosity."

Darwin is among very few scientists who have maintained that animals feel love for one another. Naturalists regularly describe anger and fear in other creatures. They see animals frolic and believe these beasts are feeling joy. They describe expressions of surprise, timidity, curiosity, and disgust. They even report moments of empathy and jealousy. Yet scientists rarely say that animals love, even though descriptions of animal courtship are filled with references to behaviors that are akin to human romantic passion.

African elephants are good examples. The female African elephant comes into an estrus (or heat) for about five consecutive days at any time during the year. If she conceives during this mating romp, her sexuality is suppressed during her twenty-two months of pregnancy and the following two years of nursing. Most do not mate again for about four years. So these females are particular about their mating partners. They *prefer* some; they refuse others. And female elephants have many admirers to choose from. Male African elephants leave their matriarchal natal group shortly after puberty (which occurs between ages ten and twelve) to wander with other males in small "all-bull" communities. But not until around age thirty does a male come into "musth," or male heat.

Musth is a dramatic advertisement of sexuality. If you think women in tight short skirts, low-cut blouses, and high-heeled shoes are flaunting their erotic desire, you should see male elephants. As a male comes into musth, which generally lasts two to three months of every year, he begins to excrete a viscous fluid from bulging glands that lie midway between his eye and ear on either side. He dribbles urine continually. His penis sheath becomes thick with green-white scum. He exudes an odor so pungent that females can smell him before they see him. And as he approaches a female herd he starts his courtship strut, his "musth walk." Head high, chin tucked in, ears tensely waving, trunk aloft, he emits a low rumble of confidence as he strides by.

Female elephants find all these drippings, this male perfume, and the "musth walk" exceedingly attractive. Those in estrus draw close like girls to rock stars. Such was Tia. During the many years that naturalist Cynthia Moss followed Tia's matriarchal group of African elephants across the Amboseli National Park in Kenya, she saw many females choose their mates the way Tia did.

Tia showed no interest in any of the young males who began to crowd around her as her period of estrus became noticeable. Off she trotted as they pursued her across the grass. Because female elephants are about half the size of males, an experienced one can outrun or outmaneuver almost any male she wishes to avoid. Tia did just that. But when Tia saw Bad Bull, a dominant, older male in the height of musth, she changed her elephant mind.

Tia wanted Bad Bull the moment he swaggered into view—with ooze dripping from his cheeks, urine streaming down his legs, and foam spraying from his penis sheath. One whiff of this stud and the younger males moved off. Not Tia. Tia looked up at Bad Bull, holding her ears high in an estrous pose. Then she, too, began to move away. But unlike her conduct with her young male suitors, Tia looked over her shoulder as she departed, glancing repeatedly to see if Bad Bull was following. He was. Off Tia sped with Bad Bull in pursuit.

Now nature's timeless dance would start. As Bad Bull caught up to Tia, his almost-four-foot penis emerged from its long gray sheath. Then delicately he placed his trunk along her back. She stopped; stood still; then backed toward him and braced herself, motionless, legs apart. He mounted energetically and, using his versatile penile muscles to direct his thrust, he sank his organ into her vulva. Together they stood for some forty-five seconds before Bad Bull dismounted. Withdrawing, he gushed his remaining semen onto the dirt. Tia turned to stand beside him. Repeatedly she emitted long low rumbles at him; then she rubbed her head along his shoulder.

Tia and Bad Bull were inseparable for the next three days, patting and stroking constantly between bouts of copulation. But when Tia's estrus waned, Bad Bull departed to search for other fertile females. As Moss wrote in her marvelous book, *Elephant Memories,* "Personally, I cannot imagine why Tia wanted to mate with Bad Bull, but then she may have seen something in him that I did not."[3]

Could it be love? A temporary crush? An infatuation? Tia and Bad Bull focussed their attention entirely on each other. Both displayed intense energy. Neither ate or slept as regularly as elephants do. And they touched and "talked" in low, soft, long, rumbling elephant conversation. Tia seemed to feel a genuine, if temporary, attraction to this proud, healthy, virile male.

The love lives of beavers are less visible. But these creatures also show signs of intense attraction as they court and mate. Take Skipper, for example. Skipper grew up on Lily Pond in Harriman State Park, New York, under the tutelage of his father, the "Inspector General," and his mother, "Lily."

Beavers live in small family groups. They work and romp at night. And kits stay with their parents for about two years before they waddle off some spring night to find mates and build homes of their own. Skipper did just that; he departed with his sister, Laurel, one moonstrewn April evening. Inbreeding is common among beavers, and that evening the two siblings moved to a nearby valley to construct a dam and grow a pond. Soon the water rose. Insects began to hatch, attracting frogs, waxwings, and king birds. Fish spawned, a dinner bell to hungry grebes. Willows, alders, and yellow iris spread along the banks. And Skipper and Laurel settled in. But alas, one night Laurel failed to return from her foraging among the maples, oaks, and conifers that nestled in the valley; she lay dead on a nearby road.

The following evening Skipper returned to Lily Pond. All summer he helped his parents fortify their dam, dredge channels, collect lilies, and frolic with their newest infants, Huckleberry and Buttercup. But as the leaves turned red and gold, Skipper once again departed and returned to his abandoned pond. Meticulously he rebuilt his dilapidated dam. Methodically he shoved mud onto the shore, then arranged it into pyramids, then sprayed these hillocks with scented oil from his anal glands and castoreum from his genital opening. These pungent advertisements, he hoped in beaver ways, would entice a "wife."

Nature did her work. A few evenings later, naturalist Hope Ryden saw Skipper in the moonlight. He popped from the rising water—followed by a little brown female beaver. The two touched noses, then swam about together, gathering sticks to fill the dike. Like most beavers, Skipper and his tawny maiden had surreptitiously bonded in the dead of night, then settled into a lifelong partnership—months before she would come into estrus.

Were they "in love"? In *Lily Pond,* Ryden writes, "Beaver pairing is based on an attraction that is as mysterious as it is compelling, one that is unrelated to any immediate urge to copulate."[4] Ryden's remark is important: among beavers, feelings of attraction and attachment were distinct from those of sex.

One April evening, however, the pair consummated their beaver marriage. Skipper and his little female emerged from their moonlit pond holding the same stick between their teeth. They tumbled over and over each other with such gusto that it looked to Ryden like foreplay. They dove and paddled and chattered together in dulcet, almost human tones. They were inseparable. And they must have mated under water—for in early August Skipper's little companion produced two fat kits.

Like elephants, these beavers expended tremendous energy as they wooed. Like elephants, they focussed all of this courtship energy on a "special" other. Like elephants, Skipper and his tiny mate nuzzled affectionately and played flirtatiously in tender, dare I say "loving," ways.

## *"Mad with Delight"*

There are so many descriptions of attraction among animals that it is impossible to recount them all. I have read about the amorous lives of some hundred different species, and in every animal society, courting males and females display traits that are central components of human romantic love.

To begin with, they express wild energy. The American marten and his female chase each other madly, dodging, hopping, scampering, and swirling with what looks like glee. Weasels chase so vigorously that naturalists call it "play fighting." The male dashes along the ground "making excited trilling calls" while his mate "may leap playfully around him."[5] In fact, the female keeps leaping around her partner long after they have finished copulating and he has sunk into a slumber. Mating civit cats vigorously chase each other. The male white-lined bat exuberantly shakes his wings at a female prior to coitus. The mating badger paws the ground as he purrs loudly. When an estrous female rat smells a courting male she hops and darts and hops some more, all the while flicking her ears and glancing over her shoulder in what can only be called a "come hither" gesture.

Big animals also become energized at mating time. As a female "common" chimpanzee comes into estrus, males begin to crowd around her. A courting male "displays" vigorously, rising to his hind legs with penis erect, swaggering before her on two feet, stamping the ground, rocking from side to side, shaking branches and staring at his intended. Male and female grizzly bears pace back and forth at a prescribed distance from one another in perfect synchrony, swinging their hulking bodies to and fro. Hyenas circle one another as they emit an excited crackling vocalization known as "laughing." Mysticete whales rise from the sea and wave their pectoral fins or flukes so rapidly that it looks as if they vibrate. Bottlenose dolphins leap out of the water, then plunge and swim frantically in all directions, often upside down. But perhaps the most enchanting account of this rapturous energy comes from naturalist Malcolm Penny, describing the black rhino. The black rhino circles the estrous female, prancing back and forth on stiff legs, snorting, spraying urine, twirling his tail, shredding nearby bushes with his horn, tossing foliage in the air, and stepping in place—"looking," as Penny put it, "for all the world as if he were dancing."[6]

"Only a mountain has lived long enough to listen objectively to the howl of a wolf," it has been said.[7] There is, however, much we can now say objectively about the wolf. One outstanding trait of this magnificent creature is that, like human beings, a male and female form a pair-bond to rear their young. And their courtship is intense. As George Rabb describes this, "The male starts dancing around the female, lowering his front quarters like a playful dog, and wagging his tail."[8]

Even amphibians and fish dance energetically as they woo. Diurnal terrestrial male frogs do a "toe dance," jumping up and down in front of the female to display themselves. And Darwin wrote that when a courting male stickleback fish sees a female he "darts round her in every direction . . . mad with delight."[9] Mad with delight: this is certainly true of men and women when they fall in love.

### *Nervousness*

Animal suitors are also nervous and restless. If teenage boys are fidgety on dates, so are savannah baboons—as primatologist Barb Smuts has demonstrated. For years, Smuts followed these creatures along their daily routes in the grasslands of Kenya and she writes a touching description of the courtship between Thalia and Alexander.

It all began as Thalia, an adolescent, reached the height of estrus. For months she had avoided Alexander, another adolescent who had joined the baboon troop only a few months before. But on this early evening Thalia and Alexander sat about two meters apart on the cliffs where members of the troop often assembled to sleep. Observes Smuts:

"Alexander was facing west, his sharp muzzle pointing toward the setting sun, watching the rest of the troop make their way up the cliffs. Thalia was grooming herself in a perfunctory manner, her attention elsewhere. Every few seconds she glanced out of the corner of her eye at Alexander without turning her head. Her glances became longer and longer and her grooming more and more desultory until she was staring for long moments at Alexander's profile. Then, as Alexander shifted and turned his head toward Thalia, she snapped her head down and peered intently at her own foot. Alexander looked at her, then away. Thalia stole another glance in his direction, but when he again glanced her way, she resumed her involvement with her foot. . . . This charade continued. . . . Then without looking at her, Alexander began slowly to edge toward Thalia. . . . Thalia froze, and for a second she looked into Alexander's eyes. Then, as he began to approach her, she stood, presented her rear to him, and, looking back over her shoulder, darted nervous glances at him."[10]

Thalia and Alexander were together still at dawn.

Many of Nature's courters get edgy. Describing a pair of shorebirds, European avocets, Niko Tinbergen writes, "Both male and female stand and preen their feathers in a hasty, nervous fashion.[11] Giraffes, among the world's most graceful creatures, "walked about restlessly" when they courted.[12] And naturalist George Schaller depicts the queen of the jungle, saying, "A lioness fully in heat is restless, changing her position often and sinuously rubbing herself against the male."[13]

## *Loss of Appetite*

Many animal suitors lose their appetites—yet another characteristic of human romantic love. When a sexually primed male elephant finds a female in peak estrus, for example, he dispenses almost entirely with food; he concentrates solely on copulating and guarding his prize from other males.[14] In fact, a mating male elephant gradually becomes so thin and tired that he goes out of "musth." He must rejoin his bachelor herd where he will recover—eating and resting for several months.

The courting male northern elephant seal loses almost half his body weight. As the three-month mating season approaches, males appear along the coast of California to claim sections of the beach. They fight viciously to stake their claims; indeed sometimes the shoreline waves are red with blood. Why so much fuss? Because females soon arrive to bear their pups and then return into estrus—briefly. The males who own the best pieces of real estate will have sexual access to the largest harems. So males are unwilling to leave their territory undefended for even an hour. Food, sleep: these essentials simply lose appeal.

Orangutans also lose their gourmand habits. These orange shambling relatives of ours live high in the jungle trees of Borneo and Sumatra, some sixty feet above the ground. When a male has grown the impressive cheek pouches that advertise his maturity, he begins to mark and defend a large territory full of fruiting trees. Several females set up smaller home ranges within his acreage. Each morning he wakes the neighborhood with a salad of grumbles followed by a bellowing roar to announce his whereabouts and sexual availability. Then when one of the females comes into estrus he begins to follow her tenaciously along her leafy trails. The female will only remain fertile for about five days. And if she conceives during this mating bout, she won't return into estrus for more than seven years. So the male must stay near her constantly while she is in heat, as well as fight off rivals. To make matters worse, male orangs are twice the size of females; they move far more slowly and eat much more. Consequently a suitor has to skip meals to keep up with his agile little partner.

These demands of courtship were no problem for Throatpouch, a wild orangutan living in the Tanjung Putting Reserve, in Borneo. Here primatologist Birute Galdikas came to study these wild orange beasts in the 1970s. TP, as she called Throatpouch, was middle-aged, grouchy, irascible, beady-eyed, and huge. "By orangutan standards, however," Galdikas writes, "TP probably was a decidedly handsome fellow." Galdikas goes on to explain: "The object of TP's adoration was Priscilla. When I saw Priscilla with Throatpouch, she was even dowdier than I remembered. I thought that TP would have chosen a more comely female. But from the way Throatpouch pursued her, Priscilla had sexual charm to spare. TP was smitten with her. He couldn't take his eyes off her. He didn't even bother to eat, so enthralled was he by her balding charms."[15] Even when Throatpouch did have time to eat, Galdikas reports, he took the gentlemanly attitude: ladies first.

The courting male lion even gives what little food he can acquire to his beloved. George Schaller wrote a charming description of this. Apparently a wooing male noticed a gazelle at a nearby waterhole. So he interrupted his courtship to fell this prize. Then he carried this luscious gift to the female and sat nearby to watch as she ate it all, "a touching and striking token considering the fact that he was hungry."[16]

I suspect the brain chemistry of attraction had overcome this male's need to eat.

### *Persistence*

Animals are also tenacious. Most have only a few chances in their lives to triumph over rivals, court available mates, and breed. So they persevere.

A male giraffe follows a female for hours until she submits to his overtures. The lioness purrs at the male, rolls suggestively on the ground before him, swats at him coyly, then flounces off, rejecting his touch. Only patient courters eventually mount this huge pussycat. The male tiger is equally persistent. He never takes his eyes off his mate; "even the slightest flicker of her tail receives his attention."[17] Perhaps the most amusing looking suitor is the male shrew. He pursues an estrous female relentlessly, scampering behind her with his nose pressed over her rump.[18]

Darwin even noted this focussed determination among butterflies. "Their courtship appears to be a prolonged affair," he wrote, "for I have frequently watched one or more males pirouetting round a female until I was tired, without seeing the end of the courtship."[19]

This persistence, seen in so many creatures—from butterflies to rhinos—is a hallmark of human romantic love.

### *Affection*

Most courting animals also show signs of tenderness, the most charming aspect of human romance.

Writing of a pair of courting beavers, biologist Lars Wilsson said, "They sleep curled up close together during the daytime and at night they seek each other out at regular intervals to groom one another or just simply to sit close side by side and 'talk' for a little while in special contact sounds, the tones and nuances of which seem to a human expressive of nothing but intimacy and affection."[20]

The male grizzly bear nuzzles the female's flanks and snuffles in her ear, whimpering for acceptance. A male giraffe rubs his head along a female's neck and trunk. The tigress nips at her mate, biting him gently on the neck and face as she rubs her body against his. A mating pair of harbor porpoises swim together, sometimes over or under one another, but always in tandem as they stroke, rub, "kiss," or mouth each other. Chimpanzees hug, pat, and kiss each other's thighs and belly. They even kiss with the deep "French kiss," inserting their tongue gently into the mouth of a mating partner. Bats stroke each other with their velvety wing membranes. Even the lowly male cockroach strokes his partner's antennae with his own.

## *Puppy Love*

In her groundbreaking book, *The Hidden Life of Dogs,* Elizabeth Marshall Thomas maintained that dogs show deep romantic passion for one another. She arrived at this conclusion moments after she introduced Misha, a handsome Siberian husky, to her daughter's young and beautiful dog of the same breed, Maria. Thomas had agreed to house Misha while his owners were on an extended trip to Europe.

The day arrived. Misha's owners delivered this vibrant male to the Thomas home. Misha pranced into the living room to look about, settling his gaze immediately on the gorgeous Maria. In an instant he bounded to her feet and skidded to a stop. At once, Thomas writes, Maria "dropped to her elbows in an invitation to play. *Chase me,* her gesture said. And he did. Quickly, lightly, the two delighted creatures spun around the room. Misha and Maria were so taken with each other that they noticed nothing. Misha didn't even notice when his owners left."[21]

These two joyous dogs were immediately inseparable. Together they ate and slept and roamed; together they bore four hearty pups; together they reared them—until the dark day when Misha's owners gave him away to people in the countryside. For weeks Maria sat in the window seat of the Thomas home in the very spot where she had watched her beloved Misha being forced into a car. Here she pined. Eventually she gave up waiting for him to return. But "Maria never recovered from her loss," Thomas writes. "She lost her radiance . . . and showed no interest in forming a permanent bond with another male, even though, over the years, several eligible males joined our household."[22]

## *Animals Are Choosy*

Excessive energy; focussed attention on a particular individual; motivation to pursue this "special" partner; loss of appetite; persistence; tender stroking, kissing, licking, snuggling, and coquettish playing: all are striking traits of human romantic love. Call it what you will, many creatures seem to have an attraction to one another.

But animals are choosy.

Of all the characteristics of human romantic love that other creatures display, perhaps none is more revealing than this choosiness. Just as you or I are unwilling to hop into bed with anyone who winks at us, no other creature on this planet will expend precious time and energy mating indiscriminately. They rebuff some; they choose others.

Such is the female African hammerhead bat. During the dry season, males regularly congregate at a "lekking ground," a specific mating area along the forested banks of the Ivindo River in Gabon, Africa. The males arrive at dusk to set up temporary evening positions. Once settled, they sing with a loud, metallic, throaty honk as they flap their half-opened wings double-time to their singing beat.

The point: to draw attention to themselves. Soon the females arrive and cruise among them, hovering to inspect one, then another. As a female examines a particular male he intensifies his display, flapping wildly as he steps up his singing to sound a staccato buzz. Amid the cacophony, each female eventually makes her selection, lands near a particular male, and copulates.[23]

Among the "common" chimpanzees that primatologist Jane Goodall has studied for more than forty years in Tanzania, Flo was the most popular. When she came into estrus in 1983, Flo was followed everywhere she went by as many as fourteen adult males, many of whom were even willing to go directly into Goodall's campsite to be near this preferred mating partner. Fifi, Flo's daughter, was also sought after—much more so than her girlfriend, Pom. Chimps have favorites.

One is inclined to think these animal attractions are due merely to hormonal cycling; that the physiology of estrus draws males to choose one female rather than another. But Goodall, a famed scientist, would not agree. She writes that "partner preferences, independent of hormonal influences, are clearly of major significance for chimpanzees."[24] In fact, she believes that males of many primate species "show clear-cut preferences for particular females, which may be independent of cycle stage."[25] Animal behaviorist Frank Beach made this same observation in 1976, writing: "The occurrence or non-occurrence of copulation depends as much on individual affinities and aversions as upon the presence or absence of sex hormones in the female."[26]

As males prefer certain females regardless of their sexual condition, females are drawn to particular males despite their lower rank and status, as Darwin noted over a hundred years ago. He wrote in *The Descent of Man* that even in exceedingly aggressive species, females are not necessarily drawn to the strongest, most courageous, or even the most victorious males at mating time. Instead, "it is more probable that the females are excited, either before or after the conflict, by certain males, and thus unconsciously prefer them."[27]

Lions, baboons, wolves, bats, probably even butterflies distinguish between suitors, assiduously avoiding mating with some and doggedly focussing their courtship energy on others.

Animals of different species are drawn to different types of partners, of course. Females of many species (including women) are often attracted to males of high rank. Some prefer those residing on the best piece of property.[28] Some want a male who will defend them or help them rear their young instead. Some like the male with the most symmetrical tail feathers or the reddest face. Moreover, males are often sensitive to the age of the female, as well as her health, size, and shape. But as Goodall writes of primates, "personality" is also highly significant.[29]

*All* animals are choosy. In fact, this favoritism is so common in nature that the animal literature regularly uses several terms to describe it, including "mate preference," "selective proceptivity," "individual preference," "favoritism," "sexual choice," and "mate choice."

Choosy though they are, most animals express their preferences fast.

## *Love at First Sight*

"From the moment she set eyes on him, she adored him. Wanting only to be near him, to lavish her affection on him, she followed everywhere he went. The sound of his voice made her bark."[30] Violet, the panicky little pug who lived with Elizabeth Marshall Thomas in Cambridge, Massachusetts, was in love with Bingo, their other pug.

Violet showed all the symptoms of love at first sight.

And her behavior is common in nature—for an important reason: most female creatures have a breeding season or other specific cyclic period when they are physiologically ripe. They have only a few minutes, hours, days, or weeks to breed, conceive, and spread their genes. They cannot afford to spend months reviewing each suitor's résumé. Moreover, wooing can be dangerous. Coitus puts one in a compromising position: predators or competitors can pounce. Equally important, mating consumes valuable time and energy. So instant attraction enables males and females of many species to focus their precious courtship energy on particular individuals and begin the breeding process swiftly.

Perhaps we humans inherited this phenomenon—because love at first sight is common to men and women. In a recent survey of one hundred American couples, 11 percent of these men and women had fallen in love the moment they set their eyes on their partner; and in a survey of 679 men and women done in the 1960s, some 30 percent of respondents reported they had fallen in love at an initial glance.[31]

This instant attraction also happened to the American president Thomas Jefferson. Historian Fawn Brodie writes, "What Jefferson was told in advance about Maria Cosway is irrelevant, for if ever a man fell in love in a single afternoon it was he."[32] A similar experience occurred to a contemporary woman living in Caruaru, a town in northeast Brazil. To an anthropologist, she confided, "I had never seen this man. And when we saw each other, I don't know what it was that happened, if it was love at first sight or what it was. After one week I eloped with him."[33] A woman on the South Seas island of Mangaia expressed the same feeling. "When I saw this man, I wished that he would be my husband, and this feeling was a surprise because I had never seen him before."[34] She married him. Years later she reflected on the experience, saying the meeting had been "nature's work."

Love at first sight is nature's work.

## *Love at First Smell?*

People have asked me whether the smell of someone can trigger this instant attraction. Certainly many animals are immediately attracted to the odors of particular mating partners. But I doubt that love at first smell happens regularly to people—for an evolutionary reason.

Our primate ancestors lived high in the trees for at least 30 million years. To avoid falling to the ground as well as to select ripe fruit, they needed acute vision—rather than a keen sense of smell. As a result, monkeys and apes have a comparatively reduced sense of smell and large regions of the brain devoted to the perception of visual stimuli. We humans inherited these faculties. And these vision networks are superbly connected to the other senses and to our thoughts and feelings. In fact, as primates we gather over 80 percent of our knowledge of the world around us with our eyes. This is undoubtedly why so many Internet romances end when partners actually meet face-to-face. Visual stimuli are important to romance.

So I doubt that many humans fall in love when they catch a whiff of a suitor at a party. But I do think that once a partner becomes familiar—and cherished—his or her smell can become a kind of aphrodisiac. I have known several women who liked to sleep in the T-shirt of a sweetheart because they liked its perfume, for example. And Western literature is full of male characters who are stimulated by the fragrance of a beloved's handkerchief or glove.

But no matter what triggers attraction, this magnetism can be instant. When human beings and other creatures are psychologically and physically ready and a relatively suitable partner appears before them, the simplest exchange can fire up attraction.

Then most animals become exceedingly possessive of their prize.

*Possessiveness*

"Yourself—your soul—in pity give me all / Withhold no atom's atom or I die." Keats wanted to possess every bit of his beloved. Many other creatures share his sentiment. Some birds and mammals will fight almost until death to possess a lover exclusively.

During the June mating season, for example, the male grizzly bear attends a female for several days or even weeks, although he will depart after a while if he sees other mating opportunities. Observing a veteran male grizzly in Yellowstone National Park, naturalist Thomas McNamee writes, "In the nest of leaves and branches that was their day bed, he would lie with a protective and possessive paw across her shoulder. When other male grizzlies came near . . . the merest grunt would usually suffice to send any would-be contender off."[35]

An unhappy example of this possessiveness was observed in mountain bluebirds by zoologist David Barash.[36] The mating season had begun and a male and female mountain bluebird had built their nest and settled in. While the male was off foraging, however, Barash placed a stuffed male mountain bluebird on a tree limb beside the nest. Bedlam ensued. When the "husband" returned and saw the intruder, he viciously and repeatedly attacked the dummy. Then he turned on his mate, brutally attacking her, tearing out two of her primary flight feathers. She fled. The male soon appeared with a new female with whom he reared a brood.

While possessiveness drives some creatures to violence, jealousy plunges others into depression. Remember Violet, the little pug dog who was in love with Bingo, another pug? Violet doted on her "husband." They were partners. "Like two little married people, they had their private arrangements," writes Elizabeth Marshall Thomas, even "the way they liked to sleep." Violet's troubles started the day the young and beautiful husky, Maria, came to live in the Marshall household. Thomas writes of Violet's jealousy, "What bothered Violet most about Maria, though, was that Bingo liked her so much. Ignoring Violet, Bingo spent time every day trying to make a conquest of Maria by parading back and forth beside her with his ears low, his expression soft and his tail very faintly wagging. Violet often tried to stop him." No luck. Eventually Violet "would withdraw to a distant corner and sit down, chastened and depressed."[37]

Our closest relatives, "common" chimpanzees and bonobos, can also be highly possessive—even though they are promiscuous by nature. At the height of estrus, a female often visits one male, then another, sometimes copulating with over a dozen suitors in a day. Most calmly wait their turn. But some male chimps become possessive. And as their passion grows, they try to establish an exclusive partnership with a particular female.

Such was Satan, a chimp living in the Gombe Stream Reserve, Tanzania. Jane Goodall writes of Satan's budding liaison with Miff. Miff had just come into "heat" and all the males knew it. The morning had started noisily as she passed from one male to the next, presenting her buttocks and coupling with each. But the day drew on and one by one, the males shuffled off through the bushes to eat or rest. Satan waited until the last of the other admirers had departed. Then as Miff roused herself to follow them, Satan jumped in front of her in the trail and walked casually in a direction not taken by the other males. He continually looked over his shoulder to see if she was following him. She was.

After half an hour Miff heard the other males calling through the foliage. For a moment she looked toward the voices, then directly at Satan, who was shaking branches impatiently to distract her. She paused, as if weighing her alternatives. Then she followed Satan over a ridge to a nearby valley—far from all the other males.[38]

Often an estrous female chimp stays in the community to copulate with almost all the males. If she is attracted to an admirer, however, she may accompany this "special" individual to the periphery of their home range, remaining with him from three days to almost three months. Goodall calls these temporary partnerships "going on safari."

## *Mate Guarding*

Because possessiveness is so common in nature, animal behaviorists have given it a name: mate guarding.[39] They regard this taste for sexual exclusivity as a primary aspect of courtship in many species. Generally it is the male who guards the female—from poachers, and from defection by the female. For sound evolutionary reasons. If a male can sequester a female during her ovulation, she may bear his offspring and pass his genes toward eternity.

Males of species that form pair-bonds to rear their young have a second Darwinian motivation to be sexually possessive. It is not adaptive for a male to expend his vital time and energy building a nest, protecting a female, battling intruders, even feeding young—unless these babies carry his DNA. If his female cavorts with another male, he risks being cuckolded. So in socially monogamous species, males tend to be highly sensitive to intruders as they court and "wed." Some male monkeys bite a female's neck if she wanders off or herd her with taps or shoves; males of many other species fiercely defend a territory where a mate resides instead.

The men and women who participated in my survey (discussed in chapter one) also showed this tendency toward mate guarding, particularly the men. Men were much more likely than women to disagree with the statement: "It is good to be out of touch with _____ for a few days so that the anticipation can build up again" (Appendix, #4). This could be because women generally have more friends, more connections, more family ties, and more responsibilities outside of their love relationship. But men are probably also unconsciously driven to guard the vessel that may bear their seed.

They have good reason. In a recent poll of American men and women, 60 percent of men and 53 percent of women admitted to "mate poaching"; they had tried to woo another's lover away to make a new committed partnership with them.[40] In fact, a study of thirty cultures showed how common mate poaching is around the world.[41] So like mountain bluebirds, humans are possessive.

The human tendency to stalk, even murder a straying lover probably comes from this animal tendency to guard a mate.

## *An Immodest Proposal*

All these data have led me to believe that animals big and little are biologically driven to prefer, pursue, and possess specific mating partners: there is chemistry to animal attraction. And this chemistry must be the precursor of human romantic love.

But what brain chemicals are involved?

Two closely related natural stimulants in the mammalian brain appear to play a role: dopamine and norepinephrine. All birds and mammals are endowed with similar forms of dopamine and norepinephrine, as well as similar structures in the brain to produce and respond to these natural "uppers"—although these brain structures and circuits vary from one species to the next.

More important, dopamine and norepinephrine play a crucial role in sexual arousal and heightened motivation in birds and mammals.[42] For example, female laboratory rats express their amorous intentions by hopping and darting, behaviors associated with increased levels of dopamine.[43] And in prairie voles, little creatures much like field mice, elevated levels of dopamine in the brain are directly associated with a *preference* for a particular mating partner.[44]

Please meet the prairie vole. These tiny animals live in a maze of tunnels and burrows on the grasslands of the American Midwest. Voles form pair-bonds to rear their young. The male leaves home soon after puberty to find a "spouse." When he sees a likely candidate, he begins to court her avidly. Sniffing, licking, nuzzling, mounting: a vole couple copulates over fifty times in roughly two days. After this sex marathon, the male starts to behave like a new husband, building a nest for their forthcoming infants, ferociously guarding his mate from rival males, and defending their mutual home range. Some 90 percent of prairie voles live in lifelong unison with a single partner.[45]

But prairie voles are choosy, as this study showed. Scientists paired an estrous female prairie vole with a male. As the female copulated with this suitor, she formed a distinct partiality for him, a favoritism that was accompanied with a 50 percent increase of dopamine in the nucleus accumbens, a part of the mammalian brain associated with craving and addiction in people.[46]

Equally telling, when scientists injected a specific region of the female prairie vole's brain with a substance that reduced levels of dopamine, she no longer preferred this partner over other males. And when the female was injected instead with compounds that increased brain levels of dopamine, she began to prefer the male who was present at the time of infusion—even though she had never mated with this individual.[47]

Dopamine appears to play a key role in animal attraction.

Norepinephrine may contribute to this magnetism. When scientists put a drop of male urine on the upper lip of a female prairie vole, levels of norepinephrine elevate in the brain. This contributes to the release of estrogen and stimulates courting behavior.[48] Is the female prairie vole "attracted" to this scent?

Levels of norepinephrine (and dopamine) also spike as an estrous female sheep looks at slides of male sheep's faces.[49] Maybe these ewes are temporarily infatuated with these rams.

Norepinephrine is even linked with a specific mammalian courting pose: lordosis—the female habit of crouching, arching her back, and tipping up her buttocks toward her suitor to advertise sexual availability.[50] Women do this, too. A woman will look coyly over her shoulder at a man as she gracefully arches her back and tips her buttocks in his direction.

These data led me to suspect that dopamine and/or norepinephrine play a role in animal attraction.

More brain chemicals are undoubtedly involved. As elephants, foxes, squirrels, and many other animals sift through their mating opportunities, they must distinguish colors, shapes, and sizes, listen for seductive tones, remember past successes and disasters, and sniff, touch, and taste to gather information about their potential consorts. A lot of chemical systems undoubtedly coordinate in some sort of chain reaction to trigger feelings of animal attraction.

But animals love. Tia, Bad Bull, Skipper, Misha, Maria, Violet, Thalia, Alexander, Miff, Satan, and just about every other mammal and bird on this planet has probably felt drawn to *specific* others. Temporarily charmed, these lovers step to a universal beat, croaking, barking, flapping, trilling, strutting, staring, nuzzling, patting, copulating—and adoring—their preferred mating partners.

When the brain chemistry for animal attraction first evolved no one knows. I suspect that by the time the first primitive mammals were scampering beneath the feet of dinosaurs, these primordial whiskered brethren of humankind had evolved a simple brain network to motivate them to distinguish among suitors and prefer particular ones. With this rudimentary equipment, they went forth to multiply, spreading this chemistry to myriad swimming, flying, creeping, hopping, leaping, trotting, swinging beings, including the ancestors of apes and humans.

Men and women of ancient India called romantic love "the eternal dance of the universe."[51] They were right. How long a chipmunk, a zebra, or a whale actually feels attracted to a special mate obviously varies, however. Environments vary. Needs vary. And species vary. In rats, attraction probably lasts only seconds. Elephants appear to be "in love" about three days. Dogs often show attraction for months and attachment for many years. Some scientists question how "conscious" these creatures are of their emotions.[52] No one knows. But animals express heightened energy, focussed attention, euphoria, craving, persistence, possessiveness, and affection: animal attraction. And data suggest that this attraction is associated with two common brain chemicals—dopamine and norepinephrine.

Could these chemicals also play a role in human romantic love? To understand the chemistry of this "eternal dance," I decided to look inside the human brain.

# 3

# Chemistry of Love:
## *Scanning the Brain "in Love"*

For love is as strong as death.
Its passions are as cruel as the grave
And its flashes of fire are the very flame of God.

The Song of Songs (c. 900–300 B.C.E.)

"There is the heat of Love, the pulsing rush of Longing, the lover's whisper, irresistible—magic to make the sanest man go mad."[1] This magic that Homer sang of in *The Iliad* has started wars, sired dynasties, toppled kingdoms, and generated some of the world's finest literature and art. People sing for love, work for love, kill for love, live for love, and die for love. What causes this sorcery?

As you know, I have come to believe that romantic love is a universal human feeling, produced by specific chemicals and networks in the brain. But exactly which ones? Determined to shed some light on this magic that can make the sanest man go mad, I launched a multipart project in 1996 to collect scientific data on the chemistry and brain circuitry of romantic love. I assumed that many chemicals must be involved in one way or another. But I focussed my investigation on dopamine and norepinephrine, as well as a related brain substance, serotonin.

I looked into the nature of these chemicals for two reasons: the attraction animals feel for particular mates is linked with elevated levels of dopamine and/or norepinephrine in the brain. More important, all three of these chemicals produce many of the sensations of human romantic passion.

## *Rock On, Sweet Dopamine*

Take dopamine. Elevated levels of dopamine in the brain produce extremely focussed attention,[2] as well as unwavering motivation and goal-directed behaviors.[3] These are central characteristics of romantic love. Lovers intensely focus on the beloved, often to the exclusion of all around them. Indeed, they concentrate so relentlessly on the positive qualities of the adored one that they easily overlook his or her negative traits;[4] they even dote on specific events and objects shared with this sweetheart.

Besotted lovers also regard the beloved as novel and unique. And dopamine has been associated with learning about novel stimuli.[5]

Central to romantic love is the lover's *preference* for the beloved. As you recall from chapter two, among prairie voles, this favoritism is associated with heightened levels of dopamine in specific brain regions. And it is not a leap of logic to suggest that if dopamine is associated with mate preference in prairie voles, it can play a role in partiality in people. As you recall, all mammals have basically the same brain machinery, although size, shape, and placement of brain parts definitely vary.[6]

Ecstasy is another outstanding trait of lovers. This, too, appears to be associated with dopamine. Elevated concentrations of dopamine in the brain produce exhilaration, as well as many of the other feelings that lovers report—including increased energy, hyperactivity, sleeplessness, loss of appetite, trembling, a pounding heart, accelerated breathing, and sometimes mania, anxiety, or fear.[7]

Dopamine involvement may even explain why love-stricken men and women become so dependent on their romantic relationship and why they crave emotional union with their beloved. Dependency and craving are symptoms of addiction—and all of the major addictions are associated with elevated levels of dopamine.[8] Is romantic love an addiction? Yes; I think it is—a blissful dependency when one's love is returned, a painful, sorrowful, and often destructive craving when one's love is spurned.

In fact, dopamine may fuel the frantic effort a lover musters when he/she feels the love affair is in jeopardy. When a reward is delayed, dopamine-producing cells in the brain *increase* their work, pumping out more of this natural stimulant to energize the brain, focus attention, and drive the pursuer to strive even harder to acquire a reward: in this case, winning one's sweetheart.[9] Dopamine, thy name is persistence.

Even the craving for sex with the beloved may be indirectly related to elevated levels of dopamine. As dopamine increases in the brain, it often drives up levels of testosterone, the hormone of sexual desire.

## *Norepinephrine's High*

Norepinephrine, a chemical derived from dopamine, may also contribute to the lover's high. The effects of norepinephrine are varied, depending on the part of the brain it activates. Nevertheless, increasing levels of this stimulant generally produce exhilaration, excessive energy, sleeplessness, and loss of appetite—some of the basic characteristics of romantic love.

Increasing levels of norepinephrine could also help explain why the lover can remember the smallest details of the beloved's actions and cherished moments spent together. This liquor is associated with increased memory for new stimuli.[10]

A third chemical may also be involved in that "irresistible" feeling of magic Homer spoke of: serotonin.

### *Serotonin*

A striking symptom of romantic love is incessant thinking about the beloved. Lovers cannot turn off their racing thoughts. Indeed, this single aspect of being in love is so intense that I use it as the litmus test of romantic passion. The first thing I ask anyone who tells me they are "in love" is, "What percentage of your waking hours do you think about your sweetheart?" Many say "over 90 percent." Some bashfully admit they never stop thinking about "him" or "her."

Lovers are obsessed. And doctors who treat individuals with most forms of obsessive-compulsive disorder prescribe SSRIs (selective serotonin reuptake inhibitors) such as Prozac or Zoloft, substances that *elevate* levels of serotonin in the brain.[11] So I came to suspect that the lover's persistent, involuntary, irresistible ruminations about a sweetheart might be associated with *low* levels of some type (there are at least fourteen variations) of this chemical compound.[12]

There is some support for my reasoning. In 1999, scientists in Italy studied sixty individuals: twenty were men and women who had fallen in love in the previous six months; twenty others suffered from unmedicated obsessive-compulsive disorder (OCD); twenty more were normal, healthy individuals who were not in love and were used as controls. Both the in-love participants and those suffering from OCD were found to have significantly lower levels of serotonin than did the controls.[13]

These scientists examined serotonin levels in components of the blood, however, rather than the brain. Until scientists document the activity of serotonin in specific brain regions, we cannot be sure of the role of serotonin in romantic love. Nevertheless, this experiment has established, for the first time, a possible connection between romantic love and *low* levels of bodily serotonin.

All those countless hours when your mind races like a mouse upon a treadmill may be associated with reduced levels of serotonin coursing through the highways of the brain.

And as a love affair intensifies, this irresistible, obsessive thinking can increase—due to a negative relationship between serotonin and its relatives, dopamine and norepinephrine. As levels of dopamine and norepinephrine climb, they can cause serotonin levels to plummet.[14] This could explain why a lover's increasing romantic ecstasy actually intensifies the compulsion to daydream, fantasize, muse, ponder, obsess about a romantic partner.

## *A "Working" Hypothesis*

Given the properties of these three related chemicals in the brain—dopamine, norepinephrine, and serotonin—I began to suspect that all played a role in human romantic passion.

The feelings of euphoria, sleeplessness, and loss of appetite, as well as the lover's intense energy, focussed attention, driving motivation, and goal-oriented behaviors, his/her tendency to regard the beloved as novel and unique, and the lover's increased passion in the face of adversity might all be caused, in part, by heightened levels of dopamine and/or norepinephrine in the brain. And the lover's obsessive cogitation about the beloved might be due to decreased brain levels of some type of serotonin.

Now for the caveats. This theory is complicated by many facts: different doses of these chemicals can produce different effects. These substances do different things in different brain parts. Each interacts with the others in different ways under different circumstances. And each harmonizes with many other bodily systems and brain circuits, setting up complex chain reactions. Moreover, passionate romantic love takes a variety of graded forms, from pure elation when one's love is reciprocated to feelings of emptiness, despair, and often rage when one's love is thwarted. These chemicals undoubtedly vary in their concentrations and combinations as the relationship ebbs and flows.

Nevertheless, the distinct correlation between numerous characteristics of romantic love and the effects of these three brain substances led me to the following hypothesis: *this fire in the mind is caused by elevated levels of either dopamine or norepinephrine or both, as well as decreased levels of serotonin.* These chemicals form the backbone of obsessive, passionate, romantic love.

## *Scanning the Brain in Love*

Next, I needed to find the regions of the brain involved in Homer's "pulsing rush of Longing." I knew that dopamine, norepinephrine, and serotonin were much more prevalent in some brain regions than in others. If I could establish which regions of the brain become active while one is feeling romantic rapture, that might confirm which primary chemicals were involved. It was time to embark on the project to scan the brains of love-struck men and women.

With neuroscientist Greg Simpson, then at the Albert Einstein College of Medicine, I developed a scheme. We would collect data on brain activity while love-smitten subjects performed two separate tasks: looking at a photograph of his or her beloved, and looking at a "neutral" photograph of an acquaintance who generated no positive or negative romantic feelings. Moreover, we would use a functional magnetic resonance imaging (fMRI) machine to take pictures of the brain.

The fMRI machine records blood flow in the brain. It is based, in part, on a simple principle: brain cells that are active suck up more blood than quiescent brain parts—in order to collect the oxygen they need to do their job. Using this machine I would not need to inject my subjects with colored dye or intrude on their bodies in any other way. No pain. That appealed to me. Then to analyze our data, we would compare the brain activity that occurred while our subjects gazed at a photo of their sweetheart with their brain activity as they looked at the neutral image.

A good beginning, we thought. In 1996 we scanned four subjects, two young men and two young women. All were madly in love. The results were encouraging. But my colleague had to withdraw from the experiment due to other professional commitments. Fortunately I had already invited Lucy Brown, an accomplished neuroscientist at the Albert Einstein College of Medicine, to interpret the scanning results—a technologically sophisticated, time-gobbling, and intellectually demanding task. With time we were joined by Art Aron, a talented research psychologist at the State University of New York in Stony Brook, and the gifted Deb Mashek, then a graduate student in the SUNY Stony Brook psychology department.

I had one concern about the design of the experiment. As you recall, lovers have a hard time ***not*** thinking about their beloved. I was afraid that the lover's passionate romantic thoughts, generated as he/she looked at the photo of a sweetheart, would carry over and contaminate their passive thoughts as they looked at the neutral photo. When I discussed this with Art and Deb, Art recommended a "distraction task," a standard psychological procedure used to wash the brain clean of emotion. We settled on a particular "distraction task" that amuses me to this day.

Between looking at the positive photo of the sweetheart and the neutral photo of some boring acquaintance, subjects would be shown a large number (like 8,421) on the screen and be required to mentally count backward from this number in increments of seven. The point: to cleanse the mind of strong feelings between exposure to the beloved and exposure to the neutral stimulus. Try it the next time you are upset, very upset. Pick any large number; then really concentrate on counting backward in increments of seven starting with that number. It's demanding. But it works. At least briefly, feelings simply fade away as you struggle to count accurately.

Before we started to scan more brains of love-stricken men and women, however, we had to be certain of one thing: that a photograph of the beloved would actually stimulate feelings of romantic love more effectively than would a smell, song, love letter, memory, or other object or phenomenon associated with the beloved.

Poets and artists have always known the power of visual images, of course. As William Butler Yeats wrote, "Wine comes in at the mouth / and love comes in at the eye."[15] Most psychologists also assume that the visual image triggers romantic passion. We were convinced of this ourselves. But before we attempted to generate feelings of romantic ecstasy with a photograph, Art, Deb, and I wanted to be positive that love "comes in at the eye" more intensely than through some other sense.

To find out, we launched an ingenious experiment with a device we came to call the love-o-meter.

## *The Love-o-meter*

On a bulletin board for psychology students on the SUNY Stony Brook campus, Art and Deb solicited men and women who were in love. The announcement began with bold letters: "Have you just fallen madly in love?" "Just" and "madly" were the operative words. We sought only candidates who were so intensely in love that they could hardly eat or sleep.

Lots of volunteers contacted Deb at the Stony Brook psychology department, then arrived in person. She selected those who seemed genuinely in love, and gave each several questionnaires designed to provide insights into their personality, their feelings about the beloved, and the duration, intensity, and status of their love affair. Then she asked each to return to the lab a week later, bearing items that made them feel intense romantic passion for their adored one. Back these students came with photographs, letters, e-mails, birthday cards, music tapes, colognes, memories written on sheets of paper, and notes about anticipated future events. They carried them like glass flowers.

Then each subject was prepared for the experiment. First Deb glued three electrodes to different regions of the scalp, thereby connecting the participant to an electroencephalograph (EEG). She told each subject that these wires would record their brain waves during the experiment. Actually, this wasn't true; the machine was not turned on. But we hoped this deception would stimulate each volunteer to be honest. Then, the participant sat in front of a computer screen displaying an icon that looked like a vertically standing thermometer and was given a handheld rotating dial, arching from zero to thirty degrees. By turning this spring-loaded dial, the subject could raise the "mercury" in the thermometer. When he/she released the dial, it returned to zero. We jokingly called this computer-based response device our love-o-meter.

The experiment began. First the subject was shown the photograph of his/her beloved, then a neutral photo of someone else of the same sex or a photograph of nature. Second, each participant read a love letter from the beloved, then a paragraph from a statistics book. Third, each smelled a scent that reminded them of the beloved, then water with weak rubbing alcohol. Fourth, the subject was asked to "think back" to a wonderful moment with the sweetheart, then recall some mundane event such as the last time they washed their hair. Fifth, each heard a song they associated with their sweetheart, then a song sung by characters on the American children's television show *Sesame Street*. Last, each participant was asked to imagine an exhilarating future event with the beloved, then a mundane incident such as brushing teeth. And each assignment was interspersed with our distraction task: mentally counting backward in increments of seven, starting with one from a sequence of large numbers.

The subject's job was to respond to each task by twisting the love-o-meter dial to reflect the intensity of his/her feelings of romantic passion. Eleven women and three men participated; their average age was eighteen and a half. When their responses were recorded and statistically analyzed, the results were revealing: feelings of intense romantic love were triggered almost equally by photographs, songs, and memories of the beloved.[16]

## *Photographs Stimulate Love*

I was not surprised that photographs elicit romantic passion. After all, most of us keep a picture of our true love on our desk. Moreover, as you recall, this visceral reaction to visual images has an anthropological explanation. Humans evolved from tree-living ancestors who needed exceptional vision to survive high above the ground. Those with bad eyesight must have misjudged where fruit and blossoms hung, then missed their mark as they leapt from one branch to another and fell and broke their necks. As a result, all higher primates have large brain regions devoted to the perception and integration of visual stimuli. In fact, for decades psychologists have emphasized the important role of visual appearances in stimulating feelings of romantic attraction.[17]

This experiment confirmed for us that photographs of the beloved actually do elicit romantic bliss. Our experimental design was sound. We could begin to put lovers into the brain scanner and search for the circuitry of romantic ecstasy.

## *The Experiment*

"Have you just fallen madly in love?" We used this line again when we placed a new advertisement on the psychology bulletin board on the SUNY Stony Brook campus. But this time we called for men and women who were willing to recline in a long, dark, cramped, noisy machine while we scanned their brains. Once again, we sought only those who had fallen crazily in love within the last few weeks or months, people whose romantic feelings were fresh, vivid, uncontrollable, and passionate.

They were not difficult to find. In John Donne's words, "Love, all alike, no season knows, nor clime, / Nor hours, days, months, which are the rags of time."[18] Love springs up everywhere, at any time. Students immediately began to call Art's psychology lab to volunteer. Deb weeded out those who had metal in their heads (such as lip, tongue, nose, or face jewelry, or braces on their teeth) that would affect the magnet in the fMRI machine. She also excluded those who were claustrophobic, those taking any kind of antidepressant medication that could affect brain physiology, and men and women who were left-handed. Brain organization can vary with "handedness" and we needed to standardize our sample as much as possible.

At this point, I interviewed each candidate, sometimes for as long as two hours. My first question was always the same: "How long have you been in love?" My second question was the most important: "What percentage of the day and night do you think about your sweetheart?" Because obsessive thinking is a central ingredient of romantic passion, I sought only participants who thought about their beloved almost all of their waking hours. I also looked for men and women who laughed and sighed more than usual during the interview, those who could recall tiny details about their sweethearts, and those who honestly appeared to be yearning for, indeed craving, their beloved.

If a potential subject showed these and other signs of romantic passion, I invited him or her to participate. We acquired two photographs from the subject: one of the beloved and one of an emotionally neutral individual. Generally the latter was someone they had known casually in high school or college. Then we set a date to put each into the brain scanner.

### *The Brain Scanning Procedure*

Not, of course, without a great deal of discussion about what would happen to them while in the fMRI brain scanning machine. I started by telling each participant that I had gone through the experiment myself three times, which I had. I explained that I was somewhat claustrophobic but felt I needed to experience this process before I ushered others through it. I described what would happen in the machine, minute by minute. And I assured each of them there would be no surprises. I needed these men and women to trust me; without this trust, we might end up measuring feelings of suspicion or panic rather than romantic love.

When all seemed ready, we set a time for the scanning. What joy, what anxiety, what curiosity I felt as we made that date.

The procedure was simple, but not easy. First Deb and I made the participant as comfortable as possible in the scanner—a large, horizontal, cylindrical, cream-colored plastic tube that is open at both ends and extends from above the head to about the waist. The subject reclined on a stretcher in this tubular machine in the semidark with one to two feet of space above and alongside them, depending on their size. We put pillows under their knees to relax the back, warmed them with a blanket, nestled their head in a stiff pillow to help them remain motionless during the experiment, and suspended a slanted mirror over their eyes. This way the subject could look out of the scanner to see a screen on which we would show successively each photo, as well as the large number—the distraction task.

After taking preliminary scans to establish basic brain anatomy, the twelve-minute experiment started. First, the subject looked at the photograph of the beloved on the screen for thirty seconds as the scanner recorded blood flow in various brain regions.

Next, the subject viewed a large number, such as 4,673. These numbers changed with each new viewing but each was the same distraction task. For forty seconds the subject was required to mentally count backward from this number in increments of seven.

The participant then looked at the neutral photograph for thirty seconds while the brain was scanned again.

Finally, the subject viewed another large number, this time for twenty seconds, and mentally counted backward from this number in increments of seven.

This cycle (or its reverse) was repeated six times—enabling us to collect some one hundred forty-four scans or pictures of different brain regions across these four conditions for each participant. After the experiment was over, I interviewed each subject again, asking how they felt and what they were thinking about during all parts of the test. And to express our gratitude, we gave each participant $50.00 and a picture of their brain.

We scanned twenty men and women who were deeply and happily in love. Then we scanned twenty more, of a different type—individuals who had recently been jilted, those suffering from rejection in romance. By studying romantic rejection, a devastating aspect of love that happens to just about everybody at one time or another,[19] we hoped to identify the full range of brain regions associated with romantic passion. (My discussion of unrequited love appears in chapter seven.)

## *The Passionate Love Scale*

There was one more part to this experiment. Before our subjects entered the brain scanner, we asked each to fill out several questionnaires, including the one my other colleagues and I had given to 839 Americans and Japanese and a similar survey designed by psychologists Elaine Hatfield and Susan Sprecher called the Passionate Love Scale.[20]

The Passionate Love Scale had fifteen questions about romantic love. Most were very similar to those on my questionnaire. Among them were: "I would feel deep despair if _____ left me." And "Sometimes I feel I can't control my thoughts; they are obsessively on _____." The subject was asked to respond to each statement, noting his/her reaction on a nine-point scale from "not at all true" to "definitely true."

We wanted to compare the brain activity of each subject to what each subject reported on these questionnaires, to see if those who scored high on these love surveys also had more activity in the brain. This way we hoped to answer a question that survey-makers have long puzzled over: Does what a person reports on a questionnaire accurately reflect what is going on in their brain?

We didn't know it at the time, but the Passionate Love Scale would prove remarkably informative about the brain in love.

## *Happily in Love*

I remember distinctly all of the men and women who were scanned, each for some special reason.*

*All names of participants in this experiment have been changed.

One was Bjorn, a young man from a Scandinavian country who was studying in New York. He was in love with Isabel, a woman originally from Brazil who was currently working in London. They talked every day on the phone, he told me, and saw each other on vacations. They had been "dating" for a little less than a year and planned to marry. I mention Bjorn because I learned something valuable from him. This was a blond, bushy-haired, self-contained man with a warm smile, a quiet charm, a sharp intelligence, and a flashing sense of humor. I liked him immediately. But when I first asked him to describe his beloved, he fell silent, utterly mute. For a moment I thought I had lost the phone connection. I recall rather frantically saying to him, "Well, you must like something about Isabel." His reply: "Yawwww."

I had to cajole Bjorn into saying anything whatsoever about his beloved! Eventually he shyly revealed that he daydreamed about Isabel constantly, loved her passionately, and thought about her as much as 95 percent of the day and evening. But Bjorn never expressed that urgent excitement so characteristic of the love-possessed. So I was later astonished when I saw the results of his brain scanning session. When this reserved young man looked at the picture of his sweetheart, his brain "lit up" like a fireworks display. Do still waters run deep?

Bjorn rattled me. His dour countenance masked his inner passion. I didn't think he was consciously trying to deceive me. Instead, he expressed himself in a way that was molded by his biology, his upbringing, and his culture. Yet his outward expressions did not reflect his inner world. This raised a serious question in my mind: How was I to choose appropriate candidates?

I thought about this a lot. Finally, I got a penetrating glimpse of the obvious: I had no choice. I simply had to ask potential participants as many questions as possible, listen carefully to their words, and note any physical signs of elation, energy, focussed attention, possessiveness, and obsessive thinking. And I had to pray that my social skills were good enough to pick people who were genuinely in love.

Our most dramatic subject was Barbara, a tall, fair, red-headed, handsome, and extremely verbal woman in her early twenties. She had met Michael on the beach in New Jersey five months earlier. She was so in love that she was having trouble sleeping. Her mind raced. She felt shy in his company. At times her heart pounded when they spoke on the phone. She obsessively replayed in her mind their times together. She spoke of the "electricity" she felt. She reported that she would "go crazy" when he didn't call. She was wildly jealous, too. Apparently he had lots of women friends and she didn't even like him to talk with one on the phone. When I asked her if she would consider having a second romantic relationship "on the side," she was dumbfounded. Characteristic of almost all lovers, Barbara couldn't conceive of spending time with anyone but Michael. And when I asked her what she liked most about him, she replied, "Chemistry." It was the first time Barbara had been in love. She glowed.

The most arresting response of our happy lovers was that of William. William was quick to understand, intensely smart, amiable, eager to participate, curious about the machine, and interested in my theories about romantic love. We talked easily together before the experiment. But he missed his girlfriend terribly. She had moved to Oregon. And although they were very much in love and in frequent contact, he was suffering from her absence. This was a good sign; I suspected that this adversity had increased his passion. But it was something William said during the post-scanning interview that impressed me most. When he emerged from the machine, I asked him how he felt. William said he felt "incomplete."

Incomplete. To me, no single word better describes love-smitten men and women. Although Aristophanes was joking, he hit upon this fundamental truth about lovers some twenty-five hundred years ago. In Plato's *Symposium,* the Athenian dramatist maintained that originally every human being was a rounded hermaphroditic whole, with four hands and four legs, two faces on one head, four ears, and both sets of genitals. These primal human beings "were terrible in their strength and vigour."[21] One day these monsters tried to outdo the gods. So Zeus sliced each human into two—man and woman. "That's how, long ago, the innate desire of human beings for each other started," Aristophanes explained. "Each one of us is looking for his own matching half."[22] Like William, most lovers feel incomplete until they have achieved emotional union with a beloved.

Bjorn, Barbara, William, and all of our other participants told me a great deal about their personal lives; to all of them I am very grateful. But their brains told us much more about this primordial passion, romantic love.

## *The Brain in Love*

"In the composition of the human frame there is a great deal of inflammable matter, however dormant it may lie for a time, and . . . when the torch is put to it, that which is within you must burst into a blaze."[23] In 1795, President George Washington wrote these lines of advice in a letter to his young step-granddaughter. We have begun to understand that blaze.

Before we could comprehend the results of our scanning, however, we had to make an in-depth analysis of the brain pictures. Here my colleagues did a yeoman's job. There were literally hundreds of intricate steps in this process. And because the technology of brain scanning is so new and so complex, things constantly went wrong—and the analysis had to be redone. But with time, Greg Strong, another talented psychology graduate student at SUNY Stony Brook who had joined our team, was able to put the data in the proper order; Lucy studied the brain scans and determined which areas became active; Art did many statistical analyses. And Art and Lucy did ingenious comparisons between various sectors of the material. All this took enormous time, dedication, knowledge, creativity, insight, and skill.

Finally we saw the results: beautiful pictures of the brain in love. When I first looked at those brain scans, with the active brain regions lit up in bright yellow and deep orange, I felt the way I feel on a summer night when I gaze at the sparkling universe: overwhelming awe. But to understand what I saw, you must know a little bit about the furniture in your head.

The brain is composed of many parts or regions. Each has particular functions. And each communicates with other brain regions via nerve cells or neurons—some 10 billion of them. These nerve cells produce, store, and distribute neurotransmitters of different types; some, for example, synthesize dopamine, norepinephrine, and/or serotonin. When a neuron is electrically stimulated by a nearby neuron, the impulse often prompts these neurotransmitters to exit from a nerve cell, sail across a tiny gap, or synapse, and dock at "receptor sites" on the next nerve cell. This way neurotransmitters send an electrical impulse along, cell by cell.

Each nerve cell has about one thousand of these synaptic connections; and there are some 10 trillion synapses between nerve cells in the human brain. Some machine! Each nerve cell communicates only with specific others, however, producing nerve networks that connect specific brain parts and integrate our thoughts, memories, sensations, emotions, and motivations. Scientists call these networks of nerves and brain parts "circuits," "systems," or "modules."

The fMRI machine that we were using only shows blood flow activity in specific brain regions. But because scientists know which kinds of nerves connect which kinds of brain regions, they can surmise which brain chemicals are active when specific brain regions begin to glow with increased activity.

Many brain parts became active in each of our love-struck subjects.[24] However, two regions appear to be central to the exquisite experience of being in love.

## *The Reward System of the Brain*

Perhaps our most important finding was activity in the caudate nucleus. This is a large C-shaped region that sits deep near the center of your brain (see diagram on page 70). It is primitive; it is part of what is called the reptilian brain or R-complex because this brain region evolved long before the mammals proliferated some 65 million years ago. Our brain scans showed that parts of the body and the tail of the caudate became particularly active as a lover gazed at the photo of a sweetheart.[25]

I was astonished. Scientists have long known that this brain region directs bodily movement. Only recently have they come to realize that this enormous engine is part of the brain's "reward system," the mind's network for general arousal, sensations of pleasure, and the motivation to acquire rewards.[26] The caudate helps us detect and perceive a reward, discriminate between rewards, *prefer* a particular reward, anticipate a reward, and expect a reward. It produces motivation to acquire a reward and plans specific movements to obtain a reward. The caudate is also associated with the acts of paying attention and learning.[27]

Not only did our subjects exhibit activity in the caudate, but the more passionate they were, the more active their caudate was.

We discovered this in a curious way. Remember the Passionate Love Scale that our subjects filled out before entering the brain scanning

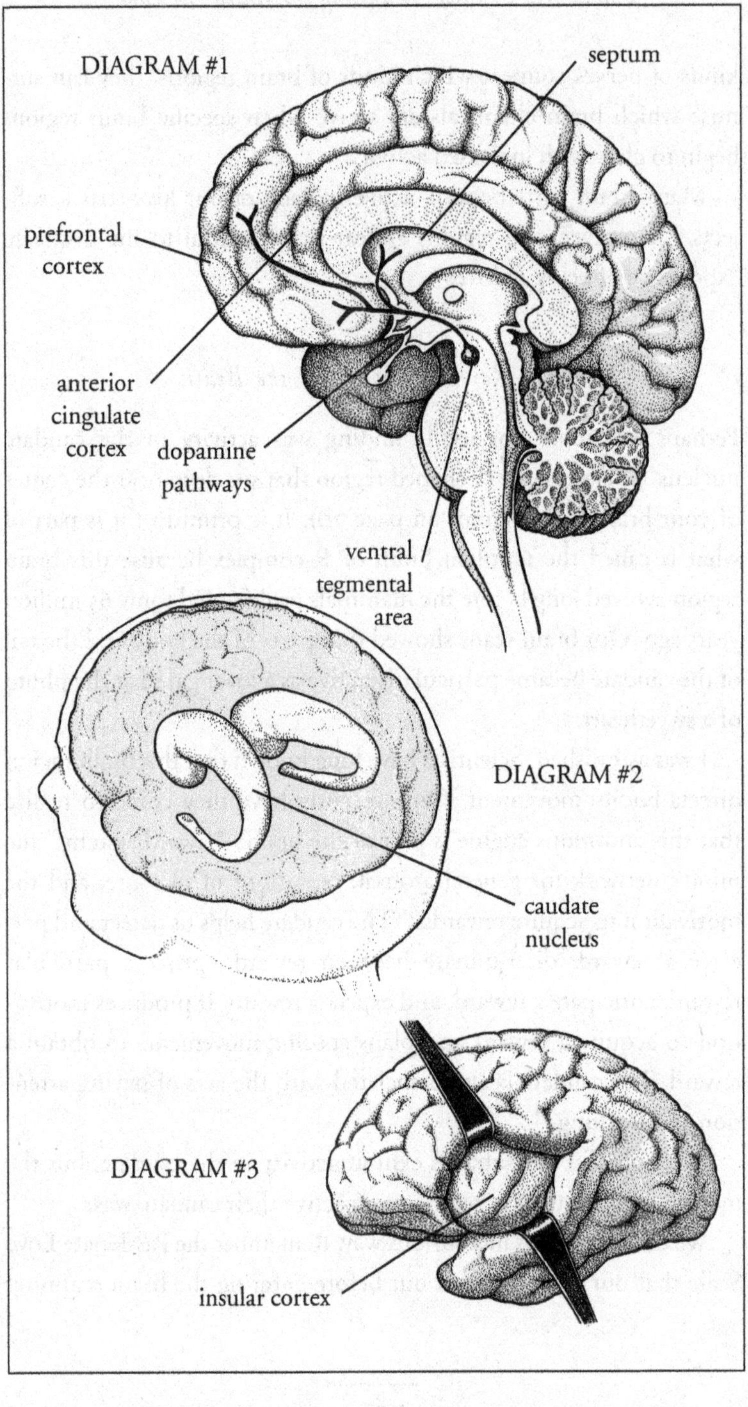
DIAGRAM #1
septum
prefrontal cortex
anterior cingulate cortex
dopamine pathways
ventral tegmental area
DIAGRAM #2
caudate nucleus
DIAGRAM #3
insular cortex

machine? When we compared each subject's responses on this questionnaire with the activity shown in their brains, we found a positive correlation: those who scored higher on the Passionate Love Scale also showed more activity in a specific region of the caudate when they looked at the picture of their sweetheart.

How remarkable. Scientists and businesspeople have long wondered whether self-report questionnaires actually reflect one's inner feelings. In this case, the answer was yes. Our team would be among the first to show a direct link between responses to a survey questionnaire and a specific pattern of brain activation.

We also found activity in other regions of the reward system, including areas of the septum and a brain region that becomes active when people eat chocolate.[28] Chocolate can be addictive. In chapter eight I will maintain that romantic love is addictive, too.

### *The Dopamine Mother Lode*

Another striking result from our fMRI experiment was activity in the ventral tegmental area (VTA), a central part of the reward circuitry of the brain.[29]

This result was what I was looking for. I had hypothesized, as you know, that romantic love is associated with elevated levels of dopamine and/or norepinephrine.[30] The VTA is a mother lode for dopamine-making cells. With their tentacle-like axons, these nerve cells distribute dopamine to many brain regions, including the caudate nucleus (see diagram).[31] And as this sprinkler system sends dopamine to many brain parts, it produces focussed attention,[32] as well as fierce energy, concentrated motivation to attain a reward, and feelings of elation, even mania[33]—the core feelings of romantic love.

No wonder lovers talk all night or walk till dawn, write extravagant poetry and self-revealing e-mails, cross continents or oceans to hug for just a weekend, change jobs or lifestyles, even die for one another. Drenched in chemicals that bestow focus, stamina, and vigor, and driven by the motivating engine of the brain, lovers succumb to a Herculean courting urge.

That "inflammable matter" that Founding Father George Washington spoke of is, at least in part, dopamine churning up the caudate nucleus and other parts of the brain's reward system—a primordial brain network that drives the lover to focus his or her attention on life's grandest prize—a mate who may pass their DNA toward eternity.

## *How Love Changes*

During our experiment we also discovered one way in which love changes over time. Our insight was due to a remarkable coincidence. In 2000, while we were in the middle of our project, scientists at University College, London, announced the completion of a similar experiment.[34] Using an fMRI brain scanner, Andreas Bartels and Semir Zeki examined brain activity in seventeen subjects who reported being "deeply, truly and madly in love." Eleven were women; all were between the ages of twenty-one and thirty-seven; and all looked at a photograph of their beloved, as well as photos of three friends of similar age, sex, and length of friendship.

The London experiment was a distinct achievement. Bartels and Zeki found several brain regions that become active while subjects gaze at pictures of a sweetheart. Particularly important, they found activity in one of the same regions of the caudate nucleus. What joy. Two research teams on different continents, with different subjects from different ethnic groups and of different general ages, in somewhat different experiments, found activity in the same brain structure. The caudate nucleus—with its supercharge of dopamine—must be the furnace of human romantic love.

However, the London data also told us something about how love develops across time. We hadn't planned to investigate how love changes. But the London study subjects were in love for an average duration of 2.3 years while ours were in love a mean duration of seven months. And their men and women showed activity in two regions—the anterior cingulate cortex and the insular cortex—whereas ours showed none (see diagram on page 70). These differences provoked us to compare the subjects in our study with one another.

Sure enough, our subjects who were in *longer* relationships showed activity in the anterior cingulate cortex and the insular cortex, just like the London study.

We don't know what this actually means. The anterior cingulate gyrus is a region where emotions, attention, and working memory interact.[35] Some parts are associated with happy states; others involve awareness of one's own emotional state and the ability to assess other people's feelings during social interactions; and some are associated with split-second emotional reactions to a win or loss, thereby judging a reward's value.[36] The insular cortex collects data from the body regarding external touch and temperature, as well as internal pain and activities of the stomach, gut, and other viscera. With this brain part we register "butterflies" in the stomach, a pounding heart, and our many other bodily reactions. Parts of the insular cortex also process the emotions.

So we established that as a relationship lengthens, brain regions associated with emotions, memory, and attention begin to respond in new ways. Exactly what these brain parts are doing, no one knows. Is the brain laying down and consolidating emotional memories of the love relationship?[37] Are we using our emotions to analyze the relationship? We all know love changes over time; when we come to understand these results, they may tell us how and why.

Our New York team also found several gender differences in romantic passion. But I will discuss these findings and their implications in chapter five.

## *The Drive to Love*

All these data had a definite effect on me—they changed my understanding of romantic love. For many years I had regarded this wonderful experience as a constellation of related *emotions* that ranged from elation to despair. But psychologists distinguish between emotions and *motivations*—brain systems oriented around planning and pursuit of a specific want or need. And our colleague, Art Aron, was wedded to the idea that romantic love was not an emotion but a motivation system designed to enable suitors to build and maintain an intimate relationship with a preferred mating partner.[38]

Indeed, because of Art's dedication to this idea, we had begun our brain scanning project with two hypotheses: my hypothesis that romantic love is associated with dopamine and/or other closely related neurotransmitters in the brain; and Art's theory that romantic love is primarily a motivation system, rather than an emotion.

As it turns out, our results suggest that both hypotheses are correct. Romantic love does seem to be associated with dopamine. And because this passion emanates from the caudate nucleus, motivation and goal-oriented behaviors are involved.

In fact, these findings prompted me to come to an even broader consideration: *I came to believe that romantic love is a primary motivation system in the brain—in short, a fundamental human mating drive.*

Neuroscientist Don Pfaff defines a drive as a neural state that energizes and directs behavior to acquire a particular biological *need* to survive or reproduce.[39] We have lots of drives. They lie along a continuum. Some, like thirst and the need for warmth, cannot be extinguished until satisfied. The sex drive, hunger, and the maternal instinct, on the other hand, can often be redirected, even quelled with time and effort. I think the experience of falling in love lies somewhere along this continuum.

First of all, like drives, romantic attraction is tenacious; it is very hard to extinguish. Emotions, on the other hand, come and go; you can be happy in the morning and angry in the afternoon.

Like drives, romantic love is focussed on a specific reward, the beloved, in the same way that hunger is focussed on food. Emotions, like disgust, pin themselves to an immense variety of objects and ideas. In fact, romantic love is linked with many diverse emotions depending on whether this urge is being satisfied or frustrated.

Like drives, romantic love is not associated with any particular facial expression. All of the primary emotions—among them anger, fear, joy, surprise, and disgust—have stereotypic facial looks.

Like drives, romantic love is exceedingly difficult to control. It is harder to curb thirst, for example, than it is to control an emotion, such as anger.

Very important, all of the basic drives are associated with elevated levels of central dopamine.[40] So is romantic love.

And like all the other drives, romantic love is a need, a craving. We need food. We need water. We need warmth. And the lover feels he/she *needs* the beloved. Plato had it right over two thousand years ago. The god of love "lives in a state of need."[41]

## *Love's Complex Chemistry*

Undoubtedly many other brain systems contribute to this "pulsing rush of Longing," as Homer called it. As you remember, I initially hypothesized that norepinephrine might be involved because it is so closely related to dopamine and produces so many of the same feelings and behaviors. I still suspect norepinephrine contributes to the passion of romance; we just haven't yet devised the appropriate experiment to establish this.

Low levels of serotonin produce obsessive thinking—a central component of romantic love. So I think someday we may find that this chemical contributes to romantic ardor, too.[42]

The prefrontal cortex must be involved. This assemblage of brain regions that lie behind the forehead is called the "central executive" because it collects data from our senses, weighs them, integrates thoughts with feelings, makes choices, and controls our basic drives (see diagram on page 70). It is here that we reason, deliberate, and decide. With various regions of the prefrontal cortex we also monitor rewards. And several parts have direct connections to the caudate nucleus.[43] Someday someone will identify those regions of the prefrontal cortex that help to orchestrate romantic love.

But we are coming to some understanding of the drive to love.

And what an elegant design. This passion emanates from the motor of the mind, the caudate nucleus; and it is fueled by at least one of nature's most powerful stimulants, dopamine. When one's passion is returned, the brain tacks on positive emotions, such as elation and hope. When one's love is spurned or thwarted instead, the brain links this motivation with negative feelings, such as despair and rage. And all the while, regions of the prefrontal cortex monitor the pursuit, planning tactics, calculating gains and losses, and registering one's progress toward the goal: emotional, physical, even spiritual union with the beloved.

"The BRAIN—is wider than the sky—," wrote Emily Dickinson.[44] Indeed, this three-pound blob can generate a need so intense that all the world has sung of it: romantic love. And to make our lives even more complex, romantic passion is intricately enmeshed with two other basic mating drives, the sex drive and the urge to build a deep attachment to a romantic partner. Ah, the web of love. How these forces feed the flame of life.

# 4

# Web of Love:

## *Lust, Romance, and Attachment*

O love is the crooked thing,
There is nobody wise enough
To find out all that is in it,
For he would be thinking of love
Till the stars had run away
And the shadows eaten the moon.
Ah, penny, brown penny, brown penny,
One cannot begin it too soon.

William Butler Yeats
"Brown Penny"

Love is "as sweet and musical / As bright Apollo's lute, strung with his hair. / And when Love speaks, the voices of all the gods / Makes heaven drowsy with the harmony."[1] Love is a harmony, as Shakespeare wrote, sometimes even a cacophony of sensations. Exuberance, tenderness, compassion, possessiveness, rapture, adoration, longing, despair: romance is a kaleidoscopic pattern of shifting needs and feelings all tethered to a celestial being on whose slightest word or smile one dangles, spinning with hope and joy and craving. Complexity, thy name is love.

Yet with time and circumstance, nature has built a few major chords within this symphony. Romantic love is deeply entwined with two other mating drives: *lust*—the craving for sexual gratification; and *attachment*—the feelings of calm, security, and union with a long-term partner.[2]

Each of these basic mating drives travels along different pathways in the brain. Each produces different behaviors, hopes, and dreams. And each is associated with different neurochemicals. Lust is associated primarily with the hormone testosterone in both men and women. Romantic love is linked with the natural stimulant dopamine and perhaps norepinephrine and serotonin. And feelings of male-female attachment are produced primarily by the hormones oxytocin and vasopressin.

Moreover, each brain system evolved to direct a different aspect of reproduction. Lust evolved to motivate individuals to seek sexual union with almost *any* semi-appropriate partner. Romantic love emerged to drive men and women to focus their mating attention on a preferred individual, thereby conserving invaluable courtship time and energy. And the brain circuitry for male-female attachment developed to enable our ancestors to live with this mate at least long enough to rear a single child through infancy together.[3]

All three of these brain networks—lust, romantic attraction, and attachment—are multipurpose systems. In addition to its reproductive purpose, the sex drive serves to make and keep friends, provide pleasure and adventure, tone muscles, and relax the mind. Romantic love can stimulate you to sustain a loving partnership or drive you to fall in love with a new person and initiate divorce. And feelings of attachment enable us to express genuine affection for children, family, and friends, as well as a beloved.

Nature is conservative. When she has a good design, she sticks with it, expanding its uses to suit many situations. But the primary purpose of these interlocking drives is to motivate us to seek an array of sexual partners, choose one to dote upon, then remain emotionally engaged with "him" or "her" at least long enough to rear a child together—the basics of the mating game.

To understand how romantic passion affects the sex drive and feelings of long-term attachment, I embarked on a research project with Jonathan Stieglitz, then a student at Rutgers University. We mined MedLine, PubMed, and other search engines on the Internet for academic articles illustrating how the chemistry of these three mating drives—lust, romantic attraction, and attachment—affect one another.

Indeed, romantic love weaves its way through these other brain networks in ways that both enrich and tear the fabric of our lives.

## *On Lust*

"What arms and shoulders did I touch and see, / How apt her breasts were to be pressed by me, / How smooth a belly under her waist saw I, / How large a leg, and what a lusty thigh. / To leave the rest, all liked me passing well; / I clinged her naked body, down she fell: / Judge you the rest, being tired she bade me kiss; / Jove send me more such afternoons as this!"[4] Ovid, the Roman poet, was one of countless millions who have savored lust.

Lust is a primordial human feeling. It is unpredictable, too. The craving for sexual fulfillment can pop up in your mind as you are driving in your car, watching a movie on TV, reading in the office, or daydreaming on the beach. And this urge is very different from the feeling of romantic love. In fact, few people in Western societies confuse the elation of romance with the longing for sexual release.[5]

People in far different cultures also easily distinguish between these feelings.[6] On the Polynesian island of Mangaia, "real love" is called *inangaro kino,* a state of romantic passion quite distinct from one's sexual desires. In their native language, the Taita of Kenya call lust *ashiki* while they refer to love as *pendo*.[7] And in Caruaru, a town in northeast Brazil, locals say, "*Amor* is when you feel a desire to always be with her, you breathe her, eat her, drink her, you are always thinking of her, you don't manage to live without her."[8] *Paixao,* on the other hand, is "horniness" and *tesao* is "a very strong sexual attraction for a person."[9]

These people are correct to regard these feelings as distinct. Scientists have recently established that lust and romantic love are associated with different constellations of brain regions.[10] In one study researchers scanned the brains of a group of young heterosexual men using the fMRI brain scanner. The men were shown three types of videos: some were erotic, some relaxing, some related to sports.[11] Each volunteer wore a custom-built pneumatic pressure cuff around his penis to record firmness. The pattern of brain activity was quite different from the one we found among the love-sick subjects in our brain scanning project.

Lust and romantic love are not the same.

And just as people everywhere have concocted love potions to spur romance, they have tried all sorts of potions to trigger lust—what an Italian proverb calls "the oldest lion of them all."

## *The Hormone of Desire*

"Candy is dandy, but liquor is quicker," quipped Ogden Nash. Everywhere humankind has used what they hoped was an aphrodisiac to trigger lust. When the tomato first crossed the Atlantic from the Americas, the Europeans thought this juicy red fruit would spark the sexual appetite; they called it the "love apple." Shark's fins, bird's nest soup, powdered rhinoceros horn, curry, chutney, mandrake root, chocolate, hyena eyes, caviar, clams, oysters, lobsters, dove brains, goose tongues, apples, bananas, cherries, dates, figs, peaches, pomegranates, asparagus, garlic, beer, perspiration: scents and tastes and ointments of dazzling variety have been employed to charm reluctant partners into bed.

The Elizabethans served free prunes in brothels because they were convinced this spurred lust. In past centuries Arabs tried to lure hesitant women into sampling a bit of camel hump to pique their sexual desire. Pliny wrote that hippopotamus snouts would do the trick. The Aztecs saw sexual magic in goat and rabbit parts because these animals were fast breeders. Sea slugs caught the fancy of the Chinese, largely because these strange animals enlarge when touched. And Europeans historically pulverized a certain type of beetle found in southern Europe to incite sexual desire; they called it Spanish fly.[12]

Eating increases blood pressure and the pulse rate, raises body temperature, and sometimes makes us sweat, physiological changes that also occur with sex. Perhaps this is why men and women have long associated different foods with sexual excitement. But nature has made only one true substance to stimulate sexual desire in men and women—testosterone, and to a lesser degree, its kin, the other male sex hormones.

This is well established. Men and women who have higher circulating levels of testosterone tend to engage in more sexual activity.[13] Male athletes who inject testosterone to elevate their strength and stamina have more sexual thoughts, more morning erections, more sexual encounters, and more orgasms. And women who take testosterone in middle age boost their sexual desire. The male libido peaks in the early twenties, when levels of testosterone are highest. And many women feel more sexual desire around ovulation, when levels of testosterone increase.[14]

As elevated levels of testosterone stimulate the sex drive, declining levels dampen it. Both sexes have fewer sexual fantasies, masturbate less regularly, and engage in less intercourse as they age.[15] Poor health, unhappiness, overwork, lack of opportunity, laziness, and boredom undoubtedly contribute to this waning lust. But with age, levels of testosterone decline, often depressing sex desire.

Some two-thirds of middle-aged women do not experience any decline in libido, however.[16] This, too, may be due to testosterone. As the estrogens decline with menopause, levels of testosterone and the other androgens become unmasked: these potent hormones can finally express themselves more fully. Indeed, they do. In one study of middle-aged women, almost 40 percent complained that they were not having enough sex.[17]

When it comes to sexual desire, people vary, in part because levels of testosterone are inherited.[18] Levels also fluctuate according to the day, the week, the year, and the life cycle. Moreover, the balance of testosterone, estrogen, and other bodily ingredients, as well as social circumstances and a host of other factors, all play a role in when, where, and how often we feel lust.[19] Nevertheless, testosterone is central to this appetite. And this primordial chemical can swamp the thinking brain. As poet Tony Hoagland said of lust, "As long as there is desire, we are not safe."[20]

Men and women are often sexually stimulated by different things, however. Men like to look. They are sexually turned on by visual stimuli. Even when men fantasize, they conjure up vivid images of body parts and copulation.[21] This lascivious peering probably boosts levels of testosterone. When male monkeys see a sexually available female or watch a companion copulate with a female, their levels of testosterone soar.[22] So the men who go to strip bars or look at "girlie" magazines are probably boosting levels of testosterone and triggering lust.

Women are generally more turned on by romantic words, images, and themes in films and stories. Women's sexual fantasies also include more affection, commitment, and sex with familiar partners.[23] And women like to yield. About 70 percent of American men and women fantasize while making love.[24] But as conquest is at the core of most men's mental plots, active surrender is prevalent in women's sexual reveries.[25]

These tastes for conquest and surrender have nothing to do with rape. Less than half of 1 percent of men enjoy forcing a woman into coitus; and less than half of 1 percent of women want to be coerced into copulation.[26] Still, American women are twice as likely as men to actively fantasize about being "done to" as opposed to "doing."[27]

Danger, novelty, particular smells and sounds, love letters, candy, endearing conversations, sexy clothes, swaying music, elegant dinners: many cues can trigger that "eternal thirst," as poet Pablo Neruda called the sex drive. How do feelings of romantic love affect this primordial brain circuit, lust?

## *Romance Triggers Lust*

Surely you have noticed that when you fall in love, your ardor stimulates the sex drive. Novelists, dramatists, poets, and songwriters all rhapsodize about this urge to kiss, cuddle, and make love to someone you adore.

Why do we feel lust when we fall in love?

Because dopamine, the liquor of romance, can stimulate the release of testosterone, the hormone of sexual desire.[28]

This relationship between elevated levels of dopamine and sexual arousal, frequency of intercourse, and positive sexual function is common in animals.[29] When dopamine is injected into a male rat's bloodstream, for example, it stimulates copulatory behaviors.[30] Moreover, when a male laboratory rat is placed in an adjacent cage where he can see or smell an estrous female, he becomes sexually excited; with this, levels of dopamine also rise.[31] And when the barrier is removed and he is allowed to copulate, levels of dopamine rise even higher.[32]

Dopamine can also stimulate lust in humans.[33] When men and women who are depressed take drugs that elevate levels of dopamine in the brain, their sex drive regularly improves.[34]

A friend of mine in her thirties told me a remarkable story regarding this. She had been mildly depressed for several years, so recently she began to take one of the newer antidepressants (one without negative sexual side effects) that elevates levels of dopamine in the brain. A month after starting this drug she not only thought more about sex, but she had also begun to have multiple orgasms with her boyfriend. I suspect her sudden change in sexual desire and sexual function occurred because the pill she was taking daily to enhance dopamine triggered the release of testosterone as well.

This positive relationship between dopamine and testosterone may also explain why people feel so sexy when they go on vacation, try some new trick in the bedroom, or make love to a new partner. Novel experiences drive up levels of dopamine in the brain—hence they can also trigger the brain chemistry of lust.

Norepinephrine, another stimulant that probably plays a role in romantic love, also stimulates the sex drive. Addicts who take amphetamines, known as "uppers" or "speed," say their sex drive can be constant. This lustiness probably stems from the same biological equation: amphetamines largely boost norepinephrine (as well as dopamine). And norepinephrine can stimulate the production of testosterone.[35]

Once again some caveats: the dosage of all these chemicals, as well as the timing of their release in the brain, makes a difference. None of these interactions are direct or simple. But generally speaking, dopamine and norepinephrine spark sexual desire,[36] most likely by elevating levels of testosterone. No wonder new lovers stay up all night caressing. The chemistry of romance ignites the most powerful urge of nature: the drive to copulate.

This chemical connection between romantic love and lust makes evolutionary sense. After all, if romantic love evolved to stimulate mating with a "special" other, it *should* trigger the drive to have sex with this beloved, too.

## *Does Lust Trigger Romance?*

But is the reverse true? Can lust stimulate amour? Can you climb in bed with "just a friend" or even a stranger, then suddenly fall in love with him or her?

Ovid, a man who had many love affairs, believed that a strong sexual attraction could often provoke a person to fall in love.[37] But lust does not always trigger romantic ardor, as many people know. Most sexually liberated contemporary adults have had sex with someone they were not in love with. Many have even copulated with this "friend" regularly. But, alas, they never felt the exhilaration of romantic passion for this bed partner. Lust does not necessarily lead to the passion and obsession of romantic love.

In fact, there is a great deal of data to the contrary. Athletes who inject synthetic androgens to build muscles don't fall in love as they take their drugs. When middle-aged men and women inject testosterone or apply testosterone cream to various body parts to stimulate their sex drive, their sexual thoughts and fantasies increase.[38] But they don't fall in love either. The brain circuitry of lust does not necessarily ignite the furnace of romance.

This is not to say that lust never triggers romantic love. It can. A middle-aged friend of mine is a good example. She had been having sex with "just a friend" for almost three years. These were sporadic events, she told me; she and her friend had sex no more than two or three times annually. Then one summer evening, about five minutes after coupling with him, she fell profoundly in love with him. At that moment the obsessive thinking, the pining, and the rapture started.

In the weeks and months that followed, she told me, she lay awake at night and thought of him constantly, waited by the phone to hear his voice, dressed attractively to win him, and fantasized about a life together. Fortunately he loved her, too.

"*Naso pasyo, maya basyo.*" Women in rural western Nepal use this off-color saying to express the same phenomenon. It means, "The penis entered and love arrived."[39]

I think biology contributes to this spontaneous love for a sex partner. Sexual activity can increase brain levels of dopamine and norepinephrine in male rats.[40] Even without sexual activity, increasing levels of testosterone can elevate levels of dopamine[41] and norepinephrine[42] as well as suppress levels of serotonin.[43] In short, the hormone of sexual desire can trigger the release of the brain's elixirs for romantic passion. As my friend cuddled and copulated with "just a friend," I think she triggered her brain circuit for romance and fell in love.

That "ol' black magic" is a fickle force. The chemistry of romantic love can trigger the chemistry of sexual desire and the fuel of sexual desire can trigger the fuel of romance. This is why it is dangerous to copulate with someone with whom you don't wish to become involved. Although you intend to have casual sex, you might just fall in love.

Romantic passion also has a special relationship with feelings of attachment.

## *On Attachment*

"Who ordered that their longing's fire / Should be, as soon as kindled, cooled?"[44] Poet Matthew Arnold mourned the passing of romantic love.

Love changes over time. It becomes deeper, calmer. No longer do couples talk all day or dance till dawn. The mad passion, the ecstasy, the longing, the obsessive thinking, the heightened energy: all dissolve. But if you are fortunate, this magic transforms itself into new feelings of security, comfort, calm, and union with your partner. Psychologist Elaine Hatfield calls this feeling "companionate love," a feeling of happy togetherness with someone whose life has become deeply entwined with yours.[45] I call this complex feeling "attachment."

And just as men and women intuitively distinguish between the feelings of romantic love and those of lust, people just as easily distinguish between feelings of romance and attachment.

Nisa, a !Kung Bushman woman of the Kalahari Desert of Botswana, explained this feeling of man-woman attachment succinctly to anthropologist Marjorie Shostak. "When two people are first together," Nisa said, "their hearts are on fire and their passion is very great. After a while, the fire cools and that's how it stays. They continue to love each other, but it's in a different way—warm and dependable."[46]

The Taita of Kenya would agree. They say that love comes in two forms, an irresistible longing, a "kind of sickness," and a deep enduring affection for another.[47] Brazilians have a poetic proverb that distinguishes between these two feelings, saying, "Love is born in a glance and matures in a smile."[48] And for the Koreans, "*sarang*" is a word close to the Western concept of romantic love, while "*chong*" is more like feelings of long-term attachment. But perhaps Abigail Adams, the wife of America's second president, said it best, writing to John in 1793, "Years subdue the ardor of passion, but in lieu thereof friendship and affection deep-rooted subsists, which defies the ravages of time, and whilst the vital flame exists."[49]

## *The Chemistry of Attachment*

Scientists began to examine this brain system, attachment, decades ago when British psychiatrist John Bowlby proposed that humans have evolved an innate attachment system consisting of specific behaviors and physiological responses.[50] Only recently, however, have researchers begun to understand which brain chemicals produce this feeling of fusion with a long-term mate. Most now believe that vasopressin and oxytocin, closely related hormones made largely in the hypothalamus and the gonads, produce many of the behaviors associated with attachment.

But to grasp how these hormones generate the sensation of union with a sweetheart, I must reintroduce you to the American midwesterners discussed earlier: prairie voles. As you recall, these brown-gray, mouselike rodents form pair-bonds to rear their young; some 90 percent mate for life with a single partner. A few years ago neuroscientists Sue Carter, Tom Insel, and others pinpointed the cause of this attachment in males. As the male prairie vole ejaculates, levels of vasopressin increase in the brain, triggering his spousal and parenting zeal.[51]

Is vasopressin nature's cocktail for male attachment?

To investigate this hypothesis, scientists then injected vasopressin into the brains of *virgin* male prairie voles raised in the lab. These males immediately began to defend the space around them from other males, an aspect of pair formation in prairie voles. And when each was introduced to a female, he became instantaneously possessive of her.[52] Moreover, when these same scientists blocked the production of vasopressin in the brain, male prairie voles acted like cads instead—copulating with a female, then abandoning her for another mating opportunity.

Nature has given male mammals a chemical to feel the paternal instinct: vasopressin.

## *Oxytocin: Another Cocktail for Devotion?*

"So we grew together, / Like to a double cherry, / seeming parted, / But yet a union in partition; / Two lovely berries moulded on one stem."[53] Few poets write about the durable feeling of attachment, perhaps because this drive rarely compels one to compose passionate verse in the dead of night. These lines by Shakespeare are an exception. Yet the feeling of attachment must be a common sensation among all birds and mammals, because it is associated not only with vasopressin but also with oxytocin—a related hormone that is ubiquitous in nature.[54]

Like vasopressin, oxytocin is made in the hypothalamus, as well as in the ovaries and testes. Unlike vasopressin, oxytocin is released in all female mammals (including women) during the birthing process.[55] It initiates contractions of the uterus and stimulates the mammary glands to produce milk. But scientists have now established that oxytocin also stimulates bonding between a mother and her infant.

More important, many now believe that oxytocin is also involved in the feelings of adult male-female attachment.[56]

You have undoubtedly felt the power of these two "satisfaction hormones," as vasopressin and oxytocin are sometimes called. We secrete them at two poignant moments during sexual intercourse: during stimulation of the genitals and/or nipples[57] and during orgasm. At orgasm, levels of vasopressin dramatically increase in men and levels of oxytocin rise in women.[58] These "cuddle chemicals" undoubtedly contribute to that sense of fusion, closeness, and attachment you can feel after sweet sex with a beloved.

How does the chemistry of attachment affect feelings of lust and romantic love?

## *Does Lust Dampen Attachment?*

The chemical components of attachment have complex effects on both the sex drive and feelings of romantic passion.

Under some circumstances, testosterone can elevate levels of vasopressin[59] and oxytocin[60] in animals, increasing attachment behaviors such as mutual grooming, scent marking, and defending a nesting site.[61] The reverse can also happen: oxytocin and vasopressin can increase testosterone production under some conditions.[62] In short, the chemistry of attachment can trigger lust and the chemistry of lust can trigger expressions of attachment.

But all these hormones can also have negative effects on one another. Increasing levels of testosterone can sometimes *drive down* levels of vasopressin (and oxytocin) and elevated levels of vasopressin can *decrease* levels of testosterone.[63] This inverse relationship between lust and attachment is "dose-dependent"; it varies depending on the quantities, timing, and interactions among several hormones.[64] But high levels of testosterone can reduce attachment. And there is a great deal of evidence that this happens to people regularly—sometimes with disastrous effects.

Men with high baseline levels of testosterone marry less frequently, have more adulterous affairs, commit more spousal abuse, and divorce more often. As a man's marriage becomes less stable, his levels of testosterone rise. With divorce, his testosterone levels rise even more. And single men tend to have higher levels of testosterone than married men.[65]

The reverse can also happen: as a man becomes more and more attached to his family, levels of testosterone can decline. In fact, at the birth of a child, expectant fathers experience a significant decline in levels of testosterone.[66] Even when a man holds a baby, levels of testosterone decrease.

This negative relationship between testosterone and attachment is also seen in other creatures. Male cardinals and blue jays flit from one female to the next; they never stick around to parent their young. These profligate fathers have high levels of testosterone. Males of species that form monogamous pair-bonds and remain with this mate to father infants, however, have much lower levels of testosterone during the parenting phase of the breeding season.[67] And when scientists surgically pumped testosterone into monogamous male sparrows, these faithful fathers abandoned their nests, their young, and their "wives" to court other females.[68]

As I have said, the interactions between these chemical systems for lust and attachment are complex and variable. But there is data to suggest that as people grow like "two lovely berries moulded on one stem," the chemistry of attachment can dampen lust. This is probably why men and women in long stable marriages tend to spend less time in their bedroom making love.

But what about romance? How does dopamine, the fuel of romantic love, affect levels of vasopressin and oxytocin, the brain's intoxicants for attachment? Do deep feelings of union and attachment enhance or stifle romantic passion?

## *Romance* and *Attachment?*

Nature isn't tidy. She likes options. And there is no definite relationship between the neurotransmitters of romance and the hormones of attachment. As should be said of all these chemical interactions: it depends.

Under some circumstances, dopamine and norepinephrine can stimulate the release of oxytocin and vasopressin[69]—and contribute to one's growing feelings of attachment. But increasing levels of oxytocin (found in both men and women) can also interfere with dopamine and norepinephrine pathways in the brain, *decreasing* the impact of these excitatory substances.[70] Hence the chemistry of attachment can quell the chemistry of romance.

There is a great deal of anecdotal evidence for this negative chemical relationship between attachment and romantic love. People around the world say the exhilaration of romance wanes as their marriage or partnership becomes increasingly stable, comfortable, and secure. Some even go to psychiatrists or marriage counselors to try to renew romantic passion in their relationship. Some seek romance outside their marriage instead. Some divorce. And many settle into a long-term partnership devoid of romantic bliss.

I have mixed feelings about this fate nature has decreed. First, many of us would die of sexual exhaustion if romantic love flourished endlessly in a relationship. We wouldn't get to work on time or concentrate on anything except "him" or "her." Moreover, as romantic love matures, it often expands into hundreds of complex and fulfilling feelings of attachment that produce an enormously intricate, interesting, and emotionally rewarding union with another living soul.

At the same time, I think you can keep the primal flame of romantic ecstasy alive in a long-term comfortable relationship, as I will discuss in chapter eight.

But to maintain that magic you have to play a few tricks on the brain. Why? Because romantic love did not evolve to help us maintain a stable, enduring partnership. It evolved for different purposes: to drive ancestral men and women to prefer, choose, and pursue specific mating partners, then start the mating process and remain sexually faithful to "him" or "her" long enough to conceive a child. After the child is born, however, parents need a new set of chemicals and brain networks to rear their infant as a team—the chemistry of attachment. As a result, feelings of attachment often dampen the ecstasy of romance, replacing it with a deep sense of union with a mate.

## *The Trellis of Love*

In spite of this evolutionary trajectory of loving, in which romantic passion gradually transforms into feelings of deep attachment, these three brain circuits—lust, romantic love, and attachment—can ignite in any combination.

In the traditional Western course of events, you meet a man or woman. You talk and laugh and begin to "date." Rapidly or gradually you fall in love. As the camaraderie escalates to bliss, your sex drive surges into higher action. Then after months or years of joyous times together, your raging romantic passion and raw sexual hunger begin to wane, replaced by what Theodor Reik called that warm "after-glow,"[71] attachment. In this scenario, romantic love has triggered lust; then with time, these raw feelings of passion and desire have settled into a sinew of emotional union and commitment—attachment.

Lust, romance, and attachment can visit you in other sequences, however. You may begin a liaison with someone for whom you feel only sexual desire. For a few months you have sex irregularly. Then one day you begin to feel possessive. Soon you fall in love with "him" or "her." And over time you become deeply emotionally entwined. In this case, lust has preceded romance, which then led to attachment.

Then there are couples who actually begin their relationship with feelings of attachment. They quickly achieve emotional union in the college dorm, at the office, or in their social circle. They become fast friends. With time, this attachment metamorphoses into romantic passion—which finally triggers lust.

Alas, many of us also have periods in our lives when these three mating drives—lust, romantic love, and attachment—do not focus on the same person. It seems to be the destiny of humankind that we are *neurologically* able to love more than one person at a time. You can feel profound attachment for a long-term spouse, *while* you feel romantic passion for someone in the office or your social circle, *while* you feel the sex drive as you read a book, watch a movie, or do something else unrelated to either partner. You can even swing from one feeling to another.

In fact, as you lie in the dark at night you can become engulfed by feelings of attachment to your spouse; then seconds later you feel crazy romantic passion for someone you just met; then you become aware of sexual craving as an unrelated image sweeps into mind. As these three brain circuits fire interactively, yet independently, you feel as if you are having a committee meeting in your head.

"Wild is love," as the song goes. Lust, romantic love, and deep attachment can visit you in such different and unexpected combinations that many people have come to believe the mixture of sensations that draws you to another is mysterious, elusive, perhaps even heaven-sent. But once you begin to envisage lust, romantic love, and attachment as three specific mating drives, each producing many gradations of feeling that endlessly combine and recombine in countless different ways, love takes on tangibility. Even the elaborate love schemas of the classical Greeks make sense.

## *Types of Love*

The ancient Greeks were the world's masters at scrutinizing various kinds of love. They had over ten words to distinguish different types. Psychologist John Alan Lee reduced these overlapping categories into six.[72] But to my mind, each appears to be a different blend of the three basic mating circuits in the brain: lust, romantic love, and attachment.

The most celebrated is *eros,* or passionate, sexual, erotic, joyful, high-energy love for a very special partner. I think eros is a combination of lust and romantic love.

*Mania* is obsessive, jealous, irrational, possessive, dependent love. Most people are exceedingly obsessive, illogical, and possessive when they are passionately in love.

*Ludus* (rhymes with Brutus) is the Latin word for game or play. This is playful, unserious, uncommitted, detached love. These lovers can love more than one person at a time. For them, love is theater, an art form. Ludus appears to be a variation of mild lust coupled with fun and frivolity.

*Storge* (rhymes with "more gay") is an affectionate companionate, brotherly, sisterly, friendly kind of love, a deep and special friendship that lacks a display of emotion. These people prefer to talk about their interests rather than their feelings. This is "love without fever or folly," as Proudhon put it. To me, storge is a form of attachment.

*Agape* is a gentle, unselfish, dutiful, all-giving, altruistic, often spiritual love—another form of attachment. These lovers regard their sentiments as a duty, not a passion. Some are even willing to give up the relationship when it is best for the beloved; hence they will surrender willingly to a rival.

Last is *pragma,* love based on compatibility and common sense: pragmatic love. This is "shopping list" love. Pragmatic lovers keep score; they look for the perks of the relationship as well as its flaws. These men and women are not moved to excessive sacrifice or emotion. For them, friendship is a core of the relationship. I don't regard pragma as love at all.

There is a great deal of psychological literature on types of love, as well as on the various components of love and styles of loving.[73] One conceptualization of love that is popular among contemporary social scientists is that of psychologist Robert Sternberg.

Sternberg divides love into three basic ingredients: passion—including romance, physical attraction, and sexual craving; intimacy—all of those feelings of warmth, closeness, connectedness, and bondedness; and decision/commitment—the decision to love someone and the commitment to sustain that love.[74] To him, *infatuation* is composed of passion only. *Romantic love* is passion plus intimacy. *Consummate love* is passion, intimacy, and commitment. *Companionate love* has intimacy and commitment but is devoid of passion. *Empty love* has only commitment; one goes through the gestures of loving but only feelings of commitment hold the relationship together. *Liking* is based on intimacy; one feels no passion and no commitment. And *fatuous love* is often full of passion and commitment, but lacks intimacy.

## *The Mad Symphony of Romance*

"Love is such a tissue of paradoxes, and exists in such a variety of forms and shades, that you may say almost anything about it that you please, and it is likely to be correct." So claimed Queen Victoria's behavioral scientist, Sir Henry Finck.[75] Romantic love certainly has subtle variations, as well as intricate and varied relationships with its kindred reproductive drives, lust, and attachment. Love is a symphony of feelings with many notes and chords.

To make matters even more complex, the brain network for romantic love melds with many more brain systems with circuits for other basic drives, as well as with many emotions, memories, and thoughts. All these ingredients add fantastic depth, nuance, and spice to our feelings of romance.

Certainly our emotions contribute to romantic passion. Human emotions lie along a continuum, from those that are so basic that they are almost impossible to hide (such as disgust) to those like envy that we can more easily conceal. The basic emotions are universal, inherited, involuntary, rapidly expressed, portrayed everywhere with the same facial poses, hard to fake, and often difficult to control.[76] Among them are fear, anger, joy, sadness, disgust, and surprise.

Certainly the drive to love commandeers all of these basic emotions at one time or another. As you feel an irresistible urge to phone "him" or "her," you can become engulfed with fear that your lover has gone out with a rival, then overwhelmed with joy as he or she answers the phone and says, "I love you," then pummeled by surprise and disappointment as this celestial being breaks the dinner date you had planned together.

Romantic love is also linked to a host of more complex feelings. Respect, admiration, loyalty, gratitude, sympathy, apprehension, bashfulness, nostalgia, remorse, even the sense of fairness: philosopher Dylan Evans calls these "higher cognitive emotions"[77] because they are not fast-acting or associated with specific facial mannerisms; people in different societies express them in different ways and at different times; and men and women are often able to conceal and fake them. We tack on dozens of these complex emotions while we are in the throes of romantic love.

Calm, tension, contentment, anxiety, mild pain, mild pleasure, and other general bodily states also contribute to feelings of romantic love. As neurologist Antonio Damasio puts it, these "background emotions" provide the landscape of the body, the persistent mood that accompanies us as stronger emotions and motivations ebb and surge.[78] Only occasionally do these background states gush into your conscious mind. But these steady undercurrents of anxiety, pain, and pleasure certainly color our feelings for a beloved.

Most compelling, this trellis of emotions and motivations is hierarchically ordered in the brain. Fear can overcome joy, for example. Jealousy can stifle tenderness. The juxtapositions are manifold. But in this pecking order of basic and complex emotions, background feelings and powerful drives, romantic love holds a special place: close to the zenith, the pinnacle, the top. Romantic love can dominate the drive to eat and sleep. It can stifle fear, anger, or disgust. It can override one's sense of duty to family and friends. It can even triumph over the will to live. As Keats said, "I could die for you."

"How do I love thee? Let me count the ways," wrote Elizabeth Barrett Browning. There are so many ways. Like a chord on a piano, the feeling of romantic passion harmonizes with myriad other feelings, drives, and thoughts to create different melodies in different keys. Moreover, each of us is wired somewhat differently. Some are predisposed to happiness; others to calm, anxiety, fear, or anger; some are insatiably curious; others wonderfully amusing. Scientists say that about 50 percent of our temperament is inherited; the rest is molded by our upbringing and environment. But we all share this wondrous—and devilish—thing called romantic love.

How do you and I fish in the sea of varied human beings to find our "special" other? What makes us choose "him" or "her"?

# 5

# "That First Fine Careless Rapture": *Who We Choose*

Somewhere there waiteth in this world of ours
For one lone soul, another lonely soul—
Each chasing each through all the weary hours,
And meeting strangely at one sudden goal;
Then blend they—like green leaves with golden flowers,
Into one beautiful and perfect whole—
And life's long night is ended, and the way
Lies open onward to eternal day.

Sir Edwin Arnold
"Somewhere"[1]

"She was so extraordinarily beautiful that I nearly laughed out loud. She . . . [was] famine, fire, destruction and plague . . . the only true begetter. Her breasts were apocalyptic, they would topple empires before they withered . . . her body was a miracle of construction. . . . She was unquestionably gorgeous. She was lavish. She was a dark, unyielding largesse. She was, in short, too bloody much . . . those huge violet blue eyes . . . had an odd glint. . . . Aeons passed, civilizations came and went while these cosmic headlights examined my flawed personality. Every pockmark on my face became a crater of the moon."

So thought Richard Burton when he first saw nineteen-year-old Elizabeth Taylor. Why does a man walk into a room full of attractive women, speak to several he finds charming, then fall head over heels in love with one? Why does a woman with several suitors see a man for only moments before her brain circuits fire up with romantic passion? Why does one person ignite these primitive brain circuits while another perfectly lovely human being leaves us totally unmoved? Why "him"? Why "her"?

## *Timing*

"How can we know the dancer from the dance?" Yeats asked. Perhaps you have been swept away by someone at a party, in the office, or on the beach; then later wondered whether you just got caught up in the excitement of the moment. Your craving to love and to be loved altered your vision—transforming a frog into a prince or princess. You confused the dancer with the dance.

Love can be triggered when you least expect it—by pure chance. The perfect partner can sit right next to you at a party and you might not notice him or her if you are exceptionally busy at work or school, enmeshed in another relationship, or otherwise emotionally preoccupied.

But if you just entered college or moved to a new city by yourself, recently recovered from an unsatisfactory love affair, began to make enough money to raise a family, are lonely or suffering through a difficult experience, or have too much spare time, you are ripe to fall in love.[2] In fact, people who are emotionally aroused, be it by joy, sadness, anxiety, fear, curiosity, or *any* other feeling, are more likely to be vulnerable to this passion.[3]

I suspect this is because all agitated mental states are associated with arousal mechanisms in the brain, as well as with elevated levels of stress hormones. Both systems elevate levels of dopamine—thus setting up the chemistry for romantic passion.

## *Proximity*

"Ah, I have picked up magic in her nearness," wrote poet Ezra Pound. Quite right; proximity can also spark this rapture. We tend to choose those who are around us.[4]

This was elegantly expressed by Terry, a man from Canada who recently wrote me the following e-mail:

> Dear Dr. Fisher, When I was in my "dating" years, I had certain expectations with respect to the woman I would marry. She had to be this, that and the other thing too! What I overlooked was a beautiful, caring, unselfish woman with wonderful goals literally living in my back yard! She met none of my "expectations" but we started dating, lived together, fell in love and were married a year later. It's been 15 years now and our relationship has grown tremendously and continues to grow every day. I guess what I'm trying to say is, take a step back and look around you. Don't micro-analyze every detail. Maybe your soul mate is closer than you think :).

Many other hidden forces play a role in whom you choose. Among them: mystery.

## *Mystery*

Both sexes are often attracted to those they find mysterious. As Baudelaire wrote, "We love women in proportion to their degree of strangeness to us." The sense that one has a slippery grip on an elusive, improbable treasure can trigger romantic passion.

The reverse is also true. Familiarity can deaden thoughts of romantic love—as life on one Israeli kibbutz has shown. Here children grew up together in a common house where they lived, slept, and bathed with other youths of all ages. Boys and girls touched and lay together playfully. By age twelve, however, they became tense with one another. Then as teenagers, they developed strong brother-sister bonds. But none of those who started life in this common cradle married a fellow kibbutznik.[5] So scientists now think that at a critical time in childhood, sometime between ages three and six, boys and girls who live in close proximity and get to know each other well lose the ability to fall in love with one another.

This repugnance for mating with the familiar is common among mammals. Almost all individuals of all species on record have a sexual aversion to closely familiar others; they prefer to mate with strangers. So males (or females) usually leave home at puberty to find sex partners in other groups. If a young male remains in his natal community, as male rhesus monkeys do, he often behaves like a child around his mother, snuggling in his sweetheart's arms instead of courting her to copulate. And in one recorded case of attempted incest among chimpanzees, a sister violently repelled her brother—screaming, kicking, and biting him before she wiggled away and fled.

You and I inherited this natural repulsion for copulation with close family members and other individuals we know well, a distaste that undoubtedly evolved to discourage in-breeding—the destructive act of mixing one's DNA with close kin. As a result, we are more likely to become attracted to someone from outside our family or the group in which we were raised—someone with a touch of mystery.

Nature has even given us the brain wiring to find strangers exciting. Mysterious people are novel. And novelty is associated with elevated levels of dopamine—the neurotransmitter of romance.

## *Do Opposites Attract?*

Nevertheless, "that first fine careless rapture," as Robert Browning called romantic love, is generally directed toward someone much like one's self. Most people around the world do feel that amorous chemistry for unfamiliar individuals of the *same* ethnic, social, religious, educational, and economic background, who have a similar amount of physical attractiveness, a comparable intelligence, and similar attitudes, expectations, values, interests, and social and communication skills.[6]

In fact, in a new study of mate selection in America, evolutionary biologists Peter Buston and Stephen Emlen report that young men and women think of themselves as particular types of marriage partners and choose people with the same traits, ranging from financial and physical assets to intricacies of personality.[7] If a woman is blessed with a trust fund, for example, she seeks another from the upper class. Handsome men seek beautiful women. And those devoted to family and sexual fidelity select someone with these attributes. The mirror speaks. Men and women also gravitate to lovers who share their sense of humor, to those with similar social and political values, and to individuals with much the same beliefs about life in general.[8]

Remarkably, scientists have established that many of these traits, including your occupational interests, what you do in your leisure hours, many of your social attitudes, even the strength of your faith in God, are influenced by your genes.[9] So genetic types gravitate toward one another; we tend to be attracted to people like ourselves.

Anthropologists call this human propensity to be drawn to someone like yourself "positive assortive mating" or "fitness matching." The specific kind of person you actually choose, however, has been changing somewhat. The world is seeing more interracial marriages, for example. In the United States these weddings have increased some 800 percent since 1960.[10] But even in this time of the global village, that fire in the mind is still most likely to ignite when you meet an unfamiliar man or woman who is quite similar to you ethnically, socially, and intellectually.

Like our attraction to unfamiliar people, this preference for partners like oneself is probably evolutionary baggage. Why? Because a fetus and its mother are foreigners to each other. If they share a similar chemical makeup, the mother will have an easier time carrying the infant in her womb. In fact, mates who are genetically similar experience fewer natural abortions and bear more and healthier babies.[11]

It is not advantageous to be too alike, however. And humans seem to have evolved at least one mental mechanism to assure that we choose a partner who is slightly different—chemically at least. This discovery stems from what has become known as the "sweaty T-shirt" experiment. When women were asked to smell men's sweaty T-shirts and report on which they thought were the most "sexy smelling," they chose T-shirts of men with immune systems that were unlike but compatible with their own.[12] Unconsciously these women were attracted to individuals who could potentially help them produce genetically more varied young.

So opposites attract—within the limits of one's ethnic, social, and intellectual sphere.

### *Symmetry: The "Golden Mean"*

Another biological taste we have inherited from the animal kingdom is our tendency to choose well-proportioned mates. Bodily symmetry can help to trigger romantic love, as the ancient Greeks theorized. Almost twenty-five hundred years ago Aristotle maintained that there were some universal standards of physical beauty. One, he believed, was balanced bodily proportions, including symmetry. This accorded with his high respect for what he called the golden mean, or moderation between extremes.

Modern science supports Aristotle's notion. Symmetry is beautiful—to insects, birds, mammals, all of the primates, and people around the world.[13] Female scorpion flies seek mates with uniform wings. Barn swallows like partners with well-proportioned tails. Monkeys are partial to consorts with symmetrical teeth. If you walk into a village in New Guinea and point to the most beautiful man or woman sitting around the campfire, the natives will agree with you.[14] And when researchers used computers to blend many faces into a composite "average" face, both men and women liked the average face better than any of the individual ones.[15] It was more balanced. Even two-month-old infants gaze longer at more symmetrical faces.[16]

"Beauty is truth, truth beauty," Keats wrote in his "Ode on a Grecian Urn." Keats's words have puzzled many. But as it turns out, the beauty of symmetry does tell a basic truth. Creatures with balanced, well-proportioned ears, eyes, teeth, and jaws, with symmetrical elbows, knees, and breasts, have been able to repel bacteria, viruses, and other minute predators that can cause bodily irregularities. By displaying symmetry, animals advertise their superior genetic ability to combat diseases.[17]

So our human attraction to symmetrical suitors is a primitive animal mechanism designed to guide us to select genetically sturdy mating partners.[18]

And nature has taken no chances; the brain naturally responds to a beautiful face. When scientists recorded the brain activity of heterosexual men ages twenty-one to thirty-five as they looked at women with beautiful faces, the ventral tegmental area (VTA) "lit up."[19] A similar response occurred in our scanning study: those subjects who gazed at photos of better-looking partners showed more activity in the VTA. And the VTA is rich with dopamine—the neurotransmitter that provides the energy, elation, focussed attention, and motivation to win a reward.

Not surprisingly, symmetrical men and women often have many suitors to choose from. As a result, exquisitely good-looking women tend to marry higher status men,[20] Jacqueline Kennedy Onassis being a crowning example of this matching process.

Highly symmetrical men also get reproductive perks. They begin to have sex some four years earlier than their lopsided peers; they have more sex partners and more adulterous affairs as well.[21] Women also achieve more orgasms with symmetrical men,[22] even when this relationship is not emotionally satisfying to them. And when a woman has an orgasm with a well-proportioned man, her orgasmic contractions suck up more of his sperm.[23]

I suspect these sexual responses occur because as the woman looks at her symmetrical lover, the ventral tegmental area in her brain produces dopamine—which (in a series of interactions) triggers testosterone and enhances the sexual response.

Because symmetry enhances one's choices in the mating game, women go to extraordinary lengths to achieve it or at least a semblance of it. With powders they make the two sides of the face more similar. With mascara and eyeliner, they make their eyes appear more alike. With lipstick they enhance one lip to match the other. And with plastic surgery, exercise, belts, bras, and tight jeans and shirts, they mold their forms to create the symmetrical proportions men prefer.

Nature helps. Scientists have found that women's hands and ears are more symmetrical during monthly ovulation—a time when it is reproductively important to attract a man.[24] Women's breasts become more symmetrical during ovulation too.[25] Moreover, young men and young women are often quite symmetrical; we become more and more lopsided as we age.

## *"Waist to Hip" Ratio*

The golden mean of balance also applies to other bodily proportions.

To a group of American men, psychologist Devendra Singh displayed an array of line drawings of young women and asked which body types they found most attractive.[26] Most chose women whose waist circumference was about 70 percent of their hips. This experiment was then redone in Britain, Germany, Australia, India, Uganda, and several other countries. Responses varied, but many informants favored this same general waist-to-hip ratio.

When Singh measured the waist-to-hip ratio of 286 ancient sculptures from several African tribes, as well as from ancient India, Egypt, Greece, and Rome, he found that all favored a ratio that was smaller for women than for men. And in a study of 330 artworks of Europe, Asia, the Americas, and Africa, some of which date back thirty-two thousand years, scientists found that most women were depicted with a waist-to-hip ratio of these same general proportions.[27] Interestingly, *Playboy* centerfolds display these proportions, too, as do American "supermodels." Even "Twiggy," the gaunt supermodel of the 1960s, had a waist-to-hip ratio of exactly 70 percent.

A woman's waist-to-hip ratio is largely inherited; it is produced by genes. Moreover, although it clearly varies from one woman to the next, this ratio adjusts during ovulation to come closer to 70 percent. Why has nature gone to such extraordinary lengths to produce curvaceous women? And why do men around the world appreciate this particular waist-to-hip ratio in women?

Most likely for an evolutionary reason.

Women with a waist-to-hip ratio of around 70 percent are more likely to bear babies, Singh reports. They possess the right amount of fat in the right places—due to high levels of bodily estrogen in relation to testosterone. Women who vary substantially from these proportions find it harder to get pregnant; they conceive later in life; and they have more miscarriages. Egg-shaped, pear-shaped, or stick-shaped: differently shaped women also suffer more from chronic diseases, such as diabetes, hypertension, heart disease, certain cancers, and problems with circulation. They are also prone to various personality disorders.[28]

So Singh theorizes that male attraction to a specific female waist-to-hip ratio is a natural preference for healthy, fertile partners. In fact, because this preference is so deeply enmeshed in the male psyche, men of all ages express this taste, even when they have no interest in fathering young themselves or are courting women who are past the age of reproduction.

Of course, men prefer other things in women, too.

## *Who Men Choose*

In a classic study of some ten thousand people in thirty-seven societies, scientists asked men and women to rank eighteen characteristics in order of their importance in choosing a spouse.[29] Both sexes ranked love or mutual attraction first. A dependable character came next, followed by emotional stability and maturity, and a pleasing disposition. Both men and women also said they would choose someone who was kind, smart, educated, sociable, healthy, and interested in home and family.

But this study also showed a distinct gender difference in romantic tastes. When it came to sizing up potential romantic partners, men were more likely to choose women who displayed *visual* signs of youth and beauty.

These masculine predilections are documented across millennia and cultures.[30] Osiris, the legendary ruler of predynastic Egypt, was overwhelmed by the physical beauty of his beloved wife, Isis. As he wrote over four thousand years ago, "Isis has cast her net, / and ensnared me / in the noose of her hair / I am held by her eyes / curbed by her necklace / imprisoned by the scent of her skin."[31]

A Tiv tribesman of Nigeria was swept away by the shapeliness of a woman, exclaiming, "When I saw her dance she took my life away and I knew I must follow her."[32]

American men who place courtship ads in newspapers and magazines are three times more likely than women to mention that they seek beauty in a partner.[33]

And on average, men around the world marry women who are three years younger than themselves.[34] In the United States, men who remarry usually choose a woman about five years younger; if they wed a third time, they often take a bride about eight years their junior.[35]

When asked why people desire physical beauty, Aristotle replied: "No one that is not blind could ask that question." Men unquestionably find good-looking women aesthetically pleasing to look at. They also like to impress friends and colleagues with their dazzling girlfriends or trophy wives. In fact, people in general tend to regard beautiful women (and good-looking men) as warm, smart, strong, giving, friendly, polite, sexy, interesting, financially secure, and socially popular.[36]

But evolutionary psychologists now believe that men subconsciously also prefer youth and beauty because it gives them reproductive payoffs.[37] Young women with smooth skin, snow-white teeth, sparkling eyes, gleaming hair, taut muscles, a lithe body, and a lively personality are more likely to be healthy and energetic—good qualities for bearing and rearing babies. Smooth, clear skin and babylike facial features also signal elevated levels of estrogen that can aid in reproduction.

So these scientists theorize that across our long hunting/gathering past, those males who chose youthful, healthy, exuberant partners had more children. These robust babies lived—and passed along to contemporary men this male bias for youthful, good-looking women.[38]

## *The Male Brain in Love*

"Why does a woman have to be beautiful rather than intelligent?"

"Because men can see better than they can think."

It's a stale joke; I know *many* men who think very well. But this tart observation does contain a grain of truth. I say this because our fMRI study on the brain circuitry of people in love turned up some unexpected results: we found several gender differences.[39] These findings were complex and varied. Men did not fit neatly in one category and women in another; as with all gender differences, both sexes ranged in their responses to the photos of their sweethearts; some even overlapped. Moreover, these variations may not be common to all men or all women. But there were statistically significant differences between the sexes. No one knows exactly what these findings mean. But I will speculate about men for the moment and theorize about women later.

In our sample, men tended to show more activity than women in brain regions associated with *visual* processing, particularly of the face.

Could this have evolved to enhance men's ability to fall in love when they *saw* a woman who was young, symmetrical, and a good reproductive bet? Maybe. This brain activity could also help explain why men generally fall in love faster than women.[40] When the time is right and a man *sees* an attractive woman, he is anatomically equipped to rapidly associate attractive *visual* features with feelings of romantic passion. What an effective courtship device.

Indeed, we found another gender difference that could have evolved to help men court efficiently in yesteryear. When our subjects looked at their beloveds, men tended to show more positive activity in a brain region associated with penile erection. This makes Darwinian sense. The very purpose of romantic love is to stimulate mating with a "special" other. This male response directly links romantic passion with a brain region associated with sexual arousal.

Although this may be far-fetched, this male brain response may also shed light on why men so avidly support the worldwide trade in *visual* pornography; why women are more likely than men to regard their personal appearance as an important component of their self-esteem;[41] and why women go to such extraordinary lengths to advertise their assets *visually*, with all manner of clothing, makeup, and ornaments. "If you can't convince 'em, confuse 'em," maintained American president Harry Truman. Women agree. Unmercifully, women take advantage of men's fondness for—and brain response to—visual stimuli.

## *Male "Mating Effort"*

Another male penchant interests me because it also comes, I think, directly from deep history. Psychologists report that men want to help women, to solve their problems, to be useful by *doing* something.[42] Men feel manly when they rescue a damsel in distress.

No doubt millions of years of protecting and providing for women has bred into the male brain this tendency to choose women they feel they need to save. In fact, the male brain is well built to assist women. Men are, on average, more skilled at all sorts of mechanical and spatial tasks than women are. Men are problem solvers.[43] And many of men's particular skills are fashioned in the womb by high levels of fetal testosterone. Perhaps men evolved this biological machinery, at least in part, to attract, assist, and save women.

Men are also more single-minded than women when they love. Only 40 percent of the young women in my survey agreed with the statement: "Having a good relationship with _____ is more important than having a good relationship with my family," whereas a solid 60 percent of young men reported that their love relationship came first. Moreover, although most people think women are the ones who wait by the phone, change their schedules, and hang around the office or the gym to be available to a beloved, my questionnaire showed that American men reorder their priorities more frequently than women do.

This male accessibility is far from new. Even Dante, the great Renaissance Florentine poet, apparently lingered on a bridge over the Arno River for hours in hopes of speaking with his beloved Beatrice.

This male penchant may be due to the fact that men have fewer intimate connections with their natal families and friends than women. But deep evolutionary forces probably contribute. Women are custodians of the egg—a valuable commodity. And women expend much more time rearing infants and small children, a vital job. For millions of years men needed to make themselves available to potential mating partners, even risk their lives to save these precious reproductive vessels.

Men are still obliged to expend more "mating effort" to win the courtship game. In fact, men's mating efforts were clearly visible in their responses to several questions in my survey. For example, men were more worried that they would say the wrong thing on a "date." They were not as confident with their words. This is understandable. On average, women everywhere in the world are more skilled with the nuances of language, an ability linked to the female hormone, estrogen.[44] But the women in my survey were also more likely to save the cards and letters a lover sends. Women not only savored a suitor's way with words; unconsciously they were also keeping a record of his mating effort.

## *The Female Brain in Love*

Much of the psychological literature reports that both sexes feel passionate romantic love with roughly the same intensity.[45] I suspect this is true; their responses are just somewhat different. For example, my questionnaire on this passion (discussed in chapter one) showed that more American and Japanese women than men reported feeling "lighter than air" when they were certain their beloved felt passionately about them. Women also experienced slightly more obsessive thinking about an amor.

Our fMRI experiment also showed several ways in which our female subjects responded differently than our male participants. When women looked at the photo of their beloved, they tended to show *more* activity in the body of the caudate nucleus and the septum—brain regions associated with motivation and attention. Parts of the septum are also associated with the processing of emotion. Women also showed activity in some different brain regions, including one associated with retrieval and recall of memories and some associated with attention and emotion.[46]

Once again, no one knows what these results mean. But as you recall memories and register your emotions, you inform yourself about your feelings[47] and assemble information into patterns; both activities help you make decisions. And for millions of years, women needed to make appropriate decisions about a potential mating partner. If an ancestral woman became pregnant during a romance, she was obliged to incubate the embryo for nine months, then deliver the child. These were (and remain) metabolically costly, time-consuming, uncomfortable, and physically dangerous tasks. Moreover, a woman had to raise her helpless infant through a long childhood and adolescence.

While a man can *see* many of a woman's assets for bearing and rearing babies, a woman cannot see a man's "mate value" just by looking. She must compute a partner's ability to protect and provide. And these gender differences suggest that when a woman gazes at her lover, natural selection has given her specific brain responses that enable her to recall the details and emotions she needs to assess her man.

"Heredity is nothing but stored environment," wrote the great botanist Luther Burbank. The vicissitudes of rearing helpless infants in a hostile ancestral environment have unquestionably bred into women other mechanisms they use to choose a mate.

## *Who Women Choose*

In a survey of eight hundred personal advertisements placed in newspapers and magazines, American women sought partners who offered financial security twice as frequently as men did.[48] Many female doctors, lawyers, and very wealthy women are interested in men with even more money and status than themselves.[49] In fact, women everywhere in the world are more attracted to partners with education, ambition, wealth, respect, status, and position—the kinds of assets their prehistoric predecessors needed in a parenting partner. As scientists sum this up: men look for sex objects and women look for success objects.

Women are also attracted to tall men, perhaps because towering men are more likely to acquire prestige in business and politics and provide more bodily defense.[50] Women like men who sit in a carefree position, a sign of dominance, as well as men who are self-confident and assertive. Women are somewhat more likely to choose a long-term partner who is smart.[51] And women respond to men who are well-coordinated, strong, and courageous—as world literature and legend attest.

Inanna, queen of ancient Sumeria, called her beloved "my fearless one / my shining one."[52] In the Song of Songs of the Old Testament, written between 900 and 300 B.C., the woman crooned: "My love is shining and ruddy. / He is the tallest in a crowd of ten thousand men / His arms are like rods of gold / His legs are pillars of marble."[53] And in a nineteenth-century poem by an anonymous Somali woman, the poet gushed, "You are strong as woven iron. / You are poured from Nairobi gold, the first light of dawn, the blazing sun."

No wonder a man's self-respect is more tightly linked to his general status at work and in the community.[54] No wonder men are also more likely to jeopardize their health, safety, and spare time to achieve rank. Men intuitively know that to attract youthful, healthy, energetic women, they must try to appear fearless, strong as woven iron, as powerful as the blazing sun.

Women also prefer men with distinctive cheekbones and a strong jaw—for another unconscious reason. Masculine cheekbones and a rugged jawline are built with testosterone—and testosterone suppresses the immune system. Only exceedingly healthy teenage boys can tolerate the effects of this and build a rugged face.[55] Not surprisingly, around the time of monthly ovulation women become even more interested in men with these signs of testosterone. Now they can get pregnant, so they unconsciously seek males with superior genes.

Curiously, women who are likely to get pregnant are also more attracted to men with a good sense of humor—perhaps because wit has been associated with sharper general intelligence.

Biologist Randy Thornhill believes that women express two basic preferences. Around ovulation they seek men with good genes, a remnant of estrus found in all mammals. At other times of the menstrual cycle they favor men who display signs of commitment. Indeed, when instructed to manipulate computer images of male faces until they found the most attractive image, both British and Japanese women preferred more masculine male faces around the time of ovulation and softer, more feminine male faces at other times of the menstrual cycle.[56] New data suggest, however, that women without a partner still seek signs of commitment at ovulation.

To be expected, *all the time* women are attracted to men who are willing to share their rank, their money, and their position. In fact, women are more pragmatic and realistic when they love, whereas men tend to be either more cynical or more idealistic and altruistic.[57] Perhaps this feminine pragmatism explains why women fall in love more slowly than men do.

## *Casual Passion*

The sexes become more flexible in their romantic choices when they are looking for short-term love, such as when they are on vacation or seeking a temporary romance while pursuing other interests.

Historically, women looking for short-term passion choose free-spending men with resources—bestowers of gifts, lavish vacations, fancy dinners, and social or political connections.[58] Frugality was not acceptable to a woman on a fling. But today's women are wealthier and more independent than in the historical past and those pursuing casual passion are somewhat more eager to choose tall, symmetrical men with chiseled cheekbones and rugged jaws, men who are likely to have sturdy genes.[59]

Some of these women are testing their own mate value—seeing what kind of man they can attract.[60] Others use a casual relationship as a form of insurance policy; they want a backup in case their own mate defects or becomes ill and dies. But many women also use casual sex to "try out" a particular person for a longer relationship.

Psychologists know this because women are less enthusiastic than men about engaging in a one-night stand with someone who is married or involved in another love relationship. Not only is this lover unavailable but his resources are directed elsewhere. And since he is cheating on his established partner, he is likely to be unfaithful to her as well. Most women don't lower their standards for brief love affairs either. They still seek a partner who is healthy, stable, funny, kind, and generous. For women, casual sex is often not as casual as it is for men.[61]

When men seek short-term love, they tend to overlook a woman's lack of intelligence.[62] They also choose women who are less athletic, less educated, less loyal, less stable, less humorous, and of a wider age range.[63] And unlike women, they may even be attracted to a woman with a reputation for promiscuity. As Mae West so aptly put it, "Men like women with a past because they hope history will repeat itself."

As men think of committing to a long-term mate, however, they become picky about basic virtues. When it comes to wedding, both sexes are attracted to partners for reasons that arise, in part, from their primordial (and often unconscious) need to breed.

"Tell me where is fancy bred, / Or in the heart, or in the head? / How begot, how nourished? / Reply, reply."[64] We can answer much of Shakespeare's question. A taste for symmetry; men's love of youthfulness and beauty and their need to help women in distress; women's attraction to men's wealth and status: these biological predilections can potentially trigger the brain circuitry for romantic love. An element of mystery, along with similarities of background, education, and beliefs, guide our tastes. Chance, timing, and proximity can also play a part in who we choose.

But of all the forces that guide your mate selection, I think the most important is your personal history, the myriad childhood, teenage, and adult experiences that have shaped and reshaped your likes and dislikes throughout your life. All these combine to create your largely unconscious psychological chart, what is called your "love map."

## *Love Maps*

We grow up in a sea of moments that slowly sculpt our romantic choices. Your mother's wit and way with words; your father's zest for politics and tennis; your uncle's love of boats and hiking; your sister's interest in training dogs; how people in your household use silence, express intimacy and anger; how those around you handle money; the amount of laughter at the dinner table; what your older brother finds challenging; your religious education and intellectual pursuits; the pastimes of your school chums; what your grandmother finds polite; how the community you live in views honor, justice, loyalty, gratitude, and kindness; what teachers admire and deplore; what you see on television and in the movies: these and thousands of other subtle forces build our individual interests, values, and beliefs. So by the teenage years, each of us has constructed a catalog of aptitudes and mannerisms we are looking for in a mate.

This chart is unique. Even identical twins, who have similar interests and lifestyles, as well as similar religious, political, and social values, tend to develop different styles of loving and choose different types of partners.[65] Subtle differences in their experiences have shaped their romantic tastes.

This idiosyncratic psychological chart is also enormously complex. Some people seek a partner who will agree with what they say; others like a spirited debate. Some love a prank; others want predictability, order, or flamboyance. Some want to be amused; others wish to be intellectually excited. Many need a partner who will support their causes, quell their fears, or share their goals. And some choose a partner for the lifestyle they wish to lead. Søren Kierkegaard, the Danish philosopher, felt that love must be unselfish, filled with devotion for the beloved. But some are uncomfortable with a doting mate. Instead, they want a partner to challenge them to grow intellectually or spiritually.

Love maps are subtle and difficult to read. A good example is a friend of mine who grew up with an alcoholic father. She acclimated to the unpredictability around the house. But she resolved she would never marry a man like dear ol' dad. Indeed, she didn't. She married an unpredictable, chaotic artist instead—a match that suited her largely unconscious love map.

"Love looks not with the eyes, but the mind, / And therefore is winged Cupid painted blind," wrote Shakespeare.[66] This is probably why it is so difficult to introduce single friends to one another and why Internet dating services often fail: matchmakers don't know the intricacies of their clients' love templates. Often men and women don't know their own love map either.

## *The Lover's Psyche*

Hundreds of psychologists have tried to understand the dynamics between romantic partners, and many offer interesting ideas about why we choose one mate rather than another. I will review just a few.

Psychologists Elaine Hatfield and Richard Rapson believe that adults express one of six "attachment" styles.[67] "Securely attached" men and women tend to choose sweethearts they can be close to; they also make and keep friends easily. "Fickle" people get bored. If they win a lover, they become restless; if their mate departs, they pursue. Others "cling"; they prefer mates with whom they can maintain constant contact. "Skittish" types feel pushed and smothered easily;

they like their independence and flee from intimacy and deep attachments. "Casual" lovers are not willing to invest too much time or energy in loving. They like dating, but reading, traveling, or working takes precedence over commitment to a romantic partner. And a small number of men and women are uninterested in romance; they make no effort to woo or retain a sweetheart.

According to psychologist Ayala Pines, we choose a mate who is similar to the parent with whom we have unresolved childhood issues; unconsciously we are seeking to resolve this natal relationship in adulthood.[68] Harville Hendrix maintains that we choose partners who suffered similar traumas in childhood and are stuck in this same stage of development.[69] Murray Bowen believes we choose partners who display the same level of "differentiation" or independence of identity as ourselves.[70] We are seeking partners with a compatible ability to handle anxiety. And psychologists Cindy Hazan and Philip Shaver[71] build on the theories of John Bowlby[72] and Mary Ainsworth,[73] proposing that we fall in love and form attachments that mirror the type of childhood attachment we made to our mother, be it "secure," "anxious-ambivalent," or avoidant.

Elliot Aronson[74] would adhere to poet Theodore Roethke's feeling, "Love begets love."[75] He maintains that some people choose those they think love them; this belief initiates a cascade of pleasant experiences that lead to the altar. Shakespeare's Beatrice and Benedict are good examples of this; both fell in love with the other after hearing of the other's romantic ardor for them. Theodore Reik believed men and women choose mates who satisfy an important need, including qualities they lack. As Reik put it, "Tell me whom you love and I will tell you who you are and, more especially, who you want to be."[76]

There is undoubtedly some truth to all of these ideas. But they all stem from a fundamental proposition: we each have a unique personality, built by our childhood experiences and particular biology. And this largely unconscious psychic structure guides us to fall in love with one person rather than another.

Individual "love maps" probably begin to develop in infancy as we adjust to countless environmental forces that influence our feelings and ideas. As Maurice Sendak wisely noted, childhood is "damned serious business." Then as we enter school and make new friends, we engage in infatuations that further mold our likes and dislikes. As we develop more durable love affairs as teenagers, we continue to expand this personal psychological chart. And as we ride the waves of life—and experience a few romantic disasters—we trim and enrich this mental template.

So as you walk into a room of potential mating partners, you carry within your brain an extraordinary sum of infinitesimal, mostly unconscious biological and cultural preferences that can spoil or spark romantic passion.

To make matters even more complex, our suitors are, themselves, enormously varied. Do you know any two people who are alike? I don't. The variety of human personalities is remarkable. Some are brilliant musicians; others can write a touching poem, build a bridge, make the perfect golf shot, perform Shakespearean roles from memory, deliver witticisms to thousands from a bandstand, philosophize coherently about the universe, preach effectively on God or duty, predict economic patterns, or charismatically lead soldiers into battle. And that's just the beginning. Nature has provided us with a seemingly infinite variety of individuals to choose from—even within our social, economic, and intellectual milieu.

And here is the focal point of this chapter. It is my belief that along with the evolution of humanity's outstanding variety came the fundamental mechanism with which we choose a mate—the brain circuitry for human romantic love.

## *The Mating Mind*

Why are we all so different from one another?

My thinking on this matter stems from Charles Darwin's fascinating idea of sexual selection.

Darwin was annoyed by all the ornaments he saw in nature.[77] Crimson ruffs, blue penises, pendulous breasts, whirling dances, melodious trills, particularly the peacock's cumbersome tail feathers: he felt these seemingly superfluous decorations undermined his theory that all traits evolved for a purpose. As he complained, "The sight of a feather in a peacock's tail, whenever I gaze on it, makes me sick."[78]

But with time Darwin came to believe that all these flashy embellishments evolved for an important purpose: to attract mates. Those with the finest courtship displays, he reasoned, attracted more and better mating partners; these dandies disproportionately bred—and passed along to their descendants these seemingly useless decorations. He called this process sexual selection.

In a highly original book, *The Mating Mind,* psychologist Geoffrey Miller adds to Darwin's theory of sexual selection. He proposes that human beings have also evolved extravagant traits to impress potential mating partners.

As Miller reasons, our human intelligence, linguistic talent, and musical ability, our drive to create visual arts, stories, myths, comedies, and dramas, our taste for all kinds of sports, our curiosity, our ability to solve complex math problems, our moral virtue, our religious fervor, our impulse for charitable giving, our political convictions, sense of humor, need to gossip, creativity, even our courage, pugnacity, perseverance, and kindness are all far too ornate and metabolically expensive to have evolved solely to survive another day.[79] Had our forebears needed these advanced aptitudes simply to live, chimpanzees would have developed these abilities as well. They didn't.

Miller believes, therefore, that all these marvelous human capacities evolved to win the mating game. We are "courtship machines," Miller writes.[80] Those ancestors who could speak poetically, draw deftly, dance nimbly, or deliver fiery moral speeches were regarded as more attractive. These talented men and women produced more babies. And gradually these human capacities became inscribed in our genetic code. Moreover, to distinguish themselves, our forebears specialized—creating the tremendous variety in human personalities seen today.

Miller acknowledges that in their simple forms, many of these traits were also useful in order to survive on the grasslands of ancient Africa; these talents had *many* purposes. But these aptitudes, he believes, became more and more complex because the opposite sex *liked* them and chose to mate with verbal, musical, or otherwise talented men and women. He concludes: "The mind evolved by moonlight."[81]

I agree with Miller's thesis. Take language, for example. Our forebears only needed a few thousand words and simple grammatical constructions to say, "Here comes the lion" and "Pass the nuts." But our flowery poetic verse, our musical brilliance, and many of our other complex human talents probably evolved, at least in part, as men and women endlessly displayed their mating qualities.

But how did ancestral men and women come to prefer these extraordinary traits in their suitors? Some brain mechanism must have simultaneously evolved in the *display choosers* to become attracted to the fancy rhymes, lyric tunes, and other flashy traits that *display producers* paraded for them.

Darwin offered little comment on how creatures actually respond to these courtship displays and prefer one mate over another. He believed this selection process was somehow linked to an appreciation of beauty. Females of all species, he wrote, were attracted to males who displayed signs of comeliness. But Darwin could not explain how this female attraction operated in the animal brain, puzzling, "It is, however, difficult to obtain direct evidence of their capacity to appreciate beauty."[82]

Miller also notes this dilemma. Along with the evolution of traits in the human *display producer,* there must be some corresponding brain mechanisms in the *display chooser* to enable them to discriminate among these courtship signals, prefer some, and select a specific mating partner.

So he suggests that along with the evolution of our superb human mental and physical abilities came the "mental machinery" or "sexual choice equipment" to discriminate among and appreciate these wooing ploys. Hence, our forebears developed a taste for linguistic flair, for artistic drawings in the sand, for charismatic oratory, moral strength, and many other budding human talents—as well as the aptitudes to discriminate, remember, and judge these courtship cues.

But Miller offers no concrete suggestion as to what actually enables the display chooser to choose one wooing tactic rather than another, saying only that it is something like "a big pleasure meter" in the brain and that endorphins (the brain's natural painkillers) might be involved.

I propose that this pleasure meter is the brain circuitry for romantic love—orchestrated largely by dopamine networks through the caudate nucleus and other reward pathways in the brain. As ancestral men and women sifted through their array of mating opportunities, the primordial brain circuitry for animal attraction evolved into human romantic love—to help the chooser choose a specific mating partner, pursue this beloved avidly, and devote his/her courtship time and energy to this reproductive prize.

When and where and why did our forebears begin to need complex language abilities and myriad other astounding talents to win a mate? Chimpanzees don't need poetry or guitar music to bed a lover.

What triggered the evolution of these myriad special human talents and the brain circuitry to be wildly drawn to one rather than another: romantic love?

It all began, as Dryden put it, "when wild in wood the noble savage ran."

# 6

# Why We Love:
## *The Evolution of Romantic Love*

The fountains mingle with the river,
And the rivers with the ocean;
The winds of heaven mix forever,
With a sweet emotion;
Nothing in the world is single;
All things by a law divine
In one another's being mingle:—
Why not I with thine?

Percy Bysshe Shelley
"Love's Philosophy"

"I seem to have loved you in numberless forms / numberless times, / In life after life, in age after age forever . . . / Today it is heaped at your feet, it has found its end / in you, / The love of all man's days both past and forever." Indian poet Rabindranath Tagore sensed that his passion for a woman had come across the eons from a mind built long ago. Indeed, we carry embedded in our brains the whole history of our species, all the circuits that our forebears built as they sang and danced and shared their wisdom and their food to impress their lovers and their friends, then passionately fell in love with "him" or "her."

How did we come to court and love the way we do? Bad Bull didn't shower Tia with poetry to prove he was king of elephants. Skipper found his little beaver mate one spring evening; he didn't sing rock 'n' roll songs to a thousand assembled female beavers to impress them first. Misha fell in love with Maria the moment Maria wagged her doggy tail and invited him to play. All animals have mating preferences. And most have evolved courtship plumage of one kind or another to dazzle their would-be lovers. But no creatures except human beings parade about with such extravagant displays as sonnets and skydiving.

As psychologist Geoffrey Miller argues, many of our exceptional human traits, such as our ornate language skills, our affinity for all kinds of sports, our religious fervor, our humor and moral virtue, are too ornate, too metabolically expensive, and too useless in the struggle for existence to have evolved merely so we could survive another day. They must have emerged, at least in part, to help us court and win the mating game.

Moreover, I have proposed that along with all the magnificent courtship ornaments that we flaunt to persuade prospective mates, men and women have also evolved a specific brain network to respond to these traits: the circuitry for romantic love. This passion, a developed form of animal attraction, emerged to drive each of us to choose from among these myriad courtship displays, prefer a specific individual, and begin the primordial mating dance exclusively with "him" or "her."

But Miller never tells us when, where, or why human beings evolved these special talents. And I have not explained how our species transformed from creatures who felt a temporary attraction for a "special" individual into men and women who are willing to die for "him" or "her." Something happened deep in time to produce the human drive to love.

## *Love in the Trees*

Palm trees, fig trees, wild pear trees, mahogany trees, evergreen trees, trees, trees, and more trees carpeted East Africa 8 million years ago. Here lived the last of our forest-dwelling ancestors. Anthropologists have little direct evidence of their daily lives. But our first forebears probably lived much as modern chimpanzees do. We share over 98 percent of our DNA with these creatures. "Common" chimps and their smaller chimp relatives called bonobos still live in what is left of that primal African environment. And chimps display many traits that our common ancestor most likely shared.

Like today's common chimps and bonobos, our first forebears must have lived in communities, often consisting of eighty to a hundred males and females. They slept high in the forest canopy, arose after dawn, and descended to the jungle floor to wander well-worn trails in their mutual home range. Members must have met and mixed singly or in small parties, eating and socializing intensely. These human ancestors knew who was family, friend, and foe. And they chattered among themselves with at least fifty different kinds of hoots and barks, as well as with about thirty varied gestures.

Like today's chimps, they probably used stone hammers to crack nuts, toothpicks made of twigs, and napkins from wadded grass. Like chimps they probably hurled rocks and sticks to spar for dominance, hunted monkeys, shared the meat, and made war on chimp neighbors to usurp their lands. Some were pranksters, some leaders; others brave, deceptive, curious, or belligerent. And many made friends and enemies, gave twigs as gifts, defended comrades in spats, and lingered near dying relatives.

They also made love. Today's chimps and bonobos are among the most sexually active animals on earth. They kiss—sometimes with the deep "French kiss," walk arm in arm, hug, stroke, pat, groom, bow to one another, and often copulate throughout most (if not all) of the female's monthly estrus cycle. But unlike human beings, our last tree-dwelling forebears were almost certainly promiscuous—just as chimpanzees and bonobos are today.

At the height of estrus, an ancestral female may have joined a single male and left the community to copulate with him in private. But this bond was temporary; most likely they never paired for more than a few days or weeks.

Nor did they fall in love. Undoubtedly our first relatives had "favorites," like all other creatures. But these distant kin showed none of the obsessive focus on a single mate that is so characteristic of human romantic passion. And they probably never formed a partnership to rear their young. A mother didn't need a mate to help protect or provide for her and her child. So like chimps, mothers raised their infants by themselves.

Nevertheless, some of our forest-dwelling ancestors must have felt *more* attraction for a mating partner than others did, an affinity that would eventually develop into human romantic love. When, where, and why humanity started to love with new vigor, no one knows. But I think this journey began soon after our forebears began to descend from the trees of East Africa to build a new world on the perilous ground.

## *The Human Stride*

The earliest hominid fossils come from northern Chad. In 2002, anthropologists reported finding an almost complete skull as well as several jaws and teeth in this Central African country.[1]

Some ancient kin lived here, near a shallow, freshwater lake, between 6 and 7 million years ago. They may have spent most of their days in the trees that crowded along the shore. Some must have also ventured into the open plains, sticking close to ribbons of forest that wove through the prairie grass. Perhaps they followed vultures to the half-consumed carcass of an eland or wildebeest. Maybe the bravest hurled sticks and stones at feeding lions, then stole their dinner. Some must have waded into the swampy deep as well, steering clear of dunking hippos to seize a turtle or corner a gazelle that came to drink.

We know little about these relatives. Their bones don't even tell us whether they walked on two feet or four. But "Toumai," as the local people call the Chad skull, was part of our human lineage. True, his brain was no bigger than a chimp's. But he had a flatter face, a more human jaw, and more human teeth. And he and his relatives clearly courted, copulated, and bred.

Their children bred; their children's children's children also bred. Because by 3.5 million years ago many more hominids were roaming the gladed forests and the more open woodlands and savannahs that stretched across East Africa. Anthropologists have found hundreds of their fossilized bones and teeth. These folks had changed. Their feet, legs, hips, and skulls bespeak men and women who walked erect, on two feet instead of four.

I sing the human stride. As we balance our neck and spine above our hips, extend the leg, lock the knee, hit the ground with the heel, then roll onto the ball of the foot and spring off with the big toe, we almost effortlessly fall forward.

This single innovation would change much of life on earth. With walking, our ancestors could carry stones to throw at leopards or lions that stalked them in the dark. With walking, they could carry sticks to dig for roots and tubers. With walking, they could hurl rocks at small animals that nestled in the grass. Bipedalism also liberated their hands for gesturing and freed their mouths for words. With walking, collecting, and carrying, our forebears began their uncharted march toward modernity.

All this is fact. Now for theory. I think the human stride caused a problem for females: they became obliged to carry their babies in their arms instead of on their backs. In the trees, their quadrupedal chimplike ancestors had carried their infants on their backs. In that leafy universe a mother's hands were free to gather fruits and vegetables. And she could easily dash from predators to safe places high above the ground. But as our forebears began to walk along the ground beneath the trees and out onto the open plains, as well as carry sticks and stones to harvest dinner, I think females became overburdened.

How could a young mother dig for roots and catch small animals with one arm while she carried a squirming, twenty-pound infant in the other? How could she sprint away from hungry lions that licked their chops as she toted armloads of bulky things? I believe these early females began to need mates to help feed and protect them—at least while they carried and nursed a child.

As pair-bonding became essential to females, it became suitable to males. How could a male protect and provide for a harem of females? Even if he succeeded in attracting a flock of women, other males would join his group to woo them, perhaps even steal away with one or more. But a male could provision and safeguard a single female and their nursing child.

So as our forebears adopted life on the dangerous ground, pair-bonding became imperative for females and practical for males. And monogamy—the human habit of forming a pair-bond with one individual at a time—evolved.[2]

We have some evidence that monogamy evolved long ago. Recently the bones of men and women living some 3.5 million years ago and known as *Australopithecus afarensis* were remeasured for skeletal size. As it turns out, males were somewhat larger than females; in fact the sexes varied from each other in roughly the same proportions that modern men and women vary. Anthropologists regularly use size differences between the sexes of a species to gauge what sort of social group they lived in. And this size difference suggests these early relatives lived in the same sort of social units we do today: they were "principally monogamous."[3]

Scientists have even found genetic evidence of ancestral monogamy. Remember prairie voles, those mouselike creatures that form pair-bonds soon after puberty and settle into a lifetime of burrowing with a spouse? Neuroscientist Tom Insel and his colleagues discovered in these animals an *extra* bit of DNA in the gene that controls for the distribution of vasopressin receptors in the brain, a bit of DNA not present in their promiscuous, asocial cousins, montane voles. These scientists took this tiny piece of DNA out of prairie voles and inserted it into some highly promiscuous male mice. Sure enough, these mice began to form close monogamous relationships with particular females.[4]

Humans have a similar gene that codes for the activities of vasopressin. And some people (but not all) carry this same extra bit of DNA on this gene.[5] Someday we will know exactly what this genetic region does in people and why some carry it and others don't. For the moment we can say this: long, long ago humanity must have needed to pair up to rear their young—because at least one gene that codes for monogamous behaviors is embedded in our DNA.

"Two are better than one," the Bible says.[6] I think our forebears understood this aphorism more than 3.5 million years ago.

## *Evolution of Divorce*

But I don't see why these primordial pair-bonds needed to be permanent. Everywhere in the world where people are permitted to divorce (and economically can divorce), many do. If you ask them why they terminate a union, each gives a different reason. Yet human parting has some patterns—and some of this blueprint appears to have evolved in the cradle of humankind.

I arrived at this conclusion while I was gathering divorce data on fifty-eight diverse human societies recorded in the Demographic Yearbooks of the United Nations.[7] I found several surprising worldwide patterns to human separation. There were many exceptions, of course. But as a rule, couples around the world who divorced, tended to part during and around the *fourth* year of marriage, in their middle twenties and/or with a single dependent child.

At first these patterns were meaningless to me. But as I read about the mating habits of other creatures, I began to see some uncanny parallels.

Only 3 percent of mammals pair up to rear their young; humans are among them; but this habit only occurs under special circumstances. Among these: female mammals form a pair-bond when they cannot rear their infants by themselves.

Such are foxes. The dog fox and the vixen form a pair-bond in mid-February, build several dens, and rear their kits together. They do this because the female bears as many as five exceedingly helpless kits; they are born blind and deaf. And the female's milk is so thin that she must remain in the den almost constantly to feed her young. She will starve unless someone feeds her. So she and a "special" friend form a pair-bond and rear their young together. As the kits wander from the den in high summer, however, parents depart—separately. Their work is done. Next year the couple may reunite; more likely each will take a different mate.

Serial monogamy is common among our feathered friends. The robins that grace our parks each spring pair up for the breeding season. They, too, must divide their duties. Someone must incubate the eggs, then protect the chicks; the other must provide dinner for the family. Successful couples raise several broods. But when the last of the fledglings wing away, parents part. Next year, many will take new spouses.

So, in those species that pair up to rear their babies, many remain together only long enough to raise the young through infancy.

This principle also seems to apply to people. In traditional societies, the lifeway of habitual exercise, a lean diet, and low body weight coupled with the habit of nursing an infant for extended periods around the clock inhibits regular ovulation for several years after childbirth. Among these societies are the !Kung Bushmen of southern Africa, the Australian Aborigines, the Gainj of New Guinea, the Yanomamo of Amazonia, and the Netsilik Eskimos; women in these cultures tend to bear their young about four years apart. As a result, anthropologists think that four-year birth intervals were the regular pattern of birth spacing during our long human prehistory.[8]

Thus the duration of human birth spacing is similar to the general duration of worldwide marriages that end in divorce.

So here's my theory: perhaps like robins, foxes, and many other serially monogamous creatures, ancestral humans living some 3.5 million years ago paired with a mate *only long enough to rear a single child through infancy—about four years.*[9] When a mother no longer needed to nurse or carry an infant constantly and could deposit her baby with grandmother, aunts, sisters, cousins, and older youngsters while she gathered food, she no longer needed a full-time partner to ensure the survival of her child. Indeed she could "divorce" a mate if she found a new man more to her liking. Primitive divorce even had genetic payoffs: men and women who "remarried" could bear young with a different partner—creating beneficial variety in their lineages.

"Trouble is only opportunity in working clothes," wrote industrialist Henry J. Kaiser. As serial monogamy evolved over countless generations, I think this habitual human practice selected for the brain circuitry for short-term attachment. Along with this remarkable innovation came our human concepts of the "father," the "husband," and the nuclear family, our human tendency to become restless in long relationships, and our human penchant to depart a relationship and pair again: serial monogamy.

But did this primitive tendency to form short-term partnerships spark the development of human romantic love?

Perhaps it did. Perhaps the attraction that chimps and other creatures feel for a "special" mating partner became more intense and enduring as primitive men and women began to pair up to rear infants as a team. Then as this attraction slowly ebbed, feelings of intense attachment grew. When their child toddled out of infancy, however, I think many couples began to seek fresh love. A few parents may have remained together to have more children; many others sought new romance—unconsciously driven to bear more varied young.

But the courtship process must have been rather simple some 3.5 million years ago. I say this because these australopithecines had a cranial capacity of some 420 cubic centimeters, only slightly larger than the average cranial capacity of chimps. And impressions left by brain tissue on the inside of these fossil skulls indicate that the regions for human language had not begun to grow. They did not speak in human ways. Moreover, these forebears left no drawings on rock walls, no homemade flutes or drums. They didn't even make flint knives or any other kinds of stone tools for hunting—a hallmark of humankind. Our forebears had not developed the linguistic flair or other courtship tools humanity would come to flaunt. And it was in tandem with the evolution of all these magnificent human talents for wooing that I think human romantic love would bloom.

To court, these australopithecine forebears must have depended on their status in the group, their chimplike wits and charm. They probably felt deep attraction to a mate, even remained attached to a mating partner for a few years. But many went on to court and love anew.

## *"O Brave New World"*

The brave new world of humanness that Miranda wondered at in Shakespeare's *The Tempest* started to appear some 2 million years ago. New people had begun to wander the open plains of what is today Kenya and Tanzania—*Homo habilis,* or handy man.

Archaeologists have found heaps of their unfinished stone tools scattered across the plains of East Africa.[10] Generation after generation of *Homo habilis* peoples must have come to these quarry sites to make hammerstones, knives, anvils, and other tools, leaving behind slivers of flint and lumps of unfinished lava, obsidian, quartzite, and limestone. They weren't highly skilled. They only whacked off one or two sides of rocks to create a sharpened edge or point. But these implements were far superior to those made by any other creature living at the time.

Our *habilis* forebears also assembled at what appear to be meat-processing places. Here they lugged huge hunks of hunted game, then sat and stripped the bones of meat, removed the marrow and the fat, and shared and ate. Some twenty-five hundred tools and animal bones were found in these ancient garbage dumps. These ancestors evidently hunted an assortment of large animals, too. Primitive zebras, horses, pigs, monkeys, gazelles, and many other types of antelope were their prey. And because these animals are too big to be consumed alone, our kin must have shared their spoils according to social rules.

They also left what could be evidence of romantic love.

Some of these hunters left dozens of stone tools around a fallen elephant. All its bones remain except its tusks and toes. Did they remove these appendages to use as amulets for luck in hunting—or in love? Did these hunters give away these trophies to impress "special" girls instead?

I suggest these possibilities because these people were getting smarter. One *Homo habilis* individual who lived some 1.8 million years ago in what is now the badlands of Koobi Fora, Kenya, had a brain capacity of some 775 cubic centimeters. His friends and neighbors had an average cranial capacity of some 630 cubic centimeters. Equally remarkable, one skull dated 1.8 million years ago had an indentation on its inner side to accommodate a brain region we now call Broca's area. Humans use this brain region to form words and produce the sounds of human language.

Talking. There have been so many different theories on the evolution of human language that as long ago as 1866 the Linguistic Society of Paris announced it would accept no more articles on this topic. That declaration has deterred almost no one since. I won't offer another elaborate theory. Nevertheless, as Broca's area started to take a human shape by 1.8 million years ago, it seems reasonable to believe that some of our forebears were beginning to speak with some sort of primitive human tongue.

One can certainly see many purposes for language. With meaningless noises arranged and rearranged to make words, with words strung grammatically together to make sentences, *Homo habilis* men and women could frame arguments, strike deals, support leaders, dupe foes, teach skills, scold cheaters, spread news, set rules, stop tears, define kin, placate gods, and recall events that occurred years ago.

The first human conversations were probably about the weather. I say this because I am constantly amazed at how earnestly and repeatedly people converse on this matter. Unquestionably our forebears also discussed which way the zebras went, the cliffs where the baboons congregate at dusk, the ripe melons near the canyon edge, and why Mara's little baby cries at night. They probably expressed hundreds of other thoughts and feelings about today, yesterday, and tomorrow.

But with words they could also woo. Men and women could tell clever stories, chant sexy tunes, and entice would-be lovers with insightful thoughts. With words, our forebears could flatter, tempt, and tease. They could gossip, reminisce, and whisper with a beloved, too. As primitive human language gradually emerged, our forebears must have begun our endless human chat about, and with, "him" and "her."

It is at this general time in human evolution that I feel the brain circuitry for animal attraction developed into its human form: romantic love. I propose this for a series of related reasons.

## *Nariokotome Boy*

A boy died. His bones sank into the mud of a swamp some 1.6 million years ago in what today is Kenya. In 1984, paleoanthropologists retrieved almost all of his fossilized remains.[11] When they reassembled his bones and teeth, they gazed upon a child who was somewhere between the ages of eight and twelve. He looked unnervingly like you and me.

Nariokotome Boy, as anthropologists call this stunning fossil find, might have stood over six feet tall had he lived to adulthood. His hands, arms, hips, and legs were similar to ours. In fact, had he worn a mask, he could have walked along any street today without notice. Had he removed his headgear, however, we would have gasped. Nariokotome Boy had thick brow ridges above his eyes. His forehead was low and sloped. His face protruded. His teeth were big. And he had no chin.

Yet he and his *Homo erectus* relatives had evolved in many ways.

These people made fancy tools, known as Acheulean hand axes. Some were almond-shaped, others looked like a pear or teardrop; many were seventeen inches from tapered tip to rounded butt; and all were well balanced and quite symmetrical. These folk had conventions for making tools and weapons. And they left thousands of their streamlined hand axes, as well as an enormous variety of cleavers, picks, and knives, along the bogs, marshes, lakes, streams, and rivers of East Africa. They were hunters.

They felled huge creatures, too. They left hundreds of tools around the skeletons of hippos, elephants, buffalo, and zebras. To track, surround, and kill these beasts, they needed acute spatial skills. To parcel out their booty, they needed memory of their obligations and advanced linguistic skills. To appease, impress, coordinate, and cooperate as a group they must have needed humor, compassion, and many other executive social skills as well. *Homo erectus* men and women were becoming human.

Nariokotome Boy and his relatives also harnessed fire.

Not the computer, the printing press, the steam engine, or the wheel would transform humanity as did this basic technological development: controlling flame.

With fire they could harden points on spears, smoke small mammals from their burrows, drive elephants into bogs, steal a lion's supper, and frighten all sorts of creatures from their caves—and then move in. The sick, the young, the old could lounge in camp. They were able to maintain a camp. And they could extend the day into the night, talk around the flame, and sleep in its protective glow. Unchained from the circadian rhythms of all other animals, these forebears had time to sing and dance, propitiate unknown forces, mull over yesterday, decide about tomorrow—and explore beyond the horizon to the north.

Explore they did. Carrying burning embers, our *Homo erectus* ancestors moved out of Africa to explore colder climes, in part because they could. Some 1.8 million years ago the earth's temperature plunged, beginning the Glacial Ages. Periodically mountains of ice would suck up ocean waters and the world sea level would drop over three hundred feet, leaving wide land highways out of Africa. The big herd animals headed north to pastures fresh and new. *Homo erectus* families followed—leaving their bones and tools in far-flung Europe, China, and Java more than a million years ago.

## *Brain Power*

Of all the gifts bestowed by flame, however, perhaps the most remarkable was humankind's new ability to cook food. I think this innovation contributed considerably to the evolution of human romantic love.

Cooking meat hastens the release of amino acids that aid digestion.[12] Cooking vegetables destroys toxins. And cooking any food devastates microorganisms that can take up residence in the gut and kill. Cooking helped Nariokotome Boy and his relatives survive and thrive.

But cooking also spurred the evolution of the human brain, for an interesting reason. Animals must expend a great deal of metabolic energy to build and maintain their heart, liver, kidneys, stomach, and intestines. They must expend even more energy to build and feed their brain. So animals must allocate their resources. And because creatures that eat mainly leaves must devote a huge amount of energy to their digestive organs, they cannot support a complex brain as well.[13] Those who eat meat, however, have extra fuel to allot to brain power.

*Homo erectus* did just that. Nariokotome Boy had a cranial capacity of approximately 880 cubic centimeters. And some of his relatives had brain volumes as big as 1,000 cubic centimeters, not too much smaller than the modern human cranial capacity of about 1,325 cubic centimeters.

What an investment. While the human brain is only 2 percent of our body weight, it consumes 25 percent of our metabolic energy and 40 percent of our blood glucose as food. Thousands of genes, indeed one-third of our genome, direct its development. During their first year infants spend 50 percent of their metabolic energy just constructing and refining brain mechanisms.[14] Moreover, the slightest mistake in these processes can seriously impair brain function. So the evolving *Homo erectus* brain was exceedingly costly, as well as highly vulnerable to mutations and poor engineering.

This magnificent organ *must* have served crucial purposes: among them may have been to impress potential mating partners with new types of linguistic, artistic, moralistic, or other forms of seductive flair.

Bigger brains would cause trouble for women, however—an obstetrical dilemma that I believe spurred the evolution of romantic love.

## *The Obstetrical Dilemma*

How could *Homo erectus* women bear big-headed babies through their little birth canals? The size of the human pelvis must retain its basic shape to enable upright walking. So as the infant's head increased in size, ancestral women became obliged to deliver their infants in an *earlier* state of development. Anthropologists think this "obstetrical dilemma" began to occur by the time the adult human cranial capacity had reached about 800 cubic centimeters—during *Homo erectus* times.

Many women must have died as they tried to deliver their big-headed young. But nature likes variety, and some fortunate females must have been able to give birth to their infants in an earlier stage of growth. These babies lived. And rapidly our forebears evolved a hallmark of our species: exceedingly helpless, undeveloped infants.

With this remarkable evolutionary development, *Homo erectus* women must have felt overwhelmed by the job of parenting.

To make matters worse for mothers, childhood almost doubled. Chimpanzees complete puberty around age ten; we humans don't complete our growth until around age eighteen. And unlike chimps who begin to feed themselves around age four, human children depend on adults until the late teenage years. This phenomenon is known as "delayed maturation." Anthropologists believe it first developed in *Homo erectus* times.[15]

What a burden—small, weak, needy infants who often remained boisterous, willful, unskilled, and hungry for almost twenty years.

With the origin of big-game hunting, fancy tools and weapons, the harnessing of fire, our growing brains, our tiny helpless babies, our long teenagehood, and our march from Africa into chilly, dangerous northern worlds, our ancestors must have felt intense pressure to find mates they could live with for longer periods of time. Parenting had become far too much for one.

With these developments I believe courtship intensified. Individuals needed to distinguish themselves in new and special ways to attract mates with whom they were genuinely compatible. Men and women had already begun to develop a modicum of verbal ability, artistic verve, humor, inventiveness, courage, and many other human gifts in order to survive on the open plains, as well as the brain circuitry to appreciate these skills in others. Now suitors increasingly used these talents to display their usefulness and good genes to potential lovers, too. Those being wooed responded, due to their preexisting preference for these skills.[16]

With this greater need to seek and choose a *long-term* partner, I think the brain circuitry for human romantic love emerged.

## *Evolution of Human Romantic Love*

The process was probably rather simple. A million years ago, some ancestors excelled at clever remarks or charismatic speeches; others were good at athletic feats. The forerunners of our modern journalists kept track of the group's doings; they impressed potential mates with news and gossip. The first poets charmed their admirers with rhythmic tales. The ancestors of Rembrandt and Matisse drew better pictures in the dirt. And the forerunners of our rock stars and opera divas swayed potential lovers by singing tribal myths. Some cured the sick. Some communed with the spirits of the wind and night. Some were daring; some extraordinarily generous. Others made their sweethearts laugh. "When a man makes her laugh, a woman feels protected," wrote Ugo Betti. *Homo erectus* women must have adored witty fellows—and joined them in the bushes on idle afternoons.

In those demanding days of yesteryear, our forebears came to need more and more special talents to entice potential mates into long-term partnerships. Those who excelled at complex forms of language, art, or song survived and bred—passing these and many other exquisite human talents along to us. But each man and woman "advertised within their budget," because each had a limited amount of metabolic energy and brain circuitry to expend.[17] Suitors therefore specialized—and displayed their special wares to catch a mate.

This courting process continues. Einstein once asserted that "a person who has not made his great contribution to science before the age of 30 will never do so." Although all of us can list men and women who excelled later in life, Dr. Satoshi Kanazawa of the London School of Economics recently confirmed Einstein's statement and offered a Darwinian explanation. After studying 280 great male scientists, he confirmed that 65 percent of them made their biggest discoveries before age thirty-five. He also noted that most lost their creative drive after a few years of marriage. Kanazawa concludes that these young geniuses were "seeking to impress women with their virtuosity."[18]

I think young *Homo erectus* men (and women) were seeking to impress potential mates with their virtuosity more than a million years ago.

More important to our story: as suitors displayed their various special talents, those *viewing* these courtship ploys began to need advanced reasoning, judgment, insight, memory, awareness, consciousness, self-consciousness, and many other sophisticated brain mechanisms to distinguish among courters.

They also needed the brain circuitry to appreciate these courtship displays. They needed to relish morality, admire religious fervor, treasure novelty, esteem clever poems and touching rhythms, delight in good conversation, cherish honesty, applaud determination, and value myriad other aptitudes. They had to evolve the brain power to detect fakers. And they surely needed to develop brain mechanisms to decipher what potential lovers were thinking. Called "theory of mind," this ability to understand the mental states of others, their desires and intentions,[19] is particularly well developed in humans. *Homo erectus* men and women needed the mental machinery to assess personality and accomplishment in order to appraise and value their suitors a million years ago.

*They also needed a mighty biological urge to drive them to focus their courtship energy on a specific mating partner, an urge so potent they would be willing to make a long-term commitment to this special individual, even die for "him" or "her."*

"What does not destroy me, makes me strong," wrote Friedrich Nietzsche. Among *Homo erectus* people, the vicissitudes of childbirth and delayed maturation spurred the need for long-term pair-bonds and greater courtship ingenuity. And this courtship pressure gave rise to our extraordinarily fancy human aptitudes, our human mental machinery to appreciate these talents, and the brain circuitry for romantic love—the passion to drive the "courter" and the "courted" to make a deep commitment to rear their young together for years and years.

"O, I willingly stake all for you," declared Walt Whitman. Men and women needed to say these words over a million years ago.

## *The Mind Evolved by Daylight*

Of course, our *Homo erectus* forebears had other vital reasons to develop uniquely human capacities. Nariokotome Boy and his relatives needed to feel empathy for a wounded comrade, patience for a cranky child, understanding for a disgruntled teen, and to develop the social graces to get along with obstreperous or pompous members of the group. They were a band. They had to move together through the grass, a killing field for predators. So those who could perceive dangers, remember past calamities, devise strategies, articulate choices, make decisions, judge distances, foresee obstacles, and persuade comrades with convincing postures and compelling words disproportionately survived. The human mind evolved by daylight.

But after dark they must have assembled around the firelight to roast their meat, sharpen spears, rock their cooing infants, and imitate the ostrich, hog, or panther as the old folks slept. They must have sung of courage, fortitude, and conquest, leapt and wrestled to show endurance, wept to show compassion, and clowned to parade their wit. Many also slipped away to cuddle. By moonlight, our outstanding aptitudes also took their human shape.

## *Marching toward Modernity*

As time passed, our forebears left increasing evidence of their courting life. By 500,000 years ago, someone in what is now Ethiopia had a brain volume of roughly 1,300 cubic centimeters, within the modern human range. He or she certainly had a complex brain—and a mind capable of passionate romantic love.

About 250,000 years ago, a man living in what we know as England meticulously chipped a symmetrical hand axe around a fossil shell he had found embedded in a lump of flint. Perhaps it was a gift to a beloved or an advertisement to show a lover his tool-making prowess. In fact, scientists now maintain that the huge seventeen-inch hand axes our forebears chipped for over a million years were too big to serve on the hunt or to gather vegetables or roots. Because many are unwieldy and meticulously fashioned, they may well have been used to impress and woo.[20]

Sixty thousand years ago people living in the Zagros Mountains of northeastern Iraq buried someone in a shallow grave one June day and covered the corpse with hollyhocks, grape hyacinth, bachelor's buttons, and yellow flowering groundsel. Perhaps one of them yearned to see a beloved one in an afterlife. At this same time, someone in France scraped lumps of hematite and manganese to make earthy red and gray-white powders. With these, a woman may have decorated her hips and breasts for a summer dance.

By thirty thousand years ago, Cro-Magnon people sported totally modern human skulls, as well as brains like yours and mine. Now they would decorate just about everything they touched. Skilled artists descended into huge caverns beneath France and Spain to draw magnificent bulls, reindeer, ibexes, rhinos, lions, bears, and magical beasts on dank cave walls. These black, red, and yellow creatures pound along these grottos with such vigor they almost come alive. Breaking the utter silence of these vaults, musicians played flutes and drums. Hundreds stenciled their handprints on craggy walls. Sculptors left behind small bison of fired clay. And footprints in some caverns still tell of those who danced in the flickering light of oil lamps.

From Europe to Siberia, people also carved grotesquely buxom, faceless female fertility symbols out of stone, as well as realistic figurines of women they must have known. Hunters engraved the handles of ivory tools with graceful horses. And men and women bedecked themselves with beads, bracelets, and probably tattoos, as well as caps, headbands, and gowns. Wall paintings even suggest that women coiffed their hair.

Then by four thousand years ago, someone in ancient Sumeria wrote the first love letter ever found, inscribed in cuneiform on a fist-sized piece of clay. Today it sits in the Museum of the Ancient Orient in Istanbul, Turkey, a postcard from the past. This person loved. He or she felt the same rapture that lovers felt a million years before.

### *The Human Capacity to Love*

I once believed that Skipper, Maria, Tia, and the rest of the animals who have become enamored of their mating partners feel the same sensations that you and I feel when we fall in love. I reasoned that as our ancestors got smarter, humanity simply embroidered this animal magnetism with a host of cultural traditions and beliefs. I have changed my mind. What convinced me that the human experience of romantic love is far more complex—and more intense—is the impressive brain architecture that generates our intellect and feelings.

"The brain is my second favorite organ," Woody Allen reportedly joked. Had Woody thought carefully about the abilities of the human brain, he might have made it number one. We are so much smarter, so much funnier, so much more mechanically adept, artistic, spiritual, inventive, altruistic—and sexy—than any other animal that if you could somehow combine all the mental capacities of all non-human creatures, they would not equal the capabilities of a seven-year-old human child.

I think the mental equipment that produces these human talents also creates in humanity a *greater* capacity for romantic love.

To begin with, the higher primates have larger brains than most mammals, relative to body size. The human cerebral cortex (the outer rind with which we do our thinking and recognize our feelings) is almost *three times* bigger than that of the apes—gorillas, chimps, and orangutans.[21] The human brain is heavier, too. The chimp brain weighs about one pound while the human brain weighs three.[22] And size counts. Paul M. Thompson of the University of California, Los Angeles, has shown that the number of gray cells in the frontal lobes is significantly linked to intelligence.[23]

The human brain is also more complex. The number of nerve connections between specific brain regions has increased significantly over that of the apes.[24] We even have more genes to build and maintain the brain. Humans have about thirty-three thousand genes. About one-third of them construct and sustain brain functions. And although we don't have many more genes than apes, just a few hundred extra can make a qualitative difference in how the brain operates because genes interact—exponentially increasing the number of possible combinations. Known as the "combinatorial explosion," at some point our forebears acquired a few more genes and thus *much* more machinery to build and operate an elaborate brain. Some of our genes even work faster than those of our closest kin.[25]

Not only is the human brain generally bigger and more complex, but almost all of its specific regions have expanded.

For example, the prefrontal cortex, the collection of brain parts that reside directly behind your forehead, is twice as large as that of other primates (see diagram on page 70).[26] It is more convoluted, too,[27] with a cortical folding that provides extra space for thinking. These regions are central to "general intelligence."[28] Here we assemble facts, reason, weigh options, exercise forethought, generate insights, make decisions, solve problems, learn from experience, and plan ahead. We also add meaning and emotional value to our thoughts, assess our risks, and monitor the acquisition of rewards.

With this remarkable brain region, the prefrontal cortex, humans have infinitely more capacity to *think* about "him" or "her."

Our human brains also enable us to *feel* intensely. Frankly, I have long thought that nature overdid it when it comes to human emotions. We "feel" too much. Now I know why. The human amygdala, an almond-shaped region on the side of the head beneath the cortex, is more than twice the size of the amygdala in apes.[29] This brain region plays a central role in generating fear, rage, aversion, and aggression; parts produce pleasure, too. With this brain capacity for generating strong, often violent emotions, we humans have the ability to link our drive to love with an enormous collection of feelings.

We are also uniquely endowed to *remember* "him" or "her." "Memory, of all the powers of the mind, is the most delicate and frail," wrote Ben Jonson. 'Tis true. Just try to memorize a long poem or remember what you ate a week ago today. To help us remember, however, nature contrived to make our hippocampus, the brain region we use to produce and store memories, almost twice as big as that of the great apes.[30] This brain region exquisitely recalls the feelings that accompany memories as well. With this remarkable factory and storage bin, the hippocampus, we humans are able to recollect the smallest details about "him" or "her."

But of all the brain parts that evolved to intensify the experience of romance, undoubtedly the most important is the human caudate nucleus. As you may remember, the caudate became active as our lovesick subjects gazed at the photos of their beloveds. This brain region is associated with focussed attention and intense motivation to win rewards. And it is twice as large in humans as in our closest kin.[31] As the caudate enlarged among our *Homo erectus* ancestors, it may have intensified the urge to seek and win a sweetheart.

Exactly when a primitive form of animal magnetism finally

evolved into human romantic love—with all its complex thoughts and feelings—no one knows. But many scientists now think that all parts of the human brain (except the cerebellum) expanded in unison.[32] We know when this began: some 2 million years ago. A million years ago, *Homo erectus* peoples had considerably larger brains. By 250,000 years ago, some of our *Homo sapien* ancestors had skulls as big as yours and mine. And by 35,000 years ago, their brains had taken our modern shape.

Humanity had emerged from its jungle crucible. Someday we may lift off from Earth entirely and soar toward the stars. These voyagers will carry in their heads exquisite mental machinery born on the grass of ancient Africa over a million years ago. Among these special talents will be our wit, our flair for poetry, the arts, and drama, a charitable spirit, and many other courting traits, including the astonishing human ability to fall head-over-heels in love.

## *Capricious Love*

"But I am tied to very thee / By every thought I have; / thy face I only care to see, / Thy heart I only crave."[33] In the mid-1600s, Sir Charles Sedley vividly expressed this intense drive to love another. But alas, this feeling isn't always joyful.

As you know, romantic love does not necessarily go hand in hand with the urge to attach to a mating partner over a long period. You can fall in love with someone from a different walk of life whom you never wish to marry. And you can feel romantic passion for one person *while* you feel deeply attached to another, usually a spouse. Moreover, you can have sex with someone for whom you feel no romantic love, even feel romantic passion for one individual while you copulate with another. What madness—to be socially or sexually entwined with one person and wildly in love with someone else.

Why has the brain circuitry of romantic love become unlinked from feelings of lust and long-term attachment?

I think love's capriciousness is part of nature's plan. If a *Homo erectus* man had one wife and two children and meanwhile fell in love with a woman from a different band and secretly gave her two more young, he would double the number of his descendants. Likewise, an ancestral woman who was wedded to one man yet became entranced by another might bear her sweetheart's baby and/or acquire extra food and protection for the children she had already borne. In short, the fickle brain circuitry for romantic love is capricious by nature's design. It enabled our ancestors to follow *two complementary reproductive strategies in tandem.* Nariokotomi Boy and all his relatives could make a socially sanctioned mating relationship with one partner; with a clandestine lover, they could beget additional babies and/or acquire extra resources as well.

Today many men and women still pursue this dual reproductive strategy. The most recent statistics on American adultery come from a study done at the National Opinion Research Center in Chicago in 1994. Here scientists polled 3,432 Americans between the ages of eighteen and fifty-nine on many aspects of their sexuality.[34] One-fourth of these men and 15 percent of these women revealed that they had philandered during their marriage. Others may be lying, because many scientists think these figures are far too low.[35] American philanderers even have children by their clandestine partners. In a 1998 program to screen for genetic diseases, scientists were astonished to find that 10 percent of children tested were not the offspring of their legal fathers.[36]

These adulterers are hardly unique. Philandering is common in all human societies on record.[37] "Cheating" is even common among other "socially monogamous" creatures.[38] In a study of 180 species of songbirds, some 90 percent of females bore some infants that were genetically unrelated to the "father" who fed them.[39] In fact, it has been said that the only truly monogamous creature in the state of California is a particular kind of vole.

We were built to love and love again. What joy this passion brings when you are single and starting out in life, divorced in middle age, or alone in your senior years. What confusion, what sorrow this chemistry can generate when you are married to someone you admire, then fall in love with someone else.

The independence of these emotion systems—lust, romantic attraction, and attachment—evolved among our ancestors to enable men and women to maintain several relationships at once. But this brain circuitry has created tremendous turmoil today—contributing to our worldwide patterns of adultery and divorce, the high incidence of sexual jealousy, stalking, and spousal battering, and the prevalence of homicide, suicide, and clinical depression associated with spurned passion.

Lost love. Almost everyone on earth knows the agony of rejection. Why do you plummet into despair when you lose somebody you adore?

# 7

## Lost Love:
## *Rejection, Despair, and Rage*

Lie still, lie still, my breaking heart;
My silent heart, lie still and break:
Life, and the world, and mine own self, are changed
For a dream's sake.

Christina Rossetti
"Mirage"[1]

"Walking inland, inland, inland, / I am walking inland. / Nobody loves me, she least of all, so I walk inland."[2] An anonymous Inuit of the Arctic recited this sad poem in the 1890s.

Almost everyone in the world feels the agony of romantic rejection at some point in their lives. I have met only three people who claimed never to have been "dumped" by someone they adored. Two were men, one a woman. Both men were handsome, healthy, rich, and exceedingly successful in business. The woman was a young television star. These people are rare. Among college students at Case Western Reserve, 93 percent of both sexes reported that they had been spurned by someone they passionately loved. Ninety-five percent also said they had rejected someone who was deeply in love with them.[3] Almost no one in the world escapes the feelings of emptiness, hopelessness, fear, and fury that rejection can create.[4] "Parting is," as Emily Dickinson wrote, "all we need to know of hell."

Because my brain scanning colleagues and I wanted to understand the full range of romantic feelings, we embarked on a second project: scanning the brains of people who had recently been rejected by romantic partners. We found many volunteers; all were in excruciating psychological pain. In spite of their sorrow, perhaps because of it, they were willing to undergo fMRI testing. This experiment is in progress as I write, but the participants have already told me a great deal about this agony and the stages of despair the rejected lover must endure.

Poet Donald Yates once wrote, "People who are sensible about love are incapable of it."[5] As you will see, few of us are sensible when it comes to rejected romantic passion. We aren't built for it.

## *Rejected Lovers*

"Have you just been rejected in love? But can't let go?" My colleagues and I hung a flyer on the psychology bulletin board on the State University of New York at Stony Brook campus that began with these words. We were determined to scan the brains of men and women who had just been scorned in love. We sought only those who were really suffering.

Rejected sweethearts were quick to respond. As with our earlier experiment, we winnowed out those who were left-handed, had metal in their heads (such as braces on their teeth), were taking antidepressant medications, and/or were claustrophobic. Then I called the applicants and spoke to each at length, discussing the details of their unhappy love affairs and carefully explaining what would happen to them while in the brain scanner.

The procedure I described was the same as the one we used with our subjects who were happily in love. Each participant would alternately look at a photograph of his or her rejecting beloved and a neutral photo that generated no positive or negative feelings; between these tasks the subject would do the mind-cleansing job of counting backward from a large number in increments of seven. Meanwhile, the fMRI machine would record their brain activity.

I found the pre-interviews difficult to do. I was deeply moved by each story that I heard. It seemed to me that all these heartbroken men and women were deeply depressed. I had expected this. But many were also angry, and it was this unforeseen aspect of romantic rejection that made me come to realize the awful power of this passion.

I first saw this scalding "love hatred," as dramatist August Strindberg called it, directly after my brain scanning session with Barbara.

## *Love Hatred*

We had scanned Barbara's brain when she was madly and happily in love with Michael. Like all of the other subjects who were blissfully in love, Barbara had emerged from the first experiment sparkling. Her eyes danced. She giggled softly. She had gotten off the fMRI table gracefully, enthusiastically, full of optimism. And she had commented on how pleased she had been to spend that quiet time looking at the photograph of Michael, reviewing her memories of their times together. But for Barbara this euphoria would not last. Five months later Michael left her.

I learned this one morning when I walked into the psychology lab at SUNY Stony Brook and found her sobbing at a large conference table. I was horrified to see this lovely young woman so broken. Her hair was matted. She had lost weight. Her face was colorless and streaked with trails of tears. She acted as if she were carrying heavy weights on her arms; she hardly moved. And she told me she was "miserable;" that her "self-esteem was shot." "My thoughts," she said, "always go back to Michael . . . I have a lump of unhappiness in my chest." Indeed, she had spent that morning sitting on her bed, staring.

I was so touched by her sorrow that I had to leave the room. But as I stood in a darkened nearby office to collect myself, I came to realize that Barbara might be able to offer some incredibly valuable scientific information: she could show us what happens in the brain when someone has recently been profoundly disappointed in love.

So I apologetically asked Barbara if she would be willing to be scanned again, this time as a subject who had been rejected in love. I warned her that thinking about her relationship while in the brain scanner might trigger powerful feelings, and I assured her that I would talk with her after the brain scanning session to settle her down (if necessary) and that I would also like to call her at home a few days after the procedure to make sure the experiment hadn't caused her further despair. Nevertheless, I explained, this scanning session might help others who were suffering the way she was. I hesitantly suggested we do the experiment the same day.

That sweet girl agreed.

As we walked toward the scanning lab, Barbara dragged; she looked as if she were drowning in despair.

This was just the beginning. Although I had anticipated that Barbara would be upset, I was staggered by what happened directly after the experiment ended. Barbara leapt off the scanning table and bolted out the door, then out of the building altogether. She didn't give me time to talk with her or wait to collect her $50.00 compensation for participating in the project. I was even more stupefied a half hour later when she returned to get the money. She was wildly distraught. I implored her to sit with me in the waiting room. She did. There she began to talk.

She told me that while she had looked at Michael's picture during the experiment, she had recalled all of their arguments. "I will never get over him," she burst out; then she exploded into sobs. As she wept, I noticed something else about Barbara: she was furious at me. She glared at me between her tears. Suddenly she shrieked, "Why do you want to study this?" On she railed as I stared at her, too stunned to speak. Gradually I realized something important: the experience had triggered in Barbara what psychologist Reid Meloy calls "abandonment rage."[6] Barbara was not angry at me; she was furious at Michael. She had attacked me because I was available.

Was the brain circuitry for passionate romantic love, I asked myself, somehow directly connected to the brain networks for what psychologists call hate/rage?

I had long believed that the opposite of love was not hate, but indifference. Now I came to suspect that love and hate/rage might be intricately connected in the human brain, and that indifference might run along an entirely different circuit. Moreover, perhaps this brain link between love and hate/rage could help explain why crimes of passion—such as stalking, homicide, and suicide—are so common around the world: when an attachment is ruptured and the drive to love is thwarted, the brain can easily turn this powerful force to fury.

## *Abandonment Paranoia*

"No doubt this way is best. No doubt in time I'd learn / To hate you like the rest / I once loved."[7] Poet W. D. Snodgrass knew the same rage that Barbara felt. Indeed, I saw this bitter anger in several other jilted subjects as they emerged from the brain scanning machine.

I also saw paranoia—in a beautiful young woman named Karen. Karen's boyfriend, Tim, had deserted her three months earlier. They had been dating for almost two years and planned to marry. They had picked out both an engagement and a wedding ring. So when he left her for a woman at his office, she was stunned. "I lost fifteen pounds in two weeks," Karen moaned. She was still having a hard time sleeping. "I think about him constantly," she told me. "Everything makes me sad. I don't care what I look like, or who I'm with. I don't care about anything at all. It's terrible; it hurts so much." She had put all of Tim's pictures in a box and hidden them in her closet. And she was considering taking antidepressants.

My day with Karen turned bizarre. She seemed dejected when I met her at Grand Central Station in New York City the morning of the scan. But she was convivial, indeed charming, on the two-hour train ride to Stony Brook. When we got to the psychology lab, however, her mood changed from chatty to despondent. On the way to lunch she was teary-eyed. She didn't eat any of her pizza or drink any of her Coke—not a bite or swallow. And she lagged behind as we walked to the scanning lab. Later she told me that the experience had started to overwhelm her. She had begun to feel that she shouldn't have volunteered, that she hated Tim, and that she didn't want to be reminded of him. "This is all a big mistake."

Karen didn't tell me this prior to the scanning session, however. We scanned her brain without incident. But when she emerged from the machine, she was highly agitated. Then it started: she turned on the radiologist, accusing the astonished man of inserting the name "Tim" into the sounds of the MRI machine. "Tim; Tim; Tim; Tim." She told us she repeatedly heard Tim's name as she was looking at his photograph. I assured her over and over that we had not deceived her; that we could not possibly tinker with this complex multimillion-dollar machine even if we wanted to; and that I wouldn't dream of terrorizing her by inserting Tim's name into the sounds of the scanner.

She didn't seem to believe me until we got back onto the train—some two hours and several beers later. Finally, when I thought I had regained her trust, I warily asked her if anyone in her family was paranoid. "Yes," she offered, "my mother." I didn't pursue the conversation further.

I questioned every participant immediately after they emerged from the MRI machine. I wanted to know how they felt as they looked at the photograph of their beloved, what went through their minds as they gazed at the neutral photograph, and how they felt as they performed the count-back task. Apparently as Karen looked at the photograph of Tim, her melancholy and disappointment had turned to rage. Her anger must have then triggered paranoia—because, as she told me later, only after she got angry did she think she heard Tim's name constantly repeated.

Rage, paranoia; only vaguely had I anticipated these reactions. But I had fully expected our rejected subjects to emerge from the scanning machine unhappy. I was right. One young woman cried so hard during the experiment that she soaked the pillow we use to secure each subject's head. In fact, I saw this anguish in almost all our love-scorned subjects. And with each encounter I could not escape thinking about the countless other men and women in every corner of the world who have suffered the same despair.

## *Love Despair*

"Mother, I cannot mind my wheel; / My fingers ache, my lips are dry; / Oh! If you felt the pain I feel! / But oh, who ever felt as I!"[8] To answer Sappho's desperate query made over twenty-five hundred years ago: millions have felt the sorrow of rejection in love.

From the Americas to Siberia, thousands have left lyric remembrances of their heartache. An Aztec Indian left these melancholy words in the sixteenth century: "Now I know / why my father / would go out / and cry / in the rain."[9] "I look at the hand you held, and the ache is hard to bear," a Japanese poet wrote.[10] And Edna St. Vincent Millay left these wrenching lines: "Sweet love, sweet thorn, when lightly to my heart / I took your thrust, whereby I since am slain, / And lie disheveled in the grass apart, / A sodden thing bedrenched by tears and rain."[11]

Anthropologists have collected evidence of this sorrow, too. A forsaken Chinese woman confided, "I can't bear life. All my interests in life have disappeared."[12] "I was lonely and really sad and I cried. I stopped eating and didn't sleep well; I couldn't keep my mind on my work," a scorned Polynesian woman moaned.[13] Up the Sepik River in New Guinea, rejected men compose tragic love songs they call "*namai,*" songs about marriages that "might have been."[14] And in India, brokenhearted men and women have formed a club, the Society for the Study of Broken Hearts. Each year, on the third day of May, they celebrate National Broken Hearts Day, swapping stories and consoling one another.[15]

Rejection by a sweetheart plunges a lover into one of the most profound and troubling emotional pains a human being can bear. Sorrow, anger, and many other feelings can sweep through the brain with such vigor that one can hardly eat or sleep. The degrees and shades of this powerful malaise must be as varied as human beings are. Yet psychiatrists and neuroscientists divide romantic rejection into two general phases: "Protest" and "Resignation/despair."[16]

During the protest phase, deserted lovers obsessively try harder to win back their beloveds. As resignation sets in, they give up entirely and slip into despair.

## *Stage I: Protest*

As a person begins to realize a beloved is thinking of ending the relationship, they generally become intensely restless. Overcome by longing and nostalgia, they devote almost all their time, their energy, and their attention to their departing mate. Their obsession: reunion with their lover.

Many of our scanning subjects found it difficult to sleep. Several had lost weight. Some trembled. Others sighed as they spoke to me of their sweethearts during the prescanning interview. They all reminisced, fixating on the troubled times, repeatedly searching for clues as to what went wrong and pondering on how to patch up the crumbling partnership. And all of them told me they never stopped thinking about their "rejecter"; every waking hour they were plagued by thoughts of "him" or "her."

Spurned lovers also take extraordinary measures to reconnect with their former partner, revisiting mutual haunts, phoning day and night, writing letters, or incessantly e-mailing. They plead. They make dramatic entrances into a beloved's home or place of work, then storm out, only to return and renew their appeal for reconciliation. Most become so focussed on this missing partner that everything reminds them of their sweetheart. As poet Kenneth Fearing put it, "tonight you are in my hair and eyes, / And every street light that our taxi passes shows me / You again, still you."[17]

Most of all, rejected people yearn for reunion. So they protest, relentlessly seeking the slightest sign of hope.

## *Frustration Attraction*

"Love is a sickness full of woes / All remedies refusing; / A plant that with most cutting grows, / Most barren with best using, / Why so?" The seventeenth-century poet Samuel Daniel pinpointed this peculiarity of romantic love: as adversity intensifies, so does romantic passion. This phenomenon is so common in literature and in life that I coined a term for it: "frustration attraction." And I suspect that frustration attraction is associated with brain chemistry.

As you know, dopamine is produced in factories in the "basement" of the brain, then pumped up to the caudate nucleus and other brain regions where it generates the motivation to win designated rewards. If an expected reward is delayed in coming, however, these dopamine-producing neurons *prolong* their activities—increasing brain levels of this natural stimulant.[18] And very high levels of dopamine are associated with intense motivation and goal-directed behaviors, as well as with anxiety and fear.[19] The Roman dramatist Terence unknowingly summed up this chemistry of frustration attraction, saying, "The less my hope, the hotter my love."

Psychiatrists Thomas Lewis, Fari Amini, and Richard Lannon maintain that this protest response is a basic mammalian mechanism that activates when *any* kind of social attachment is ruptured.[20] They use the example of the puppy. When you remove the puppy from its mother and put it in the kitchen by itself, it begins to pace. Frantically, tirelessly it combs the floor, scratches at the door, leaps at the walls, barks and whines in protest. Baby rats that are isolated from their mother hardly sleep because their brain arousal is so intense.[21]

And these psychiatrists believe, as I do, that this protest reaction is associated with elevated levels of dopamine, as well as with norepinephrine. Rising levels of dopamine and norepinephrine, they say, serve to increase alertness and stimulate the abandoned individual to search and call for help.

Indeed, protest can be quite effective in love relationships. Those doing the abandoning often feel deeply guilty about causing the breakup.[22] So the more the rejected partner protests, the more the departing one is likely to reconsider and return to the relationship. Many do, at least temporarily. Protest works.

Not always, however. And sometimes the romantic rift can cause the abandoned partner to panic.

## *Separation Anxiety*

Like the impulse to protest, this panic response is common in nature; it is called "separation anxiety."[23] When a mother leaves a baby bird or infant mammal, these tiny creatures often become profoundly disturbed. Their discomfort starts with a pounding heart. The baby cries and makes sucking gestures. These "distress calls" are frantic and frequent. Abandoned puppies and baby otters whimper, even sob. Baby chickens cheep. Infant rhesus monkeys dolefully give out a "hoo-hoo" sound. When baby rats are separated from their mother, they emit ceaseless ultrasonic cries.[24] Neuroscientist Jaak Panksepp believes that separation anxiety is generated by the panic system in the brain—a complex brain network that makes one feel weak, short of breath, and panicky.[25]

A related brain system also kicks into action: the stress system. Stress begins in the hypothalamus where corticotropin-releasing hormone (CRH) is secreted and travels to the nearby pituitary; here it initiates the release of ACTH, adrenocorticotropin hormone. This travels through the bloodstream to the adrenal gland (which sits atop the kidney) and commands the adrenal cortex to synthesize and release cortisol, the "stress hormone." Cortisol then activates myriad brain and bodily systems to counteract stress. Among them, the immune system revs up to fight disease.[26] Despite this bodily readiness, disappointed lovers tend to get sore throats and colds. Short-term stress also triggers production of dopamine and norepinephrine and suppresses serotonin activity[27]—the combination of elixirs associated with romantic love.

How ironic: as the adored one slips away, the very chemicals that contribute to feelings of romance grow even more potent, intensifying ardent passion, fear, and anxiety, and impelling us to protest and try with all our strength to secure our reward: the departing loved one.

## *Abandonment Rage*

The attempt to win back one's sweetheart, a craving for "him" or "her," separation anxiety, and panic at the impending loss: all these reactions make sense to me. But what causes rejected people to get so fiercely angry? Even when the parting lover honors his or her responsibilities as a friend (and often co-parent) and leaves the relationship with compassion and honesty, many rejected people swing violently from feelings of heartbreak to utter fury. English poet John Lyly commented wisely on this phenomenon in 1579, "As the best wine doth make the sharpest vinegar, so the deepest love turneth to the deadliest hate."

Why so?

Because love and hate are intricately linked in the human brain. The primary circuits for hate/rage run through regions of the amygdala downward to the hypothalamus and on to centers in the periaqueductal gray, a region in the midbrain.[28] Several other brain areas are also involved in rage, including the insula, a part of the cortex that collects data from the internal body and the senses.[29] But here's the key: the basic brain network for rage is closely connected to centers in the prefrontal cortex that process reward-assessment and reward expectation.[30] And when people and other animals begin to realize that an expected reward is in jeopardy, even unattainable, these centers in the prefrontal cortex signal the amygdala and trigger rage.[31]

Known to psychologists as the "frustration-aggression hypothesis," this rage response to unfulfilled expectations is well known in animals. For example, when a cat's brain circuits for reward are artificially stimulated, they feel intense pleasure. If this stimulation is withdrawn, however, they bite. And each time the pleasure is withdrawn, the cat gets angrier. Likewise, scorned lovers just get more and more furious. "All our reasoning ends in surrender to feeling," wrote Blaise Pascal. Pascal clearly knew how victimized we can be by our emotions.

Fury need not be directed at the lost reward, however.[32] An enraged monkey will vent his ire on a subordinate monkey rather than attack a superior. In the same way, a rejected lover might kick a chair, throw a glass, or get angry at a friend or colleague rather than strike an errant sweetheart.

So romantic love and abandonment rage are well connected in the brain. And when you think about it, these passions have much in common. They are both associated with bodily and mental arousal; both produce excessive energy. Both drive one to obsessively focus one's attention on the beloved. Both generate goal-directed behaviors. And both cause intense yearning, either for union with a sweetheart or for revenge against a jilting loved one.

No wonder our scanning subject, Barbara, turned on me. Barbara must have felt deep romantic love for Michael as she looked at his photograph in the fMRI machine; then her thwarted passion turned to frustration, which triggered hate and rage. I just happened to be a convenient target.

"One of the relics of early man is modern man," wrote psychiatrist David Hamburg. Why did our ancestors evolve brain links that enable us to hate the one we cherish?

## *The Purpose of Abandonment Rage*

Rage is exceedingly expensive, metabolically. It stresses the heart, raises blood pressure, and suppresses the immune system.[33] So in ancestral times this link between romantic love and abandonment rage probably evolved to solve an important problem related to mating and reproduction.

At first, I suspected that this brain wiring might have emerged for an entirely different courtship purpose: to fight rival suitors.

"The season of love is that of battle," Darwin wrote.[34] Indeed, many male animals do two things at mating time: They court. And they fight competitors. Male sheep, male sea lions, and males of many other species *must* fight one another to win the right to woo. So I reasoned that perhaps attraction and hate/rage became closely connected in the mammalian brain in order to enable suitors to easily switch back and forth between attraction for a potential mate and rage at a rival. But this theory didn't hold up under closer scrutiny.

Combative male suitors strut and pose and attack one another like gladiators in a duel for love and honor. And when the match is over the winner regularly displays feelings of triumph while the loser slinks off in ignominy. But neither shows fury. There is even sound biological evidence that the neural system for male-male courtship competition is independent of the rage system in the brain. This rivalry is associated with elevated levels of testosterone and vasopressin instead.[35] So human abandonment rage did not evolve from the emotion/motivation systems that mammals use to fight rivals.

Then why does the human brain *easily* enable an abandoned lover to hate the person that he or she adores?

Psychiatrist John Bowlby argued in the 1960s that the anger that accompanies the loss of a loved one is part of nature's biological design to regain the lost attachment figure.[36] Undoubtedly this rage sometimes serves this purpose. But fury is not a likeable trait; I can't imagine it often entices a lover to return to a disintegrating relationship.

So I have come to think that abandonment rage evolved to serve another purpose: to drive disappointed lovers to *extricate* themselves from dead-end matches, lick their wounds, and resume their quest for love in greener pastures.

Moreover, if the rejected person has produced babies during this bankrupt partnership, abandonment rage may give them the energy to fight for the welfare of their children. You certainly see this behavior in contemporary divorce proceedings. Well-adjusted men and women turn vicious to acquire resources for their abandoned young. In fact, an American judge who regularly presides over trials of violent criminals reports that he is much more worried about his personal safety during divorce proceedings, particularly when child custody is an issue. He and other judges have even installed panic buttons in their chambers to push for help in case arguing spouses become violent.[37]

I am not surprised that abandonment rage sometimes erupts into violence. Jilted men and women have wasted priceless reproductive time and energy on a partner who is deserting them. They must start their courtship search again. Moreover, their reproductive future has been jeopardized—along with their social alliances, their personal happiness, and their reputation. Their self-esteem is severely damaged. And time is dribbling by. Nature has given us a powerful purgative mechanism to help us *release* a rejecting mate and get on with living: rage.

Alas, this rage does not necessarily cancel out one's love, one's longing, or one's sexual desire for a departing partner.

In an interesting study of 124 dating couples, psychologists Bruce Ellis and Neil Malamuth found that romantic love and what they call "anger/upset" respond to different kinds of "information."[38] One's degree of anger/upset oscillates in response to events that *undermine* one's goals, such as infidelity or lack of emotional commitment by the partner. One's feelings of romantic love fluctuate, instead, in response to occurrences that *advance* one's goals, such as a partner's social support and happy times in bed together. Hence love and anger/upset, though closely linked, are independent systems; they *can* operate simultaneously. In short, you can be terribly angry but still be very much in love. Such was Barbara.

Eventually, however, all these feelings wane. The focussed attention on the failing partnership, the drive to win back the beloved, the showdowns, the separation anxiety, the panic, even the rage: all dissipate with time. Then the rejected person must deal with new forms of torture—resignation and despair.

## *Stage II: Resignation*

"I am exhausted by longing," wrote the eighth-century A.D. Chinese poet Li Po. Eventually the disappointed lover gives up. Their beloved is gone forever and they are spent. Many plummet into hopelessness. They toss in bed and cry. Drugged by the potent liquor of sorrow, some just woodenly sit and gaze into a void. They hardly work or eat. Perhaps they feel an occasional urge to renew pursuit of their lost love or a passing flash of anger. Generally, they feel deep melancholy. Nothing pries them from their anguish—except time.

Loss of a loved one usually triggers deep sadness and depression in the human animal, what is known to psychologists as the "despair response."[39] In my love survey discussed in chapter one, 61 percent of men and 46 percent of women said that they went through periods of despair when they thought their beloved might not love them (Appendix, #53). And in a study of 114 men and women who had been rejected by a partner within the past eight weeks, over 40 percent were experiencing "clinically measurable depression"; of these, some 12 percent displayed moderate to severe depression.[40] People can also die of a broken heart. They expire from heart attacks or strokes caused by their depression.[41]

Men and women tend to handle love-sadness differently.

Men are often more dependent on their romantic partners,[42] probably because men, as a rule, have fewer ties to relatives and friends. Perhaps because of this, men are more likely to turn to alcohol, drugs, or reckless driving than to their kin or buddies when they despair over a rejecting mate.[43] Moreover, men are less likely to reveal their pain, containing their sorrow within their inner mental core.[44] Some even score low on scales of depression because they have effectively masked their suffering, even from themselves.[45]

Though many cloak their sorrow, interviews with rejected men, and observation of their work performance, their daily habits, and their interactions with friends, often reveal that they are ill—psychologically and physically.[46] Men also show their sorrow in the most dramatic way one can: men are three to four times more likely than women to commit suicide after a love affair has decayed.[47] As poet John Dryden put it, "Dying is a pleasure, / when living is a pain."[48]

Women often suffer differently. In cultures around the world, women are twice as likely as men to experience major depression.[49] They become depressed for many reasons, of course, but a common one is abandonment by a lover. And in studies of romantic rejection, women report more severe feelings of depression, particularly hopelessness.[50]

Rejected women sob, lose weight, sleep too much or not at all, lose interest in sex, can't concentrate, have trouble remembering commonplace daily things, withdraw socially, and contemplate suicide. Locked in a dungeon of despondency, they barely manage life's basic chores. Some write out their grievances. And many women talk, moping for hours on the phone with any sympathetic ear, retelling all. Although this chatter gives women some relief, these replays of shattered dreams often backfire. As a woman dwells on the dead relationship, she feeds the ghost—often inadvertently retraumatizing herself.[51]

This second phase of rejection—resignation coupled with despair—is well documented in other species. Infant mammals suffer terribly when they are separated from their mother. Remember the puppy? When you isolate it in the kitchen, at first it protests. Eventually, however, it curls up in a corner into a despondent heap. Abandoned infant monkeys suck on their fingers or their toes, clasp themselves, and often curl into a fetal position and rock.[52]

The feeling of despair has been associated with several different networks in the mammalian (including human) brain.[53] Among them is the brain's reward system and its fuel: dopamine. As the abandoned partner gradually realizes that the reward will never come, the dopamine-making cells in the midbrain (that became so active during the protest phase) now *decrease* their activity.[54] And diminishing levels of dopamine are associated with lethargy, despondency, and depression.[55] The stress system also contributes. As you may recall, short-term stress activates the production of dopamine and norepinephrine and suppresses serotonin. But as the stress of abandonment wears on, it drives levels of all these potent substances down below normal—producing profound depression.[56]

Shakespeare called the brain the "soul's frail dwelling place." It is also a frail dwelling place for romantic love.

## *Depression as an Adaptation?*

Like abandonment rage, the despair response may seem counterproductive. What's the point of suffering pain and misery when you have lost a sweetheart? Isn't it better to recover your energy than waste it crying?

Many scientists now believe, however, that there are good reasons for depression, so good that this complex brain circuitry evolved as a coping mechanism millions of years ago.[57] Some maintain it originally emerged to enable abandoned infant mammals to conserve stamina, discourage them from wandering until their mother returns, and keep them quiet and thus protected from predators. Depression thus enabled animals to conserve energy in times of stress. Depression also could have driven ancestral humans to abandon hopeless ventures and adopt more successful strategies to achieve their goals—particularly reproductive goals such as getting married.[58]

Despair is such a debilitating experience that it must have evolved for many good reasons. A related purpose I particularly like is proposed by anthropologist Edward Hagen, biologist Paul Watson, and psychiatrist Andy Thomson. These scientists believe that the very high metabolic and social cost of depression is actually its benefit: one's depression is an honest, believable signal to others that something is desperately wrong. Hence depression evolved, they say, to enable stressed ancestors to signal for and acquire social support in times of intense need,[59] particularly when they were unable to verbally persuade or use force to get friends and relatives to support their cause.

An example would be a young woman living a million years ago whose husband openly pursued and copulated with another woman in their camp. At first the young wife bitterly protested, flew into jealous rages, and tried to persuade her husband to dismiss the interloper. Furious, she also appealed to her father and other kin to support her request. Unable to influence her spouse or relatives with words or tantrums, however, she became deeply depressed. This affliction further disrupted camp life, not to mention her ability to gather vegetables and help take care of kids and other kin. So eventually her despondency galvanized her kinfolk to drive out this flagrantly unfaithful husband and console her until she could recover her vitality, find a new man, and contribute more food, child care—and gaiety—to the group.

Aeschylus, the classical Greek dramatist of the fifth century B.C., saw another merit in depression. As he proclaimed in *Agamemnon,* "He who learns must suffer. And even in our sleep, pain that cannot forget falls drop by drop upon the heart, and in our own despair, against our will, comes wisdom to us by the awful grace of god." Depression, in short, can give you insight. Scientists can now explain why. Mildly depressed people make clearer assessments of themselves and others.[60] As psychologist Jeffrey Zeig puts it, "They suffer a failure of denial." Even severe and prolonged depression can push a person to accept unhappy facts, make decisions, and resolve conflicts that will ultimately promote their survival and capacity to reproduce.[61]

So, like the protest response, the despair of rejection probably evolved for a number of reasons. Among them, depressed lovers were able to assemble familiar, loving, patient, compassionate friends and kin around them and use their heightened mental acuity to appraise themselves and their failed love affairs, set new goals, review their courtship tactics, and try their luck again—perhaps even win a more suitable mating partner. The pain rejected men and women endured probably even steered them away from making similar bad choices in the future.

In discussing the evolutionary value of despair, one must distinguish, of course, between the sorrow of romantic rejection and the depression that can accompany a severe, long-term, internal mental disorder, such as bipolar depression. What we are concerned about here is the deep grief that *normally well-balanced* men and women feel for a period of time when they are cast aside by someone they adore.

Not everyone suffers to the same degree, of course. How we react to rejection depends on many forces—including our upbringing. Some people make secure attachments as children and have the self-esteem and resilience to overcome a romantic setback relatively quickly. Others grow up in loveless homes fraught with tension, chaos, or rejection—leaving them clingy, or defenseless in other ways.[62] As we venture into life, we develop new feelings of competence or incompetence, different sorts of romantic expectations, and different coping mechanisms that affect how we weather lost love.[63] Some people have more mating opportunities than others; they easily replace a rejecting partner with amorous distractions that mitigate their feelings of protest and despair. And we are all wired differently; some are simply less angry, less depressed, more self-confident, and more relaxed about life's disasters in general or about romantic rejection in particular.

Still, we human beings are intricately wired to suffer when we have been spurned by a beloved. Everywhere on earth men and women can recall the bitter details of their distress—even many years after the turmoil has defused.[64] For a good evolutionary reason. Those who love and mate and breed will pass on their genes toward posterity, while those who lose in love and sex and reproduction will ultimately die out.

We are designed to suffer when love fails.

Alas, the feelings that accompany rejection can lead some men and women to deeds that earn the deadly mark of Cain.

## *Crimes of Passion: Jealousy*

"We must in tears / Unwind a love knit up in many years. / In this last kiss I here surrender thee / Back to thyself. Lo thou again art free."[65] Poet Henry King was able to let a departing lover go.

Some people find this impossible to do. Even before a partner actually leaves a relationship men and women can be exceedingly possessive of "him" or "her." Jealousy is common around the world.[66] In fact, as discussed in chapter two, this possessiveness is so common in all of nature that scientists call it "mate guarding."

When a relationship is threatened by a rival suitor, some jealous people sulk. Others monopolize the mate's spare time, conceal the loved one by not taking him or her to parties, or even scold a mate who talks to others in social situations. Some try to make a sweetheart jealous in return. Many also try to appear more important, sexier, richer, or smarter than a potential competitor, as well as irresistible themselves. Some shower a beloved with presents and affection to keep the beloved's undivided attention. And some threaten to kill themselves if their partner leaves them for another.

Men and women become jealous over many of the same things. When either sex sees a partner flirting with others, they can become ferociously possessive. Catching a mate kissing, fondling, or copulating with another seriously unhinges most men and women.[67] At different times in life and in different societies, men and women vary in what makes them jealous.[68] But young men and women do show some consistent differences in what triggers feelings of rejection and how they manage a jealous heart.

Men bristle over actual or imagined sexual infidelity.[69] This male bias may have an evolutionary origin. A man runs a considerable risk if he is cuckolded: he could expend an enormous amount of time and energy raising another man's DNA. And men are more likely to challenge a rival, assailing him with nasty words or heavy fists. In many societies, men are also more likely than women to divorce a spouse they believe is sexually unfaithful—which may be a reflection of the male tendency to fear cuckoldry.

If men fear being cuckolded, women fear being abandoned—emotionally and financially.[70] So if the relationship begins to founder, women take steps to overcome the obstacles. Women are more likely than men to overlook a mate's "one-night stand" or temporary sexual fling with a rival. But if a woman thinks her mate is building a serious emotional attachment to another woman, or knows he is spending valuable time and money on this competitor, she can become exceedingly jealous.

This behavior also makes Darwinian sense. For millions of years ancestral women needed mates to help them rear their young. Hence, women have evolved brain mechanisms to make them exceedingly possessive when a mate threatens to withdraw resources or emotional support or abandon the relationship for another.

"Love's like a torch, which if secured from blasts, / Will faintlier burn; but then it longer lasts. / Exposed to storms of jealousy and doubt, / The blaze grows greater, but 'tis sooner out." So wrote poet William Walsh.[71] At first glance, jealousy appears to be a death knell to a love affair. But psychologists believe it can stimulate a mate to soothe the mistrustful partner with declarations of fidelity and attachment. Indeed, these reassurances can contribute to the durability of the relationship.[72]

Jealousy can undermine a love affair, however, and this response can also be adaptive. Jealous men and women are often picking up genuine signals that the relationship is failing. And every day they remain tied to uncommitted partners, they lose opportunities to catch more suitable mates—as well as risk picking up sexually transmitted diseases.

So jealousy has reproductive payoffs. It can strengthen a partnership or destroy it. Either way, jealousy is useful. As a result, this unpleasant trait has become deeply threaded into the skein of human romantic love, part of an array of powerful feelings our forebears needed on the grasslands of ancient Africa to win the courtship game.

When a lover departs for good, however, jealousy, the drive to protest, feelings of depression, and all the other disruptive forces that accompany lost love can lead to violence—and tragedy.

## *Stalking, Battering, Killing*

Men stalk. They obsessively follow and often threaten or harass a lover who has left them.[73] Some shower a departed woman with vile or entreating messages. Some steal valuables or personal items such as underwear. Some follow a former partner in their cars. Others loiter near the partner's home or place of work to jeer or plea. In one study of American college students, 34 percent of women said they had been followed or harassed by a man they had rejected.[74] And one out of twelve American women will be stalked by a man at some point in her life, usually by a former spouse or lover. In fact, the Justice Department reports that every year over a million American women are stalked (most are between ages eighteen and thirty-nine); 59 percent of them are stalked by boyfriends, husbands, former spouses, or live-in partners.[75] One out of four women are also hit, slapped, shoved, or otherwise physically assaulted by their stalkers.[76] In fact, five independent investigators on three continents report that in some 55 percent to 89 percent of cases, stalkers became violent toward former sexual intimates.[77] Most are men.

Men also batter. One-third of all American women seeking emergency medical care, one of four women who attempt suicide, and some 20 percent of pregnant women who seek prenatal care have been battered by an intimate partner.[78] And in a study of thirty-one battered American women, twenty-nine reported that a male partner's jealousy was a frequent cause of the beatings.[79] These statistics are not surprising. The most common cause of wife battering everywhere in the world is male possessiveness.[80]

Men kill too. About 32 percent of all female murder victims in the United States die at the hands of spouses, ex-spouses, boyfriends, and ex-boyfriends, but experts believe the true numbers may be as high as 50 percent to 70 percent instead.[81] Over 50 percent of these murderers stalk their lover first.[82] Men commit the vast majority of spousal homicides in all other countries, too.[83]

The classic tale of jealous murder is Shakespeare's *Othello*. What a mess. Othello, a dark-skinned Moor, had achieved the rank of general because of his valor in the Venetian wars against the Turks. Now returned to Venice, he meets Desdemona, the beautiful daughter of a senator. The Moor and the maiden fall in love almost instantly; secretly they marry. But Othello has used a go-between, Cassio, to help court the fair Desdemona. And to reward the young soldier, he promotes him to be his chief lieutenant.

Iago, one of the most treacherous villains in all of Western literature, coveted this rank. He smolders with concealed hatred for Cassio and the Moor. And he vows revenge. Craftily, Iago begins to feed Othello false innuendos about Desdemona's sexual infidelity with Cassio. The Moor is a naive man, commanding in temperament and swift to action. He soon begins to seethe with jealousy, raging, "I had rather be a toad, / And live upon the vapor of a dungeon, / Than keep a corner in the thing I love / For others' uses."[84] Finally driven wild, Othello suffocates his adoring and faithful wife.

Historically many societies have fostered this male predilection to guard a mate from poachers or desertion. English common law regarded the slaughter of an adulterous wife as understandable, even justified—if done in the heat of passion.[85] Legal traditions in Europe, Asia, Africa, Melanesia, and among American Indians historically also condoned or overlooked murder by a jealous husband.[86] And until the 1970s, in several American states it was lawful to kill an adulterous wife.[87]

At the base of all this violence is a primordial male urge to protect oneself from cuckoldry and hold on to the vessel that may bear their DNA. Not surprisingly, American women—from all ethnic groups and economic backgrounds—are six times more likely than men to be victims in crimes of passion between intimates.[88]

## *Feminine Vengeance*

Women are far less likely to maim or murder when they are jealous of a rival and fearful of abandonment. They tend to berate themselves for their own inadequacies and try to lure and seduce instead, hoping to recapture their mate's affections and rebuild the relationship.[89] They are also more likely to try to understand the problems and talk things over. But when all this fails, some women stalk. Some 370,000 American men reported being stalked in 1997; most were between the ages of eighteen and thirty-nine—men of reproductive age.[90]

Unlike men, many female stalkers have other mental problems. Like men, however, they send e-mails or letters, phone ceaselessly, or appear unexpectedly as they obsessively follow a departed mate. I know of one woman who used to sleep on her former lover's doorstep.

Women also kill rejecting lovers. But far fewer take this drastic step. In 1998, only 4 percent of male homicide victims were killed by a former or current female partner.[91]

Of all the tales of female mayhem, the most shocking to my mind is that of Medea, the princess of ancient Colchis. As told by the Greek dramatist Euripides in the fifth century B.C., Medea was "mad with love for Jason," a Greek.[92] To help him in his quest to retrieve the Golden Fleece, she was disloyal to her father, set her sisters against her brother and had him slain, and fled her homeland. Then Medea traveled with Jason to settle in Corinth with their two young sons. Alas, the ambitious Jason deserted her to marry the daughter of Creon, king of Corinth. As Medea's children's nurse says of Medea, "She will not eat; she lies collapsed in agony, / Dissolving the long hours in tears."[93] Finally the tormented Medea sends Jason's new wife a wedding present—a poisoned dress that erupts into flames and burns the Corinthian princess and the king to death. But Medea is not through with Jason. She slaughters their two sons, too. In effect, Medea murdered Jason's living genes and destroyed his reproductive future.

Like love, hate is blind; for some, no form of violence is too extreme. And this violence is driven, in least *in part,* by brain chemistry. As you recall, when lovers are first rejected, they protest—a reaction that is accompanied by soaring levels of dopamine and norepinephrine. These elevated levels of natural stimulants probably give the stalker, the batterer, and the murderer their focussed attention and wild energy. Moreover, rising levels of dopamine often *reduce* levels of serotonin in the brain. And low levels of serotonin are associated with impulsive violence against others.[94]

Stalkers and murderers are responsible for their crimes of passion, of course. Indeed, we have evolved sophisticated brain mechanisms for *curbing* our violent impulses. Nevertheless, we do carry within us a "fatal reflex," as psychologist William James called our human ferocity. And some wretched men and women do not contain it: they slaughter their sweethearts.

Others kill themselves.

## *Love Suicide*

Human beings are the only creatures on earth who commit violent suicide in high numbers.

It is difficult to obtain accurate accounts of why healthy people kill themselves; solid statistics are lacking. Loss of money, power, status, or respect, or the realization that one will never achieve a long-sought goal can drive a person to quit this life. But most men and women don't have a lot of money, power, prestige, or goals they can't attain. They do, however, fall desperately in love. And romantic love, as you know, is associated with high levels of dopamine and probably norepinephrine—brain substances that often drive down levels of serotonin. Not coincidentally, I think, low levels of serotonin are associated with suicide.[95]

In short, when a love affair turns sour, the human brain is already chemically set up for depression—and possible self annihilation. I suspect many of the men and women around the world who kill themselves do so over lost love. For centuries, the Japanese even glorified this act, regarding "love suicide," as they called it, as an honorable statement of one's devotion.[96]

*Attempted* love suicide may even have been adaptive in ancestral times.[97] Many suicidal people, largely women, fail to actually kill themselves. And psychiatrists now believe these cases are examples of an extreme strategy that jilted women use to manipulate a lover into returning to the relationship. Alas, many misjudge their tactics and mistakenly kill themselves instead. Suicide is unquestionably maladaptive. Yet it is prevalent everywhere, particularly among men. For these unfortunate people the primordial drive to love triumphed over their will to live.

"How cruel, you say. But did I not warn you? Shall I count for you love's ways? Fear, jealousy, revenge—pain. They all belong to love's innocent game." These words come across the centuries to us from the Celtic legend of Tristan and Iseult. How can you stifle this passion for a partner who has deserted you? How can you induce romantic feelings in someone you find attractive, even jump-start a feeling of romantic rapture in yourself? Perhaps most important, how can one maintain the euphoria of romantic love in a long-term partnership?

I think we can control this passion. But one has to trick the brain.

# 8

## Taking Control of Passion:
### *Making Romance Last*

> How say you? Let us, O my dove,
> Let us be unashamed of soul,
> As earth lies bare to heaven above!
> How is it under our control
> To love or not to love?
>
> Robert Browning
> "Two in the Campagna"

"Her whole character seemed to change with her change of fortune. Her sorrows, the depression of spirits, were forgotten, and she assumed all the simplicity and vivacity of a youthful mind. . . . She was playful, full of confidence, kindness and sympathy. Her eyes assumed new lustre, and her cheeks new colour and smoothness. Her voice became cheerful; her temper overflowing with universal kindness; and that smile of bewitching tenderness from day to day illuminated her countenance." The handsome, dashing, auburn-haired Mary Wollstonecraft, founder of the British feminist movement in the late eighteenth century, had fallen in love.[1]

"Love's weather is so fair," wrote William Cavendish.[2] Indeed, we radiate when we love. We also agonize and hope. Most of all we crave;

we want to see and touch and laugh and love and to be loved in return. Fueled by one of nature's most stimulating chemicals, we galvanize our energy, focus our attention, and seek our prize. Romantic love is an urge, a want, a need—a primordial mating drive that can be, at times, more powerful than hunger.

## *Addicted to Love*

World poetry and literature even refer to romantic passion as a form of hunger. In the Song of Songs, the ancient Hebrew love poem, the woman exclaimed, "I am starved for his love."[3] In the Chinese fable "The Jade Goddess," Chang Po said to his beloved, Meilan, I "crave to see you."[4] In the Arabian tale, Majnun cried out, "My beloved, send a greeting, a message, a word. I am starving for a token, a gesture from you."[5] And Richard de Fournival in his thirteenth-century book, *Advice on Love,* said of this magic, "Love is an unquenchable fire, a hunger without surfeit."

Because romantic love is such a euphoric "high," because this passion is exceedingly difficult to control, and because it produces craving, obsession, compulsion, distortion of reality, emotional and physical dependence, personality change, and loss of self-control, many psychologists regard romantic love as an addiction—a positive addiction when your love is returned, a horribly negative fixation when your love is spurned and you can't let go.[6]

Our fMRI experiment on people in love supports this proposition: romantic love is an addictive drug.

Directly or indirectly, virtually all "drugs of abuse" affect a single pathway in the brain, the mesolimbic reward system, activated by dopamine.[7] Romantic love stimulates parts of the same pathway with the same chemical. In fact, when neuroscientists Andreas Bartels and Semir Zeki compared the brain scans of their love-stricken subjects with those of men and women who had injected cocaine or opioids, they found that many of the same brain regions became active, including the insular cortex, the anterior cingulate cortex, the caudate, and the putamen.[8]

Moreover, the bewitched lover shows the three classic symptoms of addiction: tolerance, withdrawal, and relapse. At first the lover is content to see the beloved now and then. But as the addiction escalates, they need more and more of their "drug." With time they hear themselves whispering, "I crave you," "I can't get enough of you," even "I can't live without you." When the lover is out of touch with the beloved, even for a few hours, he or she longs for renewed contact. Every phone call that is not from the beloved is a disappointment.

And if the beloved breaks off the relationship, the lover shows all the common signs of drug withdrawal, including depression, crying spells, anxiety, insomnia, loss of appetite (or binge eating), irritability, and chronic loneliness. Like all addicts, the lover then goes to unhealthy, humiliating, even physically dangerous lengths to procure their narcotic.

Lovers relapse the way drug addicts do, too. Long after the relationship is over, simple events such as hearing a particular song or revisiting an old haunt can trigger the lover's craving and initiate compulsive calling or writing to get another "high": a romantic moment with the beloved. Racine had it right when he called the lover a "slave of passion."

How can we smooth the journey back to sanity and liberation when our love has been rejected? How do we jump-start romance in someone else or in ourselves? And how can we make this passion last?

## *Love Sickness: Letting Go*

"Nothing can affection's course control, / or stop the headlong fury of his speed." Shakespeare believed romantic passion was uncontrollable. I think this addiction can be conquered; it just takes determination and time. A little knowledge of brain function and human nature can be helpful, too.

To begin with, you must remove all evidence of the addictive substance: the beloved. Throw out cards and letters or stuff them in a box and put it out of reach. Don't call or write under *any* circumstances. And depart immediately if you see your former lover in the office or the street. Why? Because as Charles Dickens said, "Love . . . will thrive for a considerable time on a very slight and sparing food." Even the briefest contact with "him" or "her" can fire up your brain circuits for romantic ardor. If you wish to recover, you must expunge all traces of the thief who stole your heart.

Meditate. Develop a few mantras and silently repeat them. Something positive about yourself and your future is best, even if it isn't true—yet. Something like, "I love being myself with a soul mate of my own." Pick something that boosts your self-esteem and projects your mind out of the failed relationship and toward one that will succeed. And when you can't stop thinking about "him" or "her," dwell on their negative traits. Write down their faults and carry the list in your purse or pocket. You might also try fantasizing. Picture yourself walking arm in arm with someone who adores you and you cherish, the perfect partner. Make it up. And make it good. Someone is camping in your brain; you must throw the scoundrel out.

The Fulbe of North Cameroon do just this. A bedeviled lover hires a shaman to perform rituals to extricate the rejecting lover from their mind.[9] The ancient Aztecs used a spell instead. Part of one has been preserved: "Come forth Tlazopilli Centeotl, you will calm down the yellow heart, the green anger, the yellow anger will come out. I shall make it leave. I shall chase it away—I, Spirit in Flesh, I, the Enchanter, through this drink Medicine Spirit, will change this heart."[10]

It is very important to stay busy.[11] It's difficult to make plans when you are too depressed to get out of bed. Force yourself. As the Bible says, "Take up your bed and walk." Do it. Distract yourself. Call friends. Visit neighbors. Go somewhere to worship. Play cards or other games. Memorize poetry or historic events. Learn to draw or to play the guitar. Listen to music. Dance. Sing. Do crossword puzzles. Get a dog or cat or bird. Take that vacation you have always thought about. Write out your plans for the future. Use deep breathing and/or other relaxation techniques. Do anything that forces you to concentrate your attention, particularly things that you do well.

Why? Because the despair of unrequited love is most likely associated with plummeting levels of dopamine. As you focus your attention and do novel things, you elevate this feel-good substance, boosting energy and hope.

Exercise is particularly good for rejected lovers. Every time you slump into a chair, sit by the phone, or stare out the window, you give your departed sweetheart time to stoke the fire in your aching heart. Exercise can starve the flame. Any kind of physical exertion will elevate your mood.[12] Jogging, biking, and other forms of strenuous physical activity are known to drive up levels of dopamine in the nucleus accumbens of the brain, bestowing feelings of euphoria.[13] Exercise also elevates serotonin and some of the endorphins, calming substances. And it increases BDNF (brain-derived neurotropic factor) in the hippocampus, the memory center, which protects and makes new nerve cells. In fact, some psychiatrists believe that exercise (aerobic or anaerobic) can be as effective in healing depression as psychotherapy or antidepressant drugs.[14]

Sunlight is another tonic for depressed lovers.[15] It stimulates the pineal gland in the brain, which regulates bodily rhythms in ways that often elevate mood. So pick a daily activity you can do in daylight, preferably out of doors.

To risk sounding like Ben Franklin in his *Poor Richard's Almanac,* I'll add these thoughts for a depressed lover: avoid sweets or drugs that you know will stress your body and your mind. Count your blessings; optimism heals. Walk with the ancient human stride (as discussed in chapter six); it's graceful and easy on your muscles—and probably your brain. And smile; put on a happy face even as you cry inside. The nerves of these facial muscles activate nerve pathways in the brain that can give you feelings of pleasure.[16] Even imagining that you are happy can spur pleasurable brain activity.

"Stay me with apples; comfort me with flagons / For I am sick with love," cried the lover in the Song of Songs. I suspect forlorn lovers sought distractions and daylight, made up soothing maxims, took herbal remedies, exercised, and smiled to alleviate love sickness a million years ago.

## *The "12-Step" Approach: Love Addicts*

One way to meet new people, learn new coping mechanisms, and develop a fresh perspective on life and love is to join a "12-Step" program. This innovative movement began in the 1930s when two Americans, "Bill W." and "Dr. Bob," agreed to conquer their addiction to alcohol by speaking with each other *any time* of the day or night they felt the urge to drink. Building on these exchanges, they created the principles and rituals of Alcoholics Anonymous (AA). Today this shrewd formula for kicking addiction has spawned over a hundred similar kinds of groups, from Gamblers Anonymous, to Over-Eaters Anonymous, to Sex and Love Addicts Anonymous (SLAA). Each group follows the same 12-Step design for living—an ingenious array of slogans, principles, and practices that have helped addicts around the world recover.

*"One day at a time"* is a basic tenet. To members of AA, it is unrealistic—if not impossible—to consider giving up alcohol for the rest of one's life, but one can resist the demon hour by hour. "Just for today," they say, "I will not drink." In the same vein, the chocoholic decides not to reach for a chocolate bar today. Gamblers decide not

to bet today. And the rejected lover can decide not to contact the beloved—today.

*"If you don't want to slip, don't go into slippery places"* is another 12-Step slogan. Applied to the love addict, it means: stay out of the restaurants where you and your lover dined. Go someplace new to shop or get your exercise. Don't play the songs you used to share. Avoid the "people, places, and things" that trigger a desire for your wayward partner.

Another maxim is, *"It's the first drink that gets you drunk."* In short, addicts know that when they have their first martini or chocolate donut, they will surely have a second and a third. In like manner, don't make that first phone call, write that first e-mail, or drive past his or her house that first time. One contact with the rejecting sweetheart will inevitably lead to more contacts—and more misery.

Perhaps the most intriguing slogan is *"Think the drink through."* To members of Alcoholics Anonymous, this means that as you stand at an elegant wedding reception and gaze at all the pretty people sipping glasses of champagne, think *past* this genteel moment to its possible end: a devastating bender that could last for months. In the same manner, the jilted lover tends to romanticize the glory days. So they pick up the phone and make contact with their rejecting sweetheart with these magnificent memories in mind. Think past those joyous moments to some horrible weekend when your "true love" never called.

"In a net I seek to hold the wind," wrote the Italian poet Petrarch.[17] He knew how impossible it is to retrieve a departed lover. Better to give up the drug and rebuild your life. And remember: your former lover won't help you. Most feel morally blameless, yet guilty for hurting you.[18] But they do not know how to handle your grief or their own feelings about the ruptured tie.[19] So although they may be friendly if you contact them, most will be perplexed, annoyed, even angry that you have intruded on their new life.

### *Taking Antidepressants*

"I turn you out of doors / tenant desire / You pay no rent / I turn you out of doors / All my best rooms are yours / The brain and heart / Depart. / I turn you out of doors / Switch off the lights / Throw water on the fire / I turn you out of doors / Stubborn desire."[20] The fifteenth-century French poet Alain Chartier knew that feelings of romantic love can take up stubborn residence in the mind. And when things go sour, you must turn them out.

Modern medicine can help.

There are many different types of depression. The woman suffering from postpartum blues is not experiencing exactly the same kind of depression as the man who just got fired. Rejected love may provoke yet another form of depression, with a specific chemical fingerprint in the brain. Moreover, people mired in the initial "protest stage" of rejected love are suffering different symptoms than those who have given up hope entirely.

Nevertheless, all forms of "clinical" depression seem to manifest themselves with four basic symptoms. Cognitive impairments include lack of concentration on business as usual, the inability to remember daily events or duties, obsessive thinking about your problems and your pain, and other abnormalities of thinking. Mood is altered; depressed men and women struggle with despair, anxiety, fear, anger, and/or other disabling mood states. Bodily problems arise; depressed people generally have trouble eating, sleeping, or engaging in sexual play. And many contemplate suicide.

Rejected men and women often express all these symptoms of major depression. Unable to cope, many turn to antidepressant medications to relieve their anguish. Currently the most popular are pills that increase brain levels of serotonin in one way or another. The most common ones are the selective serotonin reuptake inhibitors, or SSRIs. Today serotonin-enhancing medications are a $12 billion industry in the United States alone. Some 7.1 million Americans take some version of serotonin booster to counter depression, stress, bereavement, or the despair of tragic love.[21]

As the drug takes effect, the physical and psychic pain of utter sorrow begins to dissipate. You spend less time staring at the wall in what psychiatrists call a "vegetative state." You begin to sleep through the night, eat breakfast, lunch, and dinner, and go about your business in a more timely and effective manner. Eventually the incessant reflecting diminishes. You become less impulsively drawn to contact "him" or "her." And feelings of rage, despair, and longing interrupt your thinking less and less. These medications even repair some of the physical damage that has occurred. They stimulate the growth of nerve cells in the hippocampus, the brain's memory center, thereby reversing the harm often caused by prolonged stress.[22]

But these serotonin-boosting drugs often have adverse side effects. Some people gain weight. An estimated 70 percent of patients taking these medications suffer diminished libido, delayed sexual arousal, and/or the inability to achieve erection, ejaculation, or orgasm.[23] And these drugs can often induce apathy, what psychiatrists call "emotional blunting."

All these side effects are worth enduring, of course, if you feel you may kill yourself or someone else. However, it might be wise to periodically reassess your condition and consider supplementing your antidepressant medication with one that raises levels of dopamine, even switching to a dopamine enhancer. There are several on the market. These dopamine-elevating substances are not as predictable in lifting suicidal depression, but for many patients they work.[24] And unlike the serotonin-enhancing medications, they do not produce weight gain or lower sex drive. Indeed, patients regularly report that their sex drive increases.[25]

More important to our story, when rejected lovers take an antidepressant that elevates dopamine levels in the brain, they are replenishing the very substance the lack of which is most likely causing their withdrawal symptoms.

Estradiol (an estrogen) has antidepressant effects, as do testosterone and thyroid hormone.[26] Substance P seems to work as an antidepressant. I suspect an opioid antagonist might alleviate some of the craving of romantic love. Moreover, medications that block corticotropin-releasing hormone (CRH), the brain hormone released during stress, may soon come on the market to relieve chronic sorrow. These and other new drugs promise to relieve melancholy.

Of course, no antidepressant medication will relieve every patient. Users must work with their doctors to find what is right for them. Moreover, none of these drugs entirely conquers the agony of lost love. And they all have side effects of one kind or another. But if they may not prove a magic bullet in every case, these chemical products are a far better alternative than stalking a former lover in your car, sobbing uncontrollably in the dark, or sitting stupefied before the TV set, awash in rage and sorrow. And anything beats suicide.

## *"Talking Therapy"*

"For use can almost change the stamp of nature," Shakespeare wrote in *Hamlet.* What wisdom. Talking about your predicament with a therapist, and thereby modifying the ways you think and act, can change your brain activity. Studies show that psychotherapy can produce many of the same changes in brain function that antidepressant medications produce.[27] In fact, sometimes "talking therapy" can be just as effective at alleviating major depression.[28]

In one telling study, scientists compared twenty-four untreated adults suffering from the apathy, melancholy, and hopelessness of major depression with sixteen adults with no psychiatric problems. First each person's brain was scanned, using an fMRI machine. The depressed men and women showed abnormally increased activity in parts of the prefrontal cortex, the caudate, and the thalamus (a relay station of the brain); the controls did not. Then ten of the despondent subjects were administered the antidepressant paroxetine, which elevates serotonin levels. The other depressed participants attended twelve psychotherapy sessions instead. Then all of the depressed patients had their brains scanned again. Following *both* forms of treatment, activity was reduced in those brain regions that had shown abnormal activation.[29]

Interestingly, those who underwent the psychotherapy got a bonus. These men and women registered significant new activity in regions of the insula that can inhibit feelings of depression.[30]

Rather than measuring out the merits of talking therapy versus drug treatment, many psychiatrists now believe that the combination of talking therapy and antidepressant medications is more effective than either treatment by itself.

## *Time to Heal*

"All things flow; nothing abides," wrote the Roman philosopher Heraclitus. As you remove the stimuli that fan your ardor, arm yourself with a battery of slogans, build new daily habits, meet new people, take up new interests, and perhaps find the right antidepressant medication and/or the right therapist or guide, your addiction to a former lover will eventually subside. We heal. Sometimes it takes a few weeks. More normally it takes months. Often it takes more than two years of separation. But some glorious morning you will notice that you haven't thought of your hurtful partner in a week or more. Your enemy is no longer lodging in your head.[31]

People never forget a true love, of course. Despite his devotion to his wife, Martha, George Washington preserved a lifelong passion for another man's wife, Sally Fairfax. Historians believe America's first president never kissed Sally, nor was he rejected by her. They were friends. But Washington adored her. He wrote to Sally some twenty-five years after their last encounter, saying that none of the great events of his career, "nor all of them together, have been able to eradicate from my mind those happy moments, the happiest of my life, which I have enjoyed in your company."[32]

In a similar vein, Su Tung-Po, a Chinese poet of the eleventh century, wrote, "Year after year / I recall that moonlit night / we spent alone together / among hills of stunted pine."[33]

"We know well only what we are deprived of," wrote French author François Mauriac. No one forgets. Nevertheless, even those who have been brutally tossed aside begin to lose their feelings of agony, bitterness, and disappointment. You can speed your recovery; but it does take determination, sometimes medication and/or therapy, and what Shakespeare called "the inaudible and noiseless foot of Time."[34]

But of all the cures for a bad romance, by far the most effective is to find a new lover to fill your heart. "A new love drives out the old." Nothing has changed since the twelfth-century French cleric Andreas Capellanus wrote these words. Modern science agrees. As you fall in love again, you elevate levels of dopamine and other feel-good chemicals in your brain.

## *Can We Conjure Love?*

Dear Helen, I just turned 70 and have fallen in love again with a wonderful man who thinks the world of me but confesses not to love me. We have wonderful times together when we have the time (he's still in business). My question to you is do you think it's possible for someone to fall in love with you after a year of being

> together. He thinks I'm wonderful and all those good things but he was so hurt by his last broken marriage he says he doesn't know if he could fall in love again. My feeling is, you don't have a choice. I would love to hear from you because my heart is just breaking and I don't know what to do. J.C.

I received this e-mail recently from a woman in Canada. I wrote back to say I thought she could win the love of her man—with a little work.

How do you ignite mad romantic passion in another?

*Do novel things together.*

Laboratory experiments have confirmed that exciting experiences can enhance feelings of attraction. The classic study of this, done by psychologists Donald Dutton and Art Aron, is known as the "creaky bridge" experiment.[35]

Two walking bridges span the Capilano Canyon in North Vancouver; one is a flimsy suspension bridge that is five feet wide and sways and wobbles some 230 feet above the jagged boulders and river rapids. Upstream is a steady, broad, low bridge. Dutton and Aron asked dozens of men to cross either one bridge or the other. In the middle of each bridge stood a beautiful young woman (part of their research team) who asked each passing man to fill out a questionnaire. After each man completed the survey queries, she casually told him that if he had any further questions about the study, he should call her at her home. She gave each her telephone number. None knew the woman was part of the experiment.

Nine out of thirty-two men who walked the narrow, wobbly high bridge were attracted enough to call the woman in her home. Only two of those who met her on the low, solid bridge contacted her.

This spontaneous attraction is probably directly linked to a physical property of danger: danger stimulates the production of adrenaline, a bodily stimulant closely related to dopamine and norepinephrine.

As psychologist Elaine Hatfield surmised, "Adrenaline makes the heart grow fonder."[36] I would add that danger is novel to most of us. And, as mentioned, novelty elevates levels of dopamine—the chemical associated with romantic love. The men on the high, scary bridge may have also experienced elevated concentrations of this stimulant.

Several studies show that couples who do exciting things together feel more satisfaction in their relationship.[37] But in another experiment Art Aron and another colleague, Christina Norman, showed that exciting activities actually stimulate romantic love as well. They asked twenty-eight dating and married couples to fill out various questionnaires, then do an activity together, then fill out more questionnaires. One activity was exciting; the other dull. The experiment with each couple took about an hour. Interestingly, questionnaire responses indicated that the couples who did the exciting activity (as opposed to the boring task) experienced increased feelings of relationship satisfaction—*and more intense feelings of romantic love.*[38]

Perhaps my e-mail friend in Canada and other courting women and men who want to trigger romantic love in a partner should invite the slowpoke to join them in exciting, somewhat risky situations. Maybe visiting a foreign city together or walking along a perilous mountain trail would galvanize romantic passion. I recently saw a man and woman tied together with "bungee" cords plunge off a ledge atop a two-hundred-foot-high crane. When they landed they were locked in tight embrace. I don't recommend it. But how about trying a new restaurant in a different part of town, buying last-minute tickets to the theater or a sports event, dashing off to a parade, or swimming after dark. Anything rousing and unusual can potentially trigger romantic love.

Even arguments can be exciting—and potentially romantic. I am not in favor of fighting with a true love. But some couples report that arguments enliven the relationship. Inanna, queen of ancient Sumeria, first fell in love with Dumuzi during a row. As a poem of the times recorded, "From the starting of the quarrel / Came the lovers' desire."[39] With quarrels, grievances get aired, often removed; then partners must use some creativity to reknit the bond. More important, anger revs up the mind and body, triggering the release of adrenaline and other stimulants that are associated with romantic passion.

"Love is a canvas furnished by Nature and embroidered by the imagination," Voltaire wrote. Embroider life with novelty and adventure. You may win your love.

## *Sexual Intimacy*

Sex can also spark romantic ardor.

Sex is good for you, if you are with someone you are fond of, the time is right, and you enjoy this form of exercise and self-expression. Stroking and massage trigger the production of oxytocin and the endorphins, brain chemicals that can relax and produce feelings of attachment.[40] Sex helps you keep your skin, muscles, and other bodily tissues in tone. It offers the opportunity to create novelty and excitement. And with orgasm, the brain releases oxytocin in women and vasopressin in men—chemicals associated with feelings of attachment. But sex is not only good for relaxation, muscle tone, and giving and receiving pleasure; it is often associated with elevated levels of testosterone. And testosterone can promote the production of dopamine, the liquor that fuels romance.

Curiously, even seminal fluid can potentially contribute to romantic passion. Psychologist Gordon Gallup and his collaborators report that this broth that surrounds sperm contains dopamine and norepinephrine, as well as tyrosine, an amino acid the brain needs to manufacture dopamine.[41] This ejaculate also contains testosterone, which can elevate the sex drive; various estrogens, which aid feminine sexual arousal and orgasm; and oxytocin and vasopressin, which encourage feelings of union with a partner. It even deposits follicle-stimulating hormone and luteinizing hormone in the vaginal canal, substances women use to regulate menstrual cycling. Not all these substances can march directly from the bloodstream into brain tissue; some cannot cross the blood-brain barrier. Yet all can potentially contribute to feelings of romance in one way or another.

Gallup and his students Rebecca Burch and Steven Platek have determined that seminal fluid also alleviates depressive symptoms in women.[42] This could occur for several reasons. Seminal fluid contains beta-endorphins, substances that can reach the brain directly and calm the mind and body. But as you may have noticed, male seminal fluid also contains the essential ingredients for *all* three of the basic mating drives discussed in this book—lust, romantic love, and male-female attachment. No wonder women are less depressed when they make love and receive this fluid; perhaps they may even become more receptive to romance.

"Exuberance is beauty," wrote William Blake. Both sexes are attracted to happy partners. This may be because we naturally mimic those around us. When another smiles, we unconsciously smile too, albeit sometimes fleetingly. And smiling moves specific muscles in the face that send nerve signals to the brain that stimulate the brain networks for pleasure.[43] So as you concoct novel, adventurous, and sexy things to do with someone you would like to win as a romantic partner, put on a happy face. You may trigger feelings of pleasure in your lover—and start that primordial romantic blaze.

### *Reassess Your Antidepressant Medications*

Before you begin courting in earnest, you should reassess the effectiveness of any antidepressant medication you may be taking—particularly if you are experiencing sexual side effects or emotional blunting.

I say this for an important reason: as you know, the brain networks for lust, romantic love, and attachment interact in complex ways. So my colleague, psychiatrist Andy Thomson, and I believe that artificially elevating serotonin activity can endanger your ability to fall in love. As you know, romantic love is associated with elevated levels of dopamine and possibly also norepinephrine. These neurotransmitters generally have a negative relationship with serotonin. So as you artificially raise brain levels of serotonin with pills, you potentially inhibit production, distribution, and/or expression of dopamine and norepinephrine—and jeopardize your ability to fall in love.[44]

Andy points out that artificially elevated levels of serotonin can imperil your ability to appraise suitors, choose appropriate mates, and form and maintain stable partnerships as well.[45]

For example, most of these drugs blunt the emotions. When you are terribly depressed over a busted romance, you seek this effect. But as men and women continue to use these antidepressants *long after* their love affair is over, they can block their ability to respond when the perfect new partner appears. They are too emotionally dull to notice "him" or "her."

The first direct evidence of this "courtship blunting" has now been found. Psychologist Maryanne Fisher asked women taking SSRIs and women taking no medications to rate the attractiveness of men's faces in photographs. Sure enough, the women taking the serotonin boosters rated the male faces as more *un*attractive than the others did; the medicated women also looked at and appraised the male faces for a shorter time.[46]

Serotonin enhancers also dampen the sex drive and inhibit the sex response (including ejaculation) in many users.[47] As a result, people taking these pills often shy away from potential romantic alliances; they are afraid of failure in the bedroom. Hence they forgo the stroking, kissing, and lovemaking that can trigger romantic love. They miss orgasm's rush of oxytocin and vasopressin that can produce feelings of attachment. And men who can't ejaculate fail to deposit chemicals of their seminal fluid that could influence their partner's mood.

These serotonin-elevating drugs have even more hidden negative effects. Female orgasm most likely evolved to suit many purposes. But scientists have long thought it emerged, at least in part, to distinguish Mr. Right from Mr. Wrong. This "fickle" orgasmic response helped ancestral women recognize lovers who were willing to commit valuable time and energy to pleasing them. It still does. So women taking serotonin-enhancing medications jeopardize their ability to assess the emotional commitment of a partner. Perhaps worse, many people taking serotonin-enhancing medications send faulty signals of ineptness and lack of interest in the bedroom that can repel a potential mate. They are also likely to mistakenly conclude that they, themselves, are not compatible with this partner. In fact, they are just drugged.

People on serotonin-enhancing antidepressant medications potentially jeopardize their ability to assess mates, trigger romance, and form attachments—altering their love lives and the future of their genes.

## *Male Intimacy; Female Intimacy*

"Yet mark'd I where the bolt of cupid fell: / It fell upon a little western flower, / Before milk-white, now purple with love's wound, / And maidens call it love-in-idleness. / Fetch me that flower; the herb I shew'd thee once: / The juice of it on sleeping eye-lids laid / Will make or man or woman madly dote / Upon the next live creature that it sees." Oberon, King of the Fairies in Shakespeare's *A Midsummer Night's Dream,* tells of a potent blossom that would make you fall in love.

How many million men and women throughout human evolution have yearned to find such a flower? Alas, it does not exist. Even taking pills (or street drugs like cocaine or amphetamines) that raise levels of dopamine in the brain won't make someone fall in love with you if he or she is not ready or is looking for an entirely different kind of partner. But if a credible suitor has expressed some interest in you, there are still other ways to stimulate their interest, and their heart—using what is known of gender differences in the brain.

Intimacy is popular these days. Many—not only in the United States but in societies as diverse as Mexico, India, and China—regard this sense of closeness and sharing as central to romantic love.[48] But men and women often define and express this closeness differently.

Both genders think shared personal secrets and happy activities together are intimate.[49] But women often regard intimacy as talking face-to-face, while men tend to feel emotionally close when they work or play or talk side by side.[50] Indeed, men often feel mildly threatened or challenged when they look directly into another's eyes. So they sit at angles and avoid looking directly at a companion.[51] This response probably stems from men's ancestry. For many millennia men faced their enemies; they sat or walked side by side as they hunted game with friends.

Smart women appreciate this gender difference. To achieve intimacy with a male partner they do things side by side, such as walking in the woods or mall, driving in a car, sitting in a movie house, or snuggling up to watch TV—beside him.

Most men also derive intimacy from playing or watching sports. From millions of years of tracking, surrounding, and felling animals, men have become, on average, more spatially adept than women—a form of intelligence linked to the male hormone testosterone.[52] So when a woman joins a man to ski, climb mountains, play chess, or cheer at a tennis match or football game, he may feel particularly drawn to her.[53]

Women derive tremendous closeness from talking face-to-face.[54]

They sit closer than men do, and they look directly into another's eyes with what linguist Deborah Tannen calls the "anchoring gaze."[55] This taste probably also harks back to yesteryear when ancestral women held their infants in front of their faces, educating, soothing, and entertaining their little ones with words. So if you are a savvy man and you find yourself sitting on a park bench with a woman who is twisting her feet, knees, hips, chest, shoulders, neck, and face to look into your face, swivel around and look directly at her as you speak. When you look straight ahead and avoid her eyes, she feels you are evading her. By returning her anchoring gaze you give her the primordial feminine gift of intimacy. You may also ignite romantic longing.

## *Courting Talk*

If men like sports events and other activities that emphasize their spatial skills, women like words. Little girls speak sooner than boys, with greater grammatical accuracy and more words per utterance. In societies around the world women are, on average, more linguistically gifted than men—probably because words have been women's tools for raising young for at least a million years.[56] In fact, women's verbal ability is even linked with the female hormone estrogen.

So smart men court with words—on the phone, on a date, on the pillow. A friend of mine recently told me she fell madly in love with the man who became her husband when he started to send her his (terrible) poetry. Men don't need linguistic talent; they just need courage and words.

Women and men generally achieve intimacy by talking about different subjects, however. Many men enjoy talking about sports, politics, world affairs, and business. These are worlds of win or lose, of top dogs and underdogs, of status and hierarchy, worlds men understand because men have always jockeyed for status to win mates.[57] Women, on the other hand, are more drawn to emotion-laden, self-revealing chat about personal issues and other people,[58] probably because women evolved in an ancestral environment where social connections were crucial to survival.

Men and women become more alike in their middle age,[59] probably in part because levels of estrogen decline in women and levels of testosterone decline in men.[60] But regardless of age, observant suitors diligently engage in conversations that will captivate a lover, hoping to promote closeness that could kindle romantic love.

### *Sex as Intimacy*

Sex, too, can lead to intimacy—and potentially trigger the ecstasy of romance. Men are about four times more likely than women to equate sexual activity with emotional closeness.[61] This male perspective has Darwinian logic. Coitus is a man's ticket to posterity; if his partner gets pregnant she will send his DNA into the future. So although men often have no conscious interest in making babies, this evolutionary payoff seems to have bred into the male psyche an unconscious tendency to regard sexual intercourse as the essence of intimacy, affection, and companionship.

Women report that they feel more intimacy with a partner when they talk together just *before* making love.[62] Women probably derive intimacy from precoital chat because it shows that their lover can listen, be patient and supportive, and contain his lust, attributes ancestral women needed in a mate.

Any way you look at it, sex is immensely memorable and satisfying when things go right. And those who adroitly conduct the sexual aspects of a relationship have a potent arrow in their quiver for stimulating romantic love.

## *Buying Time*

We all know that women are attracted to men who have resources and generously share their money, time, connections, and status with a mating partner. So all those flowers, chocolates, and theater tickets might indeed topple her head over heels in love. And as you recall, men are quite drawn to women they feel they need to save.[63] So women, often unconsciously, say and do things that display their vulnerability, what I call the "broken wing" strategy. Sure enough, this neediness often triggers gallantry and romance in men.

Vulnerability is just about the last thing men like to display.[64] Why show your weaknesses when you can flaunt your strengths and accomplishments instead? Men do that. They brag. And women listen. Although women are often appalled at these bald displays of puffery, they are also impressed. So like womanly exhibitions of helplessness, men's cocky boasting may help spark that fire in the heart.

Oscar Wilde once wrote, "The essence of romance is uncertainty." It was a clever observation. We walk a fine line when we woo. If you are too eager, an undecided suitor may flee. Biology probably plays a role in this behavior. Early acquisition of a reward reduces the duration and intensity of dopamine activity in the brain, while a delay in winning stimulates it.[65] As a result, people who are "hard to get" tend to excite a suitor. Andreas Capellanus knew this long ago, reminding troubadours of twelfth-century France that "love easily obtained is of little value; difficulty in obtaining it makes it precious."[66] So those who want to trigger romance in a would-be lover might artfully create some mystery, barriers, and uncertainty in the relationship.

I know all this sounds like playing games. But love is a game, nature's only game. Just about every creature on this planet plays it—unconsciously scheming to pass their DNA into tomorrow. By counting children, nature keeps her score.

## *Making Yourself Fall in Love*

What would have happened if Shakespeare's Oberon had sprinkled the juice of that "little western flower" in his *own* eyes? Most of us have met someone we admired and enjoyed. He or she was kind, generous, honest, happy, ambitious, humorous, successful, attractive, interesting, and amorous in ways that suited us. Yet we couldn't conjure up that magic feeling for him or her. Can you make yourself fall in love?

Well, you can certainly try. Find things you really like to do with your admirer. Make them novel and exciting. Dismiss distractions, particularly other lovers. And genuinely open yourself to his or her way of thinking, feeling, and making love. You just may be able to stimulate in yourself the appropriate brain circuits for romantic love.

Psychologist Robert Epstein is trying to do just that. Editor in chief of *Psychology Today* and author of eleven books and dozens of scholarly articles, Epstein recently ran an editorial in his magazine advertising for a woman who would date him exclusively with the express intent of falling madly in love. He hoped the process would last six months to a year and end in marriage.[67] Epstein outlined several stipulations. Among them, both would seek regular counseling together; both would read extensively about love in novels and nonfiction books; both would keep a daily diary and do various exercises (such as synchronous breathing); and both would actively seek to know the other thoroughly.

Epstein believes you can learn to fall in love. Many of those who enter arranged marriages or procure mail-order brides also seem to believe you can jump-start this magic. I do, too. If you pick someone who is ready to fall in love and fits within your love map, and if you keep your heart open and do novel things together, you may just activate the brain network for romantic passion.

The juice of Cupid's "little western flower" is creativity and determination.

### *Why Romantic Passion Recedes with Time*

"There lives within the very flame of love / A kind of wick or snuff that will abate it," Shakespeare said. Romantic love often recedes with time.

In the beginning, you spend weeks or months wooing with long e-mails, intimate conversations, shared adventures at restaurants, concerts, parties, and sports events, and joyous times in bed. You work endlessly to impress and charm your beloved. At times you feel such ecstasy you can't sleep. Then as the months turn into years, your romantic bliss begins to ripen into a deeper union: long-term attachment. Romantic fervor continues in some long relationships.[68] And this passion can still become intense during vacations and at other times of novelty and adventure. But the wild ecstasy, fierce energy, and obsessive thinking generally diminish, giving way to feelings of safety and contentment.

Exactly how the brain quells the early storm of romantic passion is unknown. One of three things might occur: Either brain regions that produce and transport dopamine (and probably norepinephrine) begin to distribute less of their stimulant. Or the receptor sites for these chemicals that reside at nerve endings gradually become desensitized.[69] Or other chemicals in the brain begin to mask or counteract the chemistry of this passion. But whatever the biological cause, the body gradually settles down.

This decline of romantic love is undoubtedly evolution's doing. Intense romantic passion consumes enormous time and energy. And it would be decidedly disruptive to one's peace of mind and daily activities (including rearing children) to spend years obsessively doting on a lover. Instead, this brain circuitry evolved primarily for one purpose: to drive our forebears to seek and find special mating partners, then copulate exclusively with "him" or "her" until conception was assured. At that point, ancestral couples needed to stop focussing on each other and start building a safe social world where they could rear their precious child together. Nature gave us passion. Then she gave us peace—until we fall in love again.

## *Making Romance Last*

Still, some people do remain passionately *in love* for a lifetime.[70] Some couples married more than twenty years report that they are still in love.[71] In fact, in one remarkable survey, men and women married more than twenty years tested higher on romantic passion for one another than did those married only five years.[72] Their scores looked much like those of high school seniors.[73]

I met such a couple recently. At a business dinner I found myself sitting beside a handsome, bright, affable, middle-aged president of a major American nonprofit organization. When he discovered that I was writing a book about romantic love, he told me he was still "in love" with his wife; they had been married twenty-six years. The following month I was fortunate enough to meet his spouse, a woman of elegance and literature. Unaware of my conversation with her husband, she avowed that she was still very much in love with her mate. So when her husband joined us, I took the liberty of asking both of them how they had kept their passion percolating.

She said, "Humor." He said, "Sex."

I was not surprised with either answer. Humor is based on novelty, the unexpected—which elevates levels of dopamine in the brain. And sex is associated with elevated levels of testosterone, which, in a chain reaction, can increase dopamine as well. But I suspect this charismatic couple kept love alive in another way as well. Both had exceptionally exciting careers and did many unusual things together. I think their lifestyle stimulated dopamine levels and maintained romantic passion.

"It is not customary to love what one has," wrote Anatole France. To counteract this conventional thinking, therapists advise people to follow several standard practices: Commit. Listen "actively" to your partner. Ask questions. Give answers. Appreciate. Stay attractive. Keep growing intellectually. Include her. Give him privacy. Be honest and trustworthy. Tell your mate what you need. Accept his/her shortcomings. Mind your manners. Exercise your sense of humor. Respect him. Respect her. Compromise. Argue constructively. Never threaten to depart. Forget the past. Say "no" to adultery. Don't assume the relationship will last forever; build it one day at a time. And never give up.

These and many other wise habits can sustain feelings of long-term attachment. But none is likely to elevate levels of dopamine or maintain romantic passion. Other tactics, however, can keep this flame burning.

"Let there be spaces in your togetherness," advised Kahlil Gibran. Although the Lebanese poet probably didn't know it, this was good advice for sustaining the biology associated with romantic love. As mentioned earlier, when a reward is delayed in coming, the tardy delivery prolongs the activity of dopamine cells—speeding more of this natural stimulant into reward centers of the brain.[74] Although men appreciate privacy and autonomy more than women do, for both sexes "space" probably helps sustain romantic passion.

Given what we know of love, surely it would also be wise to engage in what therapists call "dating time." Develop an array of common interests and make a point of doing novel and exciting things together.[75] Variety, variety, variety: it stimulates the pleasure centers of the brain,[76] maintaining the climate of romance.

## *Passion and Reason*

Since the time of the ancient Greeks, poets, philosophers, and dramatists have regarded passion and reason as separate, distinct, even opposing phenomena. Plato summed up the dichotomy, saying that one's desires were like wild horses; the intellect was the "charioteer" who must subdue and direct these cravings.[77] The belief that one must employ reason to triumph over one's baser drives has trickled through the centuries. Early Christian theologians cemented this precept in Western thought: emotions and desires were temptations, sins that must be conquered by reasoning and willpower.

Neuroscientists now believe, however, that reason and passion are inexorably linked in the brain. And I think these connections say something important about controlling romantic love.

As you might remember, the prefrontal cortex of the brain lies directly behind your forehead; it expanded dramatically in size during human prehistory and is devoted to processing information. This is the business center of the mind. With the prefrontal cortex (and its connections) you collect and order data acquired through the senses, then analyze and weigh these details, reason, plan, and make decisions. But the prefrontal cortex has direct connections with many subcortical brain regions, including an emotion center, the amygdala, and a center for motivation, the caudate, as well as others. Hence thinking, feeling, memory, and motivation are closely integrated.[78] Reason and passion are inseparably linked.

In fact, one rarely has a thought without an accompanying feeling and urge; and one rarely has a feeling or want without an accompanying thought. For good reason, says neuroscientist Antonio Damasio. Without emotions and wants, we could not assign different values to different options. Our thoughts, our reasoning, our decisions would be flat, cold-blooded, lacking the vital emotional components we need to weigh variables and make choices.[79] We would be "souls on ice."[80]

Neuroscientist Joseph LeDoux has even discovered that the brain has two highways for integrating emotions and reasoning: the "high road" and the "low road."[81] And both are connected to the reward system in the brain, with its wants and drives. When the amygdala receives signals *directly* from the prefrontal cortex we control ourselves. We think before we feel and act. This is the "high road." But the amygdala also receives data directly from sensory regions of the cortex that *bypass* the prefrontal cortex, the reasoning part of the brain. This is the "low road"; it is irrational, powerfully emotional, much larger than the "high road," and very difficult to curb. This "low road" enables the lover to experience tremendous ecstasy and yearning when they see a beloved, even before they rationally think about "him" or "her." But the "low road" can engulf the disappointed lover in *unthinking*, out-of-control rage as well—provoking them to impulsively shout at, hit, even slaughter a sweetheart.

There is a silver lining to this brain wiring. We humans *can* take the "high road." The prefrontal cortex can and often does exercise control over the amygdala and the rest of the evolutionarily older brain systems that generate our emotions and urges.[82] As philosopher John Dewey said, "Mind is primarily a verb." I agree. The human prefrontal cortex, the crowning achievement of life on earth, is built to *do* things—to assemble data in unique ways, reason, make decisions, and override our basic drives. As Aristotle put it, "The brain tempers the heat and seething of the heart."

We can control the drive to love.

How will this powerful, mercurial, primordial force fare in our modern world?

# 9

# "The Madness of the Gods":
## *The Triumph of Love*

Love—thou art deep—
I cannot cross thee—
But, were there Two
Instead of One—
Rower, and Yacht—some sovereign Summer
Who knows—but we'd reach the Sun?

Emily Dickinson
"Love Thou Art High"

"These days nothing is impossible in this world. A person can do anything. I offer a prayer today to Shree Pashupatibaba that just as our love develops more and more fully, so too may it grow and develop fully in the future, may it be able to blossom and blossom." Vajra Bahadur wrote these words to Shila in a village in Nepal in the 1990s. It is one of hundreds of love letters that anthropologist Laura Ahearn collected when she lived in this community some hundred miles southwest of Katmandu.[1]

For centuries, Nepalese parents had arranged their children's marriages according to complex kin and caste connections. Often the bride and groom spoke for the first time on their wedding day. But along with electricity, Hindi romances in the movie hall, education, and literacy has come a new tradition: love letters. And since 1993, 90 percent of all who married eloped with someone they adored.

As trade, industry, communication, and education have seeped around the globe, many other men and women have shed their custom of arranged marriages to choose partners they love.[2] As you may recall, in a recent study of thirty-seven societies, from Brazil to Nigeria to Indonesia, men and women ranked love, or mutual attraction, as the primary criterion for choosing a spouse.[3] Only in India, Pakistan, and some other Muslim countries, parts of sub-Saharan Africa, and a few other places where poverty is rife and the extended family is crucial to survival, do over 50 percent of men and women still marry at their parents' bidding.[4] Even in these places, betrothed partners meet before their wedding day to approve or reject the match.[5]

Not all of these arranged marriages are loveless.

On the contrary, in India people commonly say, "First we marry, then we fall in love."[6] But most men and women around the world today choose their partners for themselves, what the Chinese call "free love."

## *The Re-emergence of Romantic Love*

The rise of romantic love in marriage, the ubiquitous celebration of this passion in movies, plays, poems, songs, and books, the worldwide flood of discussions about romance on television and radio, and the belief that romantic love is the foundation stone of male-female partnerships is the result of many social trends. But a few are particularly important. One is the ascent of individual autonomy and the concomitant surge of women into the paid labor market.

For millions of years our forebears lived in small hunting and gathering bands. Both sexes worked. As men "commuted" to do their hunting, women hiked far afield to gather vegetables and fruits—and women provided some 60 to 80 percent of the daily sustenance. Charismatic men, and probably some forceful older women, led the band. And tradition bound all to myriad social rules. But men and women were free to make most of their own personal decisions; individuals were relatively autonomous.

Life in contemporary hunting/gathering societies suggests that ancestral parents (to serve their social purposes) often chose their daughter's first husband.[7] Their obligations met, however, they put little pressure on the youngsters to sustain the match. Most of these betrothals failed. Then divorcees picked a second and often a third mate for themselves—because they could. Women were powerful, economically, sexually, and socially. And when spouses found that they could not live harmoniously together, each could afford to part. For millions of years our ancestors largely wed for love.

Some ten thousand years ago human life changed dramatically. As our forebears settled down to farm, individual autonomy and the economic balance of power between the sexes gradually eroded. Codified political and social hierarchies arose. And as men from England to China cleared and tilled the fields, bartered goods, and brought their produce to local markets, men soon owned the land, the livestock, and most of the family's other wealth. No longer able to roam and collect the evening fare, locked into second-class jobs of gardening and keeping the home, lacking property and access to education, women lost their ancient status in cultures around the world.[8] Moreover, marriage became a business venture, an exchange of property, political alliances, and social ties.[9] Neither boy nor girl could wed for love.

Romance could not be stifled. The rich took concubines or second wives; the landless poor still wed for love.[10] And undoubtedly many men and women in arranged betrothals later fell in love with one another. People also celebrated love in myths and legends, dramas, songs, poems, and paintings. But the ancient Egyptians, Greeks, Romans, early Christians, Muslims, Indians, Chinese, Japanese, and many others of the historical world usually married for duty, money, and alliances, not for love. Indeed, romantic love was feared in much of Asia and parts of Africa. This mercurial force could lead to suicide or homicide; even worse, it could upset the delicate web of social ties.

With the growth of trade and cities, and then the Industrial Revolution, more and more European and American men and women fled farm life. Unmoored from primordial local networks of blood relatives, more and more people were on their own.[11] And by the nineteenth century, many men and women began to wed for love—provided their parents agreed to the match.[12] "Cupid's fiery shaft," as Shakespeare called romantic love, had pierced the Western heart.

The steady entrance of women into the paid workforce throughout the twentieth and into the twenty-first centuries has spread the desire to wed for love far and wide. Expanding clerical jobs, the burgeoning of the legal profession, the rise of the health care industries, the flourishing global service economy, the emergence of nonprofit organizations, and the booming communications age have all drawn women into the marketplace.[13] As a result, women are gradually regaining economic power, as well as health and education, almost everywhere.[14] As they become more economically autonomous, these women want to live with partners whom they love.

"I do." In a 1991 American survey, 86 percent of men and 91 percent of women reported that they would *not* say these words to someone they were not in love with, even if that person had every other quality they were looking for in a mate.[15] The Chinese of Hong Kong are equally determined to wed for love. In a survey done in the 1990s, only 5.8 percent of these men and women said they would marry someone they were not in love with.[16] Even more remarkable, some 50 percent of American men and women now believe they have the right to divorce if romantic passion fades.[17]

Women are also refusing polygynous unions. Some 84 percent of societies worldwide permit a man to have more than one wife at a time. Traditionally only 5 to 20 percent of men actually acquired enough wealth and status to attract multiple wives. Yet women endured these unions: often it was better to be the second wife of a rich man than the first wife of a poor one. But as more women have regained economic power in recent decades, fewer are willing to weather the favoritism, jealousy, and bickering that sharing a husband brings. As eighteen-year-old Farima Sanati of Teheran, Iran, said, "A woman cannot bear these things."[18]

Not only is humankind regaining personal autonomy and social, political, and sexual equality; we also have more time.

## *Time to Love*

Men and women are living longer. Anthropologists believe the natural human lifespan has not changed in at least a million years. But today far more people survive infancy, infectious childhood diseases, accidents, childbirth, and male-male violence; many more live into old age. In 1900, only 4 percent of Americans were over age sixty-five; today 11 percent survive to this age; by 2030 some 20 percent of all Americans will be over sixty-five; by 2050, 15 to 19 percent of the world population will be over age sixty-five as well.[19]

Many older people now live alone, too, rather than with their children. And they are healthy. In fact, some demographers say we should begin to think of middle age as extending to age eighty-five, largely because 40 percent of men and women at that age are fully functional.[20] Humanity is gaining time to love.

Technology is helping. Testosterone creams and patches now keep the sex drive active. Viagra and other medications enable seniors, largely men, to perform in bed. Estrogen replacement therapy keeps women's arousal mechanisms in gear. And with a host of other innovations, from plastic surgery and unguents to clothing of every imaginable texture, shape, and style, men and women can express their sexuality and fall in love almost until they die.

We start early, too. In hunting/gathering societies children often begin to play at sex and love as early as age five or six. But because girls are thin and get a great deal of exercise, a girl generally reaches puberty around age sixteen or seventeen and bears her first child around age twenty. Kids in our modern world also play "house" and "doctor" at a young age. But with our sedentary lifestyle and diet rich in fat, girls in advanced industrial societies now reach puberty around age twelve and a half. More and more get pregnant soon after that, beginning the adult cycle of romance long before expected.

## *Ageless Love*

But nature likes opportunity. Indeed, we are built to love at any age.

Children fall in love. In one remarkable study of childhood romance, just as many youngsters aged five reported having been in love as did those aged eighteen.[21] I noticed this myself. I recently listened to an eight-year-old boy perfectly describe the symptoms of romantic love as he told me about an eight-year-old girl that he adored. He could not stop thinking about her. He recited details of her mannerisms and their times together. And he felt elated when she spoke to him at school.

Men and women in their seventies, eighties, even nineties, also feel love's magic.[22] One friend of mine fell in love at age ninety-two. He wife had died five years before and he became enchanted with an old friend of the family. His only concern was that she was a younger woman, aged seventy-six. Interestingly, in a study of 255 adolescents, young adults, middle-aged men and women, and senior citizens, scientists found no overall difference in the intensity of their romantic passion; men and women loved just as strongly when they were sixty as when they were sixteen.[23] Older people do more varied and imaginative things together.[24] But age makes no difference in feelings of romance.

## *Why We Love*

The ancient Greeks called romantic love the "madness of the Gods." Why can this passion be triggered at any age?

Because the drive to love is a multipurpose mechanism.

When children fall in love, they are practicing courtship tactics, exploring how and when and where to flirt. Boys and girls learn what attracts a partner and what does not, how to say yes and no, and the feeling of being rejected. They are preparing for life's most important act: pursuing a worthy mating partner.

Teenagers have a more difficult task. Courting time is upon them. They are taking on the primordial shapes for wooing. As they clumsily sift through their dating opportunities, they acquire knowledge about themselves and others and develop dislikes and preferences.[25]

Most men and women around the world marry in their twenties.[26] Romantic love now serves its timeless purpose of weeding out unsuitable mates, focussing one's attention on a "special" other, forming a socially visible pair-bond with this beloved, and remaining sexually faithful to "him" or "her" at least long enough to conceive a child together. In some couples, this passion then destroys this relationship as a spouse falls in love with someone else and forms a new pair-bond (unconsciously) to produce more varied young. In other couples, romantic love serves to glue spouses to each other and thereby support their mutual offspring for many years.

These long-term unions are known as "companionate marriages" or "peer marriages," marriages between equals in which both partners work and share intimacy and household duties.[27] Because women are re-emerging in the paid labor force, sociologists predict that peer marriages will become the most common marriage form of the twenty-first century.[28] And because the population is aging, divorce rates may remain reasonably steady for years to come.[29] Finding the right mixture of autonomy and closeness probably will be a central issue for many in these companionate unions.

Why do seniors fall in love? Romance among older people probably also had adaptive functions in ancestral times. This passion gave aging men and women energy, sexual afternoons that kept the body supple, a reason to remain vital members of the community, and a partner who provided physical and emotional support. Romance among the elderly still serves these timeless purposes.

Until recently older men everywhere in the world sought younger women, however. So most people expect aging women to have less luck in love. But this male taste has been changing—in part due to the expense of rearing babies. Today a working-class American family spends at least $213,000 on their child before it reaches age eighteen; a middle-class family spends more—before they pay for college.[30] So older men are becoming wary of women who wish to bear them young.[31]

Gays and lesbians in all cultures also feel romantic passion. As you may recall from chapter one, my questionnaire on romantic love showed that homosexuals experience *more* of the "sweaty palm syndrome" than did other respondents. I feel sure these men and women carry in their brains exactly the same human wiring and chemistry for romantic love as everybody else. During development in the womb or during childhood, however, they acquired a different focus for their passion.

## *The Drive to Love*

Hail the rise of romantic love—with all of its dreams and sorrows. This passion has become untethered in our modern world. And millions today are in search of it. America has some 46 million single women and 38 million single men over the age of eighteen.[32] Twenty-five percent of them have joined a dating service in a quest for true love; many more scour the personal ads in newspapers and magazines.[33] In 2002, matchmaking online and off in America became a $917 million business.[34]

But of all the ways to find romance, one of the most remarkable to me is polyamory, the taking of "many loves." Polyamorous men and women form partnerships with more than one individual at a time. They believe one person cannot suit all one's needs; yet none wish to uproot a long-term, steady, satisfying marriage. So spouses agree to be honest with each other, set some rules for discretion, and start a romance on the side. This way, they reason, each can enjoy feelings of attachment to one partner and romance with someone else.[35] Appropriately, their most prominent magazine is entitled *Loving More*.

Polyamory is utopian—and impractical. As you know, romantic love is interwoven in a host of other motivation/emotion circuits in the brain—including the other primary mating drives, lust and male-female attachment. I mentioned earlier that although these three brain systems regularly interact, they can operate independently. Indeed, you can feel deep attachment for a long-term partner, *while* you feel romantic love for someone else, *while* you feel the sex drive when you read a book, see a film, or conjure up a sexual image in your mind. This wiring probably evolved, in part, to enable ancestral men and women to maintain a long-term pair-bond *while* they took advantage of extra (often clandestine) mating opportunities. Polyamorous men and women aim to do this openly.

But humankind does not share love gracefully. As an Australian Aborigine put it, "We are a jealous people." Not surprisingly, polyamorous couples spend many hours every week sorting out their feelings of possessiveness and jealousy.

The independence of these three mating drives causes all of us turmoil at some point in our lives. High rates of adultery and divorce, the prevalence of stalking and spousal battering, and the worldwide omnipresence of love-related homicide, suicide, and clinical depression are all the fallout of our drive to love and love again.

Yet for all the tears and tantrums of romantic disappointment, most of us recover and return to courting. Romantic love has given humankind tremendous joy. It has also contributed much to society in general. The concepts of the husband, the wife, the father, and the nuclear family; our customs for wooing and marriage; the plots of our great operas, novels, plays, films, songs, and poems; our paintings and our sculptures; many of our traditions; even some of our holidays: billions of cultural artifacts stem, in part, from this ancient drive to love.

Yet we still know so little about this madness of the gods. For example, some brain process, still unidentified, must produce the sense of fusion with the beloved that the lover feels. Scientists are beginning to pinpoint the brain regions that become active when one feels fusion with a "higher power," such as God.[36] Perhaps this brain region is also involved in love. We don't know what creates the lover's craving for sexual exclusivity either. This, too, must be accompanied by some brain anatomy and functions.

Research on the brain circuitry of romantic love also raises wider questions. Should doctors medicate stalkers and spouse abusers with drugs that change brain function? Should lawyers, judges, and legislators regard those who commit crimes of passion as chemically disabled? Should divorce laws accommodate our human tendency to leave unhappy unions? The more we learn about the biology of romance (and lust and attachment), the more I believe we will come to appreciate the role of culture and experience in directing human behavior—and the more we will need to address these and many other complex issues of ethics and responsibility.

But of one thing I am convinced: no matter how well scientists map the brain and uncover the biology of romantic love, they will never destroy the mystery or ecstasy of this passion. I say this from my own experience.

People ask me how my knowledge of romantic love has affected my personal life. Well, I feel more informed. And, for reasons I can't explain, more secure. I know more about *why* I feel the various ways I feel. I can anticipate some of the behavior of those around me. And I have some tools to deal with myself and others. But my understanding of this subject has not changed *how* I feel at all. You can know every single note of Beethoven's Ninth Symphony, yet still reel with excitement every time you hear it. And you can know exactly how Rembrandt mixed and applied his paint, yet look at one of his portraits and feel overwhelming empathy for all humanity. Regardless of what one knows about this subject, we all feel the magic.

Humanity is coming full circle, forward to patterns of romance and marriage our forebears expressed a million years ago. Childhood infatuations, a series of teenage romances, marriage in one's twenties, sometimes another love affair or wedding in midlife, and romance into one's golden years. Romantic love is deeply threaded into our human spirit. If humanity survives on this planet another million million years, this primordial mating force will still prevail.

# *Appendix*

## *"Being in Love": A Questionnaire*

*Introduction*

This questionnaire is about "being in love," the feelings of being infatuated, being passionate, or being strongly romantically attracted to someone.

If you are not currently "in love" with someone, but felt very passionately about someone in the past, please answer the questions *with that person in mind.*

You do not need to have ever been in a relationship with the person whom you feel or felt passionately about.

It does not matter if this person is the same sex or opposite sex.

There are no "right" answers to the following questions.

Please circle *ONLY ONE* response to each question.

Your answers will be totally anonymous.

So *please* be honest in your responses.

*Preliminary Questions: Answer all that apply to you.*

Birthdate: ______________________________

Sex: Male 1 Female 2

S1. Have you ever been in love?

Yes 1 No 2

S2. Are you currently "in love" or are you answering this questionnaire about your feelings for someone in your past?

A current infatuation 1
A past infatuation 2

S3. When you are in love with someone, about what percent of an average day does this person come into your thoughts?

________ percent

S4. When you are in love, do you sometimes feel as if your feelings are out of your control?

I feel in control of my feelings 1
I feel out of control of my feelings 2

S5. If you are currently in love, how long have you been in love?

________ # years ________ # months ________ # days

S6. Have you declared your love to him/her?

Yes 1
No 2

S7. Has this person indicated that he/she is in love with you?

Yes, he/she told me so 1
Yes, but only indirectly 2
No 3

S8. Do/did you think the person you are/were in love with is/was just as passionate about you as you are/were about him/her?

| | |
|---|---|
| More passionate | 1 |
| Just as passionate | 2 |
| Less passionate | 3 |
| Don't know my love's feelings | 4 |

S9. Are you currently infatuated with more than one person?

Yes 1 No 2

S10. Are you married or "living with" a partner?

| | |
|---|---|
| Married | 1 |
| Living with a partner | 2 |
| Neither | 3 |

S11. If married, how long have you been married?

________ # years ________ # months ________ # days

S12. If "living with" a partner, how long have you been living with this person?

________ # years ________ # months ________ # days

S13 If you are/were married or living with a partner at the time of the infatuation, are/were you infatuated with your mate or with someone else?

| | |
|---|---|
| With your mate | 1 |
| With someone else | 2 |

## *Being in Love: Main Interview*

*Please think about the person to whom you are or were passionately romantically attracted and circle ONLY ONE answer to each question*

1. When I am in love I have a hard time sleeping because I am thinking about ______.

| 1 | 2 | 3 | 4 | 5 | 6 | 7 |
|---|---|---|---|---|---|---|
| / | | | | | | / |
| strongly disagree | | | | | | strongly agree |

2. When someone tells me something funny, I want to share it with ______.

| 1 | 2 | 3 | 4 | 5 | 6 | 7 |
|---|---|---|---|---|---|---|
| / | | | | | | / |
| strongly disagree | | | | | | strongly agree |

3. ______ has some faults but they don't really bother me.

| 1 | 2 | 3 | 4 | 5 | 6 | 7 |
|---|---|---|---|---|---|---|
| / | | | | | | / |
| strongly disagree | | | | | | strongly agree |

4. It is good to be out of touch with ______ for a few days so that the anticipation can build up again.

| 1 | 2 | 3 | 4 | 5 | 6 | 7 |
|---|---|---|---|---|---|---|
| / | | | | | | / |
| strongly disagree | | | | | | strongly agree |

5. ________ has a distinctive voice.

1 2 3 4 5 6 7
/ /
strongly disagree — strongly agree

6. When the relationship with ______ has a setback, I just try harder to get things going right.

1 2 3 4 5 6 7
/ /
strongly disagree — strongly agree

7. I try to look my best for ______.

1 2 3 4 5 6 7
/ /
strongly disagree — strongly agree

8. When I am with ______, my mind wanders to other loves I have had.

1 2 3 4 5 6 7
/ /
strongly disagree — strongly agree

9. My heart races when I hear ______'s voice on the phone.

1 2 3 4 5 6 7
/ /
strongly disagree — strongly agree

10. I love everything about ______.

1 2 3 4 5 6 7

/ strongly disagree — / strongly agree

11. I feel happy when ______ is happy and sad when he/she is sad.

1 2 3 4 5 6 7

/ strongly disagree — / strongly agree

12. I feel preoccupied by my feelings for ______.

1 2 3 4 5 6 7

/ strongly disagree — / strongly agree

13. When I am talking to ______, I am often afraid that I will say the wrong thing.

1 2 3 4 5 6 7

/ strongly disagree — / strongly agree

14. The last person I think of each day as I fall asleep is ______.

1 2 3 4 5 6 7

/ strongly disagree — / strongly agree

15. Sex is the most important part of my relationship with ______.

1 2 3 4 5 6 7
/ /
strongly disagree — strongly agree

16. It upsets me when ______ is not being treated fairly.

1 2 3 4 5 6 7
/ /
strongly disagree — strongly agree

17. I have more energy when I am with ______.

1 2 3 4 5 6 7
/ /
strongly disagree — strongly agree

18. It does not bother me too much when ______ is having a bad day.

1 2 3 4 5 6 7
/ /
strongly disagree — strongly agree

19. If ______ is unavailable, I like to go out on romantic dates with other men/women.

1 2 3 4 5 6 7
/ /
strongly disagree — strongly agree

20. The person that I am infatuated with is the center of my life.

1 2 3 4 5 6 7
/ /
strongly disagree — strongly agree

21. When I am strongly attracted to someone, I interpret their actions, looking for clues about their feelings toward me.

1 2 3 4 5 6 7
/ /
strongly disagree — strongly agree

22. Sometimes my feelings for ______ are overshadowed by passionate romantic feelings for another person.

1 2 3 4 5 6 7
/ /
strongly disagree — strongly agree

23. I will never forget our first kiss.

1 2 3 4 5 6 7
/ /
strongly disagree — strongly agree

24. When I'm in class/at work my mind wanders to ______.

1 2 3 4 5 6 7
/ /
strongly disagree — strongly agree

25. The best thing about love is sex.

1 2 3 4 5 6 7

/ /

strongly disagree — strongly agree

26. I never give up loving ______, even when things are going poorly.

1 2 3 4 5 6 7

/ /

strongly disagree — strongly agree

27. I often wonder whether ______ is as passionate about me as I am about him/her.

1 2 3 4 5 6 7

/ /

strongly disagree — strongly agree

28. Sometimes I search for alternative meanings to ______'s words and gestures.

1 2 3 4 5 6 7

/ /

strongly disagree — strongly agree

29. Sometimes I feel awkward, shy, and inhibited when I am around ______.

1 2 3 4 5 6 7

/ /

strongly disagree — strongly agree

30. I deeply hope _____ is as attracted to me as I am to him/her.

| 1 | 2 | 3 | 4 | 5 | 6 | 7 |
|---|---|---|---|---|---|---|
| / | | | | | | / |
| strongly disagree | | | | | | strongly agree |

31. I eat more when I am infatuated.

| 1 | 2 | 3 | 4 | 5 | 6 | 7 |
|---|---|---|---|---|---|---|
| / | | | | | | / |
| strongly disagree | | | | | | strongly agree |

32. When I feel certain that _____ is passionate about me, I feel lighter than air.

| 1 | 2 | 3 | 4 | 5 | 6 | 7 |
|---|---|---|---|---|---|---|
| / | | | | | | / |
| strongly disagree | | | | | | strongly agree |

33. Having a good relationship with _____ is more important to me than having a good relationship with my family.

| 1 | 2 | 3 | 4 | 5 | 6 | 7 |
|---|---|---|---|---|---|---|
| / | | | | | | / |
| strongly disagree | | | | | | strongly agree |

34. My daydreams about _____ include making love/sexual contact.

| 1 | 2 | 3 | 4 | 5 | 6 | 7 |
|---|---|---|---|---|---|---|
| / | | | | | | / |
| strongly disagree | | | | | | strongly agree |

35. I feel very self-confident when I am with ______.

1 2 3 4 5 6 7
/ /
strongly disagree … strongly agree

36. No matter where it starts, my mind always seems to end up thinking about ______.

1 2 3 4 5 6 7
/ /
strongly disagree … strongly agree

37. My emotional state depends on how ______ feels about me.

1 2 3 4 5 6 7
/ /
strongly disagree … strongly agree

38. My relationships with my closest friends are more important to me than my relationship with ______.

1 2 3 4 5 6 7
/ /
strongly disagree … strongly agree

39. ______ has special smells that I would recognize anywhere.

1 2 3 4 5 6 7
/ /
strongly disagree … strongly agree

40. I save the cards and letters that ______ sends me.

1 2 3 4 5 6 7
/ /
strongly disagree — strongly agree

41. ______'s behavior has no effect on my emotional well-being.

1 2 3 4 5 6 7
/ /
strongly disagree — strongly agree

42. Being sexually faithful is important when you are in love.

1 2 3 4 5 6 7
/ /
strongly disagree — strongly agree

43. When ______ does well, I feel so happy for him/her.

1 2 3 4 5 6 7
/ /
strongly disagree — strongly agree

44. Being infatuated helps me to concentrate on my work.

1 2 3 4 5 6 7
/ /
strongly disagree — strongly agree

45. When I think about ______ I feel calm and serene.

1 2 3 4 5 6 7
/ /
strongly disagree strongly agree

46. I remember trivial things ______ says and does.

1 2 3 4 5 6 7
/ /
strongly disagree strongly agree

47. I like to keep my schedule open so that if ______ is free, we can see each other.

1 2 3 4 5 6 7
/ /
strongly disagree strongly agree

48. ______'s eyes are quite common.

1 2 3 4 5 6 7
/ /
strongly disagree strongly agree

49. Falling in love was not really a choice; it just struck me.

1 2 3 4 5 6 7
/ /
strongly disagree strongly agree

50. Knowing that ______ is "in love" with me is more important to me than having sex with him/her.

| 1 | 2 | 3 | 4 | 5 | 6 | 7 |
|---|---|---|---|---|---|---|
| / strongly disagree | | | | | | / strongly agree |

51. My passion for ______ can overcome any obstacle.

| 1 | 2 | 3 | 4 | 5 | 6 | 7 |
|---|---|---|---|---|---|---|
| / strongly disagree | | | | | | / strongly agree |

52. I like to think about tiny moments that I have spent with ______.

| 1 | 2 | 3 | 4 | 5 | 6 | 7 |
|---|---|---|---|---|---|---|
| / strongly disagree | | | | | | / strongly agree |

53. I go through periods of despair when I think ______ might not love me.

| 1 | 2 | 3 | 4 | 5 | 6 | 7 |
|---|---|---|---|---|---|---|
| / strongly disagree | | | | | | / strongly agree |

54. I spend hours imagining romantic episodes with ______.

| 1 | 2 | 3 | 4 | 5 | 6 | 7 |
|---|---|---|---|---|---|---|
| / strongly disagree | | | | | | / strongly agree |

55. Please briefly describe the relationship you currently have or used to have with this person: Has the relationship been painful or pleasant? What other details of your infatuation are important for us to understand?

*Thank You: Now Please Answer a Few Questions about Yourself*

S14. What is your occupation?

student: ____________

other: ______________________________

S15. If you are a student:

Which numbers best describe the total annual income of the household where you grew up?

| | |
|---|---|
| Less than $15,000 | 1 |
| $15,000 to $34,999 | 2 |
| $35,000 to $54,999 | 3 |
| $55,000 to $74,999 | 4 |
| $75,000 or more | 5 |

S16. If you are not a student:

Which numbers best describe the total annual income earned by all the adults in your household?

| | |
|---|---|
| Less than $15,000 | 1 |
| $15,000 to $34,999 | 2 |
| $35,000 to $54,999 | 3 |
| $55,000 to $74,999 | 4 |
| $75,000 or more | 5 |

S17. Were you born in the USA?

Yes 1 No 2

S18. If you were not born in the USA, where were you born?

___________________________________________

S19. If you were not born in the USA, how long have you lived in America?

Months______________ Years____________

S20. Where were your parents born?

Mother______________ Father____________

S21. Where were your grandparents born?

Mother's mother______________ Father____________
Father's mother______________ Father____________

S22. Religion:

Protestant 1
Catholic 2
Jewish 3
Muslim 4
Other ________________

S23. Race/Ethnicity

| | |
|---|---|
| White | 1 |
| Black | 2 |
| Oriental | 3 |
| Latino/Hispanic | 4 |
| Multiracial | 5 |
| Other ______________ | |

S24. Please circle the number that best reflects your sexual orientation.

| 1 | 2 | 3 | 4 | 5 | 6 | 7 | 8 | 9 |
|---|---|---|---|---|---|---|---|---|
| / | | | | | | | | / |
| 100% homosexual | | | | | | | | 100% heterosexual |

Today's Date: ______/______/______.
(mo.) (day) (yr.)

# Notes

The citation numbers in each chapter refer to specific sources, groups of sources, or textual notes that appear in the endnotes. To find the complete bibliographical reference for any source, turn to the bibliography.

### *1. "What Wild Ecstasy": Being in Love*

1. Hamill 1996.
2. Wolkstein 1991, p. 51.
3. Wolkstein 1991, p. 84.
4. Wolkstein 1991, p. 150.
5. Yutang 1954, p. 73.
6. Jankowiak and Fischer 1992.
7. Neuroscientists make a technical distinction between "emotion" and "feeling." They regard the emotions as specific neural systems that produce behaviors that assist survival. Feelings, they say, are the conscious perception of these emotions (Damasio 1999; LeDoux 1996, p. 125). But I will use these terms interchangeably.
8. Tennov 1979; Hatfield and Sprecher 1986b; Harris 1995; H. E. Fisher 1998; Fehr 1988.
9. Jankowiac and Fischer 1992; Goode 1959.
10. Tennov 1979, p. 18.
11. Hamill 1996, p. 51.
12. Hopkins 1994, p. 41.
13. Tesser and Reardon 1981; Murray and Holmes 1997; Viederman 1988.
14. Hamill 1996, p. 34.
15. Hopkins 1994, p. 26.

16. Ibid., p. 40.
17. Beach and Tesser 1988; Hatfield and Walster 1978.
18. Hamill 1996, p. 25.
19. Ibid., p. 61.
20. Wolkstein 1991.
21. Lahr and Tabori 1982, p. 110.
22. Harris 1995, p. 113.
23. Hopkins 1994, pp. i–ii.
24. Ibid., p. 21.
25. Ibid., p. i.
26. Hamill 1996, p. 44.
27. *Random House Treasury,* p. 362.
28. Hatfield and Rapson 1996; Tennov 1979; Beach and Tesser 1988.
29. Plato 1999, p. 40.
30. Hamill 1996, p. 38.
31. Whittier 1988, p. 46.
32. Solomon 1990.
33. Hopkins 1994, p. 42.
34. Tennov 1979, p. 31.
35. Fowler 1994.
36. Hopkins 1994, p. 22.
37. Hamill 1996, p. 59.
38. Milton 1949.
39. Tesser and Reardon 1981.
40. Rocamora 1998, p. 84, 87, 94.
41. Shakespeare 1936, *Romeo and Juliet,* act I, scene iv, lines 41–50.
42. Ibid., act I, scene v.
43. Whittier 1988, p. 30.
44. Wolkstein 1991.
45. Ibid., p. 129.
46. Ibid., p. 101.
47. Ibid., p. 48.
48. Harris 1995, p. 110.
49. Hopkins 1994, p. 87.
50. Buss 1994; Buunk and Hupka 1987.
51. Collins and Gregor 1995.
52. Cancian 1987.
53. Yutang 1954, p. 73.
54. Hopkins 1994, p. 18.
55. Tennov 1979.
56. Flexnor 1965.

57. Plato 1999, p. 40.
58. Marazziti et al. 1999.
59. Tesser and Reardon 1981.
60. *Random House Treasury,* p. 321.
61. Hatfield and Walster 1978.
62. Darwin 1872/1965.

## 2. *Animal Magnetism: Love among the Animals*

1. Darwin 1871/n.d., p. 745.
2. Ibid., p. 744.
3. Moss 1988, p. 118.
4. Ryden 1989, p. 147.
5. King 1990, p. 127.
6. Penny 1988, p. 28.
7. Harrington and Paquet 1982, p. v.
8. Mech 1970, p. 112.
9. Darwin 1871/n.d., p. 674.
10. Smuts 1985, pp. 4–5.
11. Tinbergen 1959, p. 29.
12. Dagg and Foster 1976, p. 129.
13. Schaller 1973, p. 78.
14. Moss 1988, p. 115.
15. Galdikas 1995, pp. 144–45.
16. Schaller 1973, p. 79.
17. Sankhala 1977, p. 67.
18. Churchfield 1991, p. 27.
19. Darwin 1871/n.d., p. 653.
20. Ryden 1989, p. 51.
21. Thomas 1993, pp. 54–55.
22. Thomas 1993, p. 72.
23. Hill and Smith 1984.
24. Goodall 1986, p. 446.
25. Ibid.
26. Beach 1976, p. 131.
27. Darwin 1871/n.d., p. 704.
28. Wilson and Daly 1992.
29. Goodall 1986, p. 446.
30. Thomas 1993, p. 46.
31. Pines 1999; Kanin et al. 1970.
32. Brodie 1998, p. 257.

33. Rebhun 1995, p. 245.
34. Harris 1995, p. 122.
35. McNamee 1984, p. 19.
36. Barash and Lipton 2001.
37. Thomas 1993, p. 49.
38. Goodall 1986, p. 459.
39. Wilson and Daly 1992.
40. Schmitt and Buss 2001.
41. Schmitt 2001.
42. Melis and Argiolas 1995; Dluzen et al. 1981; Herbert 1996; Etgen et al. 1999; Etgen and Morales 2002.
43. Herbert 1996.
44. Gingrich et al. 2000; Young et al. 1998.
45. Insel and Carter 1995.
46. Wang et al. 1999; Gingrich et al. 2000.
47. Gingrich et al. 2000.
48. Dluzen et al. 1981.
49. Fabre-Nys et al. 1997.
50. Etgen et al. 1999.
51. Wolkstein 1991, p. 79.
52. Some scientists believe animals lack evolved regions of the cerebral cortex and other brain systems that produce consciousness and self-consciousness, the mechanisms that are necessary to be consciously *aware* of one's emotions. Others believe higher mammals do perceive their emotions (Humphrey 2002; De Waal 1996). I suspect conscious awareness of one's self, one's feelings, and the external world varies from a simple awareness of "here" and "now" to an extended conscious awareness of the distant past and future (Damasio 1994). Mammals are distributed along this continuum: many are aware of their emotions, including their attraction to specific others. But they do not think about these feelings with detailed self-analysis.

### *3. Chemistry of Love: Scanning the Brain "in Love"*

1. Homer 1990, p. 376.
2. Horvitz et al. 1997; Schultz et al. 1997; Schultz 2000.
3. Kiyatkin 1995; Salamone 1996; Robbins and Everitt 1996; Wise 1996; Luciana et al. 1998.
4. Murray and Holmes 1997.
5. Horvitz et al. 1997; Schultz et al. 1997; Schultz 2000.
6. Pfaff 1999; Panksepp 1998.
7. Wise 1988; Colle and Wise 1988; Post, Weiss, and Pert 1988; Kruk and Pycock 1991; Volkow et al. 1997.

8. Abbott 2002; Schultz et al. 1997; Wise 1989, 1996, 1988; Robbins and Everitt 1996.

9. Schultz 2000; Martin-Soelch et al. 2001.

10. Griffin and Taylor 1995.

11. Flament et al. 1985; Hollander et al. 1988; Thoren et al. 1980.

12. H. Fisher 1998.

13. Marazziti et al. 1999.

14. Luciana, Collins, and Depue 1998.

15. Whittier 1988.

16. Mashek, Aron, and Fisher 2000.

17. Hatfield and Sprecher 1986a; Berscheid and Reis 1998; Walster et al. 1966.

18. Whittier 1998, "The Sun Rising," p. 25.

19. Aron, Aron, and Allen 1998.

20. Hatfield and Sprecher 1986a.

21. Plato 1999, p. 23.

22. Ibid., p. 24.

23. Flexnor 1965, p. 200.

24. H. Fisher et al. 2003; Aron et al. (in preparation).

25. The brain has two halves or hemispheres. Hence you have two caudate nuclei, one in your right brain and one in your left brain. In our experiment, we found activity only in the right caudate tail and body, as well as in the right ventral tegmental area. Many neuroscientists currently believe that the positive emotions emanate largely from *left* brain structures while negative emotions arise mainly from *right* brain structures. But several experiments contradict this generality, reporting positive emotions that arise from right brain regions. We don't know why our love-sick individuals showed activity in the right caudate and VTA, rather than in the left caudate or bilaterally. My guess is that early stage romantic love is associated with underlying feelings of anxiety and craving, uncomfortable states of mind.

26. Schultz 2000; Delgado et al. 2000; Elliott et al. 2003; Gold 2003.

27. Saint-Cyr 2003; Knowlton et al. 1996.

28. Small et al. 2001.

29. Wise 1996; Volkow et al. 1997; Schultz, Dayan, and Montague 1997; Schultz 2000; Fiorillo, Tobler, and Schultz 2003; Martin-Soelch et al. 2001; Breiter et al. 2001.

30. H. Fisher 1998; H. Fisher et al. 2002a; H. Fisher et al. 2002b.

31. Schultz 2000.

32. Horvitz et al. 1997; Wickelgren 1997.

33. Damasio 1994.

34. Bartels and Zeki 2000.

35. Damasio 1994.

36. Bartels and Zeki 2000; Gehring and Willoughby 2002; Luu and Posner 2003; Richmond et al. 2003.

37. Brown, personal communication.

38. Aron and Aron 1991; Aron et al. 1995; Aron and Aron 1996.

39. Neuroscientist Donald Pfaff maintains (Pfaff 1999) that all drives have two components: (a) A *generalized* arousal system in the brain produces the energy and motivation to acquire all biological needs. (b) A *specific* constellation of brain systems produces the feelings, thoughts, and behaviors associated with each particular biological need. He reports that the general arousal component of *all* drives is associated with the action of dopamine, norepinephrine, serotonin, acetylcholine, the histamines, orexin, prostaglandin D synthase, and perhaps other brain chemicals. The specific constellation of brain regions and systems associated with *each* particular drive varies considerably. Our fMRI study appears to have uncovered the general arousal component of romantic love, associated with the ventral tegmental area and the distribution of central dopamine. However, we also found activation in the caudate body and tail, the septum, white matter of the posterior cingulate, and other areas, as well as deactivations in several brain regions (H. Fisher et al. 2003; Aron et al., in preparation). These may constitute part of the system specific to intense, early stage romantic love. A different protocol and/or more sophisticated technology will probably be necessary to establish the full set of neural correlates associated with the drive to love. However, the feelings, thoughts, motivations, and behaviors associated with romantic passion may be so varied across individuals, as well as so varied across time within each individual, that the full set of basic systems involved is impossible to record by group analysis.

40. Pfaff 1999.

41. Plato 1999, p. 40.

42. The caudate nucleus has many receptor sites for both norepinephrine and serotonin (Afifi and Bergman 1998). But further research is necessary to establish whether these and/or other regions become active as one feels romantic passion.

43. Several regions of the prefrontal cortex are associated with monitoring rewards. The orbitofrontal cortex is specifically involved in detecting, perceiving, and expecting rewards (Schultz 2000), as well as discriminating between rewards and making preferences (Schultz 2000; Martin-Soelch et al. 2001; Rolls 2000). With the nearby medial prefrontal cortex, we experience our emotions, bestow meaning to our perceptions (Carter 1998; Teasdale et al. 1999), guide our reward-related behaviors (Öngür and Price 2000), create our mood (Öngür and Price 2000, p. 216), and also make preferences (Öngür and Price 2000, p. 215). The caudate nucleus has large nerve cables that project directly to and from the orbitofrontal and medial prefrontal cortices (Öngür and Price 2000). These brain regions became active in some of our subjects, but not all of them. This

variation may be due to difficulties with fMRI technology or because our subjects were in slightly different moods that activated somewhat different brain regions. Group analyses of the sorts we performed would not uncover these subtle individual variations.

44. Dickinson 1955, #632.

## *4. Web of Love: Lust, Romance, and Attachment*

1. Shakespeare 1936, *Love's Labors Lost,* act IV, scene iii, line 341.
2. H. Fisher 1998; H. Fisher et al. 2002a; H. Fisher et al. 2002b.
3. H. Fisher 1989, 1992, 1998, 1999.
4. Hamill 1996, p. 32.
5. Tennov 1979; Hatfield and Rapson 1996.
6. Jankowiak 1995.
7. Bell 1995.
8. Rebhun 1995, p. 253.
9. Rebhun 1995, p. 254.
10. Animal studies indicate that several brain structures are associated with the sex drive and sexual expression, including the medial amygdala, medial preoptic area, paraventricular nucleus, and the periaqueductal gray (Heaton 2000). Using fMRI, Arnow and colleagues report that when male subjects look at erotic video material, they show strong activations in the right subinsular region including the claustrum, left caudate and putamen, right middle occipital/middle temporal gyri, bilateral cingulate gyrus, and right sensorimotor and premotor regions, whereas lesser activation occurs in the right hypothalamus (Arnow et al. 2002). Beauregard and colleagues also measured brain activation (using fMRI) in men as they viewed erotic film excerpts (Beauregard et al. 2001). Activations occurred in limbic and paralimbic structures, including the right amygdala, right anterior temporal pole, and hypothalamus. Using fMRI, Karama and colleagues recorded brain activity while men and women viewed erotic film excerpts (Karama et al. 2002). The blood oxygen level dependent (BOLD) signal increased in the anterior cingulate, medial prefrontal cortex, orbitofrontal cortex, insula and occipitotemporal cortices, as well as in the amygdala and the ventral striatum. Men also showed activation in the thalamus and significantly greater activation than women in the hypothalamus, specifically in a sexually dimorphic area associated with sexual arousal and behavior. In another experiment, researchers measured brain activity among eight men as these subjects experienced orgasm. Blood flow *decreased* in all regions of the cortex except one region of the prefrontal cortex, where it dramatically increased (Tiihonen et al. 1994). Perhaps this decreased activity explains why one becomes almost totally unconscious of the world at large during orgasm.
11. Arnow et al. 2002.

12. Farb 1983.
13. Edwards and Booth 1994; Sherwin 1994.
14. Van Goozen et al. 1997.
15. Edwards and Booth 1994.
16. Hâllstròm and Samuelsson 1990.
17. Tavris and Sadd 1977.
18. Meikle et al. 1988.
19. Nyborg 1994.
20. Hoagland 1998.
21. Ellis and Symons 1990.
22. Blum 1997.
23. Ellis and Symons 1990.
24. Reinisch and Beasley 1990, p. 92.
25. Laumann et al. 1994; Ellis and Symons 1990. Because this gender difference also exists in Japan and Great Britain (Barash and Lipton 1997; Wilson and Land 1981), some scientists believe these variations may be inherited. This makes sense. Female birds and mammals must remain still and cooperative for coitus to occur. And males must display some assertiveness to mate successfully. So signs of surrender by the female in conjunction with cues of dominance by the male are important mating signals (Eibl-Eibesfeldt 1989). In fact, ethologist Ireneus Eibl-Eibesfeldt proposes that these leitmotifs of human sexuality, male dominance and female surrender, arise from primitive brain regions where they evolved to ensure mating success in all reptiles, birds, and mammals.
26. Laumann et al. 1994.
27. Ellis and Symons 1990; Barash and Lipton 1997.
28. Hull et al. 1995; Hull et al. 1997; Kawashima and Takagi 1994.
29. Liu et al. 1998; Herbert 1996.
30. Ferrari and Giuliani 1995.
31. Hull et al. 1995; Wenkstern et al. 1993; West et al. 1992.
32. Hull et al. 1995.
33. Clayton et al. 2000; Walker et al. 1993; Heaton 2000.
34. Walker et al. 1993; Coleman et al. 1999; Ascher et al. 1995.
35. Mayerhofer et al. 1992; Fernandez et al. 1975; Cardinali et al. 1975.
36. Fabre-Nys 1998.
37. Hopkins 1994, p. 14.
38. Sherwin et al. 1985; Sherwin and Gelfand 1987.
39. Ahearn 1998.
40. Damsma et al. 1992; Pleim et al. 1990; Yang et al. 1996.
41. Hull et al. 1999.
42. T. J. Jones et al. 1998.
43. Netter et al. 1998; Sundblad and Eriksson 1997; Gonzalez et al. 1994.

44. Matthew Arnold, "To Marguerite." In Quiller-Couch 1919.

45. Hatfield 1988, p. 191.

46. Shostak 1981, p. 268.

47. Bell 1995, p. 158.

48. Rebhun 1995, p. 252.

49. McCullough 2001.

50. Bowlby 1969, 1973, 1980.

51. Carter et al. 1997; Young, Wang, and Insel 1998; Young et al. 1999; Wang, Ferris, and DeVries 1994; Pitkow et al. 2001.

52. Wang, Ferris, and DeVries 1994.

53. Shakespeare 1936, *A Midsummer Night's Dream,* act III, scene iii, lines 217–20.

54. Pedersen et al. 1992; Carter, DeVries, and Getz 1995.

55. Pedersen et al. 1992.

56. Young, Wang, and Insel 1998; Williams et al. 1994.

57. Damasio 1994, p. 122.

58. Young, Wang, Insel 1998; Charmichael et al. 1987.

59. Villalba, Auger, and De Vries 1999; Delville, Mansour, and Ferris 1996; Wang and De Vries 1995; Wang et al. 1994.

60. Arsenijevic and Tribollet 1998; Johnson et al. 1991.

61. Winslow and Insel 1991a; Winslow and Insel 1991b.

62. Sirotkin and Nitray 1992; Homeida and Khalafalla 1990. When a male prairie vole cohabits with a female mate, levels of vasopressin and testosterone increase (Wang et al. 1994). The vasopressin seems to elicit expressions of attachment, scent marking, and grooming behaviors (Winslow and Insel 1991b) while the testosterone probably enables the male to aggressively defend the nest from interlopers.

63. Thomas, Kim, and Amico 1996a; Thomas, Kim, and Amico 1996b.

64. Delville and Ferris 1995.

65. Booth and Dabbs 1993.

66. Berg and Wynne-Edwards 2001.

67. De Ridder, Pinxten, and Eens 2000; Raouf et al. 1997.

68. Wingfield 1994.

69. Galfi et al. 2001; Ginsberg et al. 1994.

70. Kovacs et al. 1990; Schwarzberg et al. 1981; Van de Kar et al. 1998.

71. Reik 1964.

72. Lee 1973, 1988.

73. Fehr 1988; Aron and Westbay 1996; Hatfield and Sprecher 1986a; Critelli, Myers, and Loos 1986; Hendrick and Hendrick 1986a; Hendrick and Hendrick 1986b; Zick 1970; Hazan and Shaver 1987.

74. Sternberg 1986.

75. Finck 1891, p. 224.
76. Ekman 2003.
77. Evans 2001.
78. Damasio 1994, p. 152.

### 5. *"That First Fine Careless Rapture": Who We Choose*

1. *Random House Treasury.*
2. Hatfield 1988, p. 204.
3. Walster and Berscheid 1971; Dutton and Aron 1974; Hatfield and Sprecher 1986b; Aron et al. 1989.
4. Pines 1999.
5. Shepher 1971.
6. Galton 1884; Rushton 1989; Laumann et al. 1994; Pines 1999.
7. Buston and Emlen 2003.
8. Byrne, Clore, and Smeaton 1986; Cappella and Palmer 1990.
9. Waller and Shaver 1994.
10. Laumann et al. 1994.
11. Lampert 1997.
12. Wedekind et al. 1995.
13. Gangestad and Thornhill 1997.
14. Gangestad, Thornhill, and Yeo 1994; Jones and Hill 1993.
15. Langlois and Roggman 1990.
16. Langlois et al. 1987.
17. Hamilton and Zuk 1982; Thornhill and Gangestad 1993.
18. Gangestad and Thornhill 1997.
19. Aharon et al. 2001.
20. Buss 1994.
21. Gangestad and Thornhill 1997.
22. Thornhill, Gangestad, and Comer 1995.
23. Ibid.
24. Manning and Scutt 1996.
25. Manning et al. 1996.
26. Singh 1993.
27. Singh 2002.
28. Singh 1993, 2002.
29. Buss et al. 1990.
30. Ford and Beach 1951; Ellis 1992.
31. Wolkstein 1991, pp. 6–7.
32. Jankowiak 1995, p. 10.
33. Harrison and Saeed 1977.

34. Buss 1994.
35. Guttentag and Secord 1983; Low 1991.
36. Dion, Berscheid, and Walster 1972.
37. Johnston 1999.
38. Buss 1994.
39. H. Fisher et al. 2003; Aron et al., in preparation.
40. Kanin, Davidson, and Scheck 1970; Dion and Dion 1985; Peplau and Gordon 1985.
41. Berscheid et al. 1971; Lerner and Karabenick 1974.
42. Tannen 1990; Tavris 1992.
43. Baron-Cohen 2003.
44. H. Fisher 1999.
45. Hatfield and Rapson 1996; Tennov 1979.
46. H. Fisher et al. 2003; Aron et al., in preparation.
47. Damasio 1999.
48. Harrison and Saeed 1977.
49. Ellis 1992; Buss 1994.
50. Ellis 1992; Buss 1994.
51. Kenrick et al. 1990.
52. Wolkstein 1991, p. 52.
53. Ibid., p. 103.
54. Lerner and Karabenick 1974.
55. Buss 2003, p. 242.
56. Johnston 1999.
57. Dion and Dion 1988; Hendrick and Hendrick 1986b; Sprecher et al. 1994.
58. Buss 1994.
59. Buss and Schmitt 1993; Kenrick et al. 1993; Gangestad and Thornhill 1997.
60. Buss 2003; Cristiani 2003.
61. Buss 2003.
62. Kenrick et al. 1990.
63. Buss 1994.
64. Shakespeare 1936, *The Merchant of Venice,* act III, scene ii, line 63.
65. Waller and Shaver 1994.
66. Shakespeare 1936, *A Midsummer Night's Dream,* act I, scene i, lines 241–42.
67. Hatfield and Rapson 1996.
68. Pines 1999.
69. Hendrix 1992, 1988.
70. Bowen 1978.
71. Hazan and Shaver 1987.
72. Bowlby 1969.

73. Ainsworth et al. 1978.
74. Aronson 1998.
75. Roethke, "The Motion."
76. Reik 1964.
77. Darwin (1859/1978, 1871/n.d.). Darwin (1871/n.d.) distinguished between two types of sexual selection: *intra*sexual selection, by which members of one sex evolve traits that enable them to compete directly with one another to win mating opportunities; and *inter*sexual selection or "mate choice," by which individuals of one sex evolve traits because the opposite sex prefers them. The antlers on the male moose are a good example of Darwin's first principle. This appendage developed to enable its wearer to intimidate other males during the breeding season. It is Darwin's second form of sexual selection that is central to this book: mate choice. Human female breasts are a good example. Unlike female teats, these fleshy appendages have no purpose in reproduction; they probably evolved primarily because ancestral males *liked* them. In fact, scientists now call these adornments that evolved by mate choice "fitness indicators," precisely because they are extreme, striking, metabolically expensive, hard to fake, and useless in the daily struggle to survive (Fisher 1915; Zahavi 1975; Miller 2000). Because these traits are "handicaps," only the fittest can build and maintain them (Zahavi 1975). For this reason alone, these traits impress.
78. Miller 2000, p. 35.
79. Miller 2000.
80. Ibid., pp. 3, 29.
81. Ibid., p. 7.
82. Darwin 1871/n.d., p. 743.

### *6. Why We Love: The Evolution of Romantic Love*

1. Brunet et al. 2002.
2. H. Fisher 1989, 1992, 1999.
3. Reno et al. 2003.
4. Young, Wang, and Insel 1998; Young et al. 1999, p. 768; Insel 2000.
5. Rosenthal 2002, p. 280.
6. Holy Bible 2000, Ecclesiastes I:9–12.
7. H. Fisher 1992.
8. Lancaster and Lancaster 1983.
9. H. Fisher 1992.
10. Potts 1988.
11. Walker and Leakey 1993.
12. Allman 1999.
13. Ibid.

14. Ibid.

15. Anthropologists have long proposed that delayed maturation evolved to give youngsters time to master the skills they needed as adults. Several new theories have been offered. Some hold that our long human childhood evolved along with the evolution of our big brain because complex brains need time to grow. Others argue that the genes for a long childhood emerged along with those for an extended adulthood: our forebears remained dependent for some eighteen years to conserve energy while middle-aged kin hunted and collected; then as the young matured, they provided for their aging elders. The reverse could also have occurred: parents evolved the genetic ability to live longer in order to care for their slow-maturing children. Another view is that long-lived species tend to postpone reproduction to produce higher quality young. Like all dramatic evolutionary changes, delayed maturation probably evolved for many reasons. I'll add another. Perhaps this biological trait evolved, in part, to give ancestral children more time to gain emotional experience about sex and love.

16. Ryan 1998.

17. Miller 2000.

18. Henderson 2003.

19. Povinellia and Preussc 1995.

20. Kohn 2000.

21. Falk 2000; Rilling and Insel 1999b; Stephan, Baron, and Frahm 1988; Deacon 1988.

22. Stephan, Frahm, and Baron 1981.

23. Wade 2001.

24. Rilling and Insel 1999a; Rilling and Insel 1999b.

25. Bower 2002.

26. Turner 2000; Stephan 1983; Deacon 1988.

27. Rilling and Insel 1999b.

28. Duncan et al. 2000. We have many kinds of intelligence. "General intelligence" refers to a host of related abilities, including our capacity to assemble facts, reason, contemplate options, employ forethought, produce insights, make decisions, resolve problems, think abstractly, understand complex ideas, learn quickly, learn from experience, and plan ahead (Spearman 1904; Carroll 1997). Creativity and pragmatism are forms of human braininess (Sternberg 1985). Men and women also have many specific skills, among them musical genius, spatial intelligence, and basic articulation, the ability to find the right word rapidly (Gardner 1983). "Emotional intelligence," the ability to be self-aware, control one's impulses, and act deftly in difficult social circumstances, is a human aptitude (Goleman 1995). I think "sense of humor" is a form of intelligence. And I coined the term "sexual intelligence" to describe the ability to be sensitive to a partner's needs, express one's own wants adroitly, and act appropriately while making love.

29. Stephan, Frahm, and Baron 1981.
30. Ibid.
31. Ibid.
32. Semendeferi et al. 1997; Finlay and Darlington 1995.
33. Whittier 1988.
34. Laumann et al. 1994.
35. DeLamater 1995; Cherlin 1995.
36. Morell 1998.
37. Daly, Wilson, and Weghorst 1982; Wilson and Daly 1992.
38. Black 1996; Mock and Fujioka 1990.
39. Morell 1998.

## *7. Lost Love: Rejection, Despair, and Rage*

1. Stallworthy 1973, p. 293.
2. Hamill 1996, p. 133.
3. Baumeister, Wotman, and Stillwell 1993.
4. Baumeister and Dhavale 2001.
5. Evans 2001, p. 52.
6. Meloy 1998.
7. Stallworthy 1973, p. 297.
8. Ibid., p. 275.
9. Alarcon 1992, p. 110.
10. Stallworthy 1973, p. 260.
11. Millay 1988, p. 86.
12. Jankowiak 1995, p. 179.
13. Harris 1995, p. 113.
14. Harrison 1986.
15. Jankowiak 1995.
16. Bowlby 1973; Panksepp 1998; Lewis, Amini, and Lannon 2000.
17. Whittier 1988, p. 82.
18. Schultz 2000.
19. Panksepp 1998.
20. Lewis, Amini, and Lannon 2000; Panksepp 1998.
21. Panksepp 1998.
22. Baumeister and Dhavale 2001.
23. Bowlby 1973; Panksepp 1998.
24. Lewis, Amini, and Lannon 2000.
25. Panic involves a region in the midbrain, the periaqueductal gray (PAG), a region that lies close to regions that generate physical pain. The periaqueductal gray then sends signals to many other parts of the panic system. No one

knows exactly which brain chemicals produce feelings of separation anxiety and panic (Panksepp 1998). Glutamate, the most excitatory neurotransmitter, is probably one; it contributes to everything we do. As this neurotransmitter increases, animals begin to make distress calls that are specifically associated with abandonment. Scientists know much more about what quells separation anxiety and panic than the condition itself. Opioids, such as morphine, rapidly soothe the distress calls of abandoned animals. Oxytocin, the hormone associated with social attachment and bonding, also decreases separation-induced distress. This is probably why animals tend to stop crying when they are touched; massage activates oxytocin and opioid receptors.

26. Smith and Hoklund 1988; Campbell, Sedikides, and Bossom 1994.
27. Kapit, Macey, and Meisami 2000; Nemeroff 1998.
28. Panksepp 1998.
29. Scientists still don't know exactly which brain chemicals are involved in rage, but several probably contribute (Panksepp 1998). Substance P, a neuromodulator, can produce anger. Glutamate and acetylcholine promote fury. High levels of norepinephrine and low levels of serotonin can generate anger. And low levels of serotonin contribute to the impulsivity that generally accompanies fury (Panksepp 1998; Tiihonen et al. 1997).
30. Panksepp 1998.
31. Ibid.
32. Ibid., p. 196.
33. Dozier 2002.
34. Darwin 1871/n.d., p. 703.
35. Panksepp 1998.
36. Bowlby 1973; Shaver, Hazan, and Bradshaw 1988.
37. Dozier 2002.
38. Ellis and Malamuth 2000.
39. Bowlby 1960, 1973; Panksepp 1998.
40. Mearns 1991.
41. Rosenthal 2002; Nemeroff 1998.
42. Baumeister, Wotman, and Stillwell 1993; Buss 1994.
43. Hatfield and Rapson 1996.
44. Taffel 1990.
45. Tavris 1992.
46. Hatfield and Rapson 1993.
47. Ibid.
48. Whittier 1988.
49. Ustun and Sartorius 1995.
50. Mearns 1991.
51. Hatfield and Rapson 1996.

52. Harlow, Harlow, and Suomi 1971.
53. Panksepp 1998.
54. Schultz 2000.
55. Panksepp 1998.
56. Kapit, Macey, and Meisami 2000; Panksepp 1998; Nemeroff 1998.
57. Beck 1996; Niculescu and Akiskal 2001; Price et al. 1994; Nesse 1990, 1991; Panksepp 1998; McGuire and Troisi 1998.
58. Troisi and McGuire 2002; McGuire and Troisi 1998.
59. Hagen, Watson, and Thomson, in preparation.
60. Watson and Andrews 2002.
61. Nesse 1991; Hagen, Watson, and Thomson, in preparation; Rosenthal 2002.
62. Bowlby 1969; Ainsworth et al. 1978; Hazan and Shaver 1987; Chisholm 1995.
63. Leary 2001.
64. Baumeister and Dhavale 2001.
65. Stallworthy 1973, p. 266.
66. Buss 1994; Buunk and Hupka 1987.
67. Buunk and Hupka 1987.
68. Voracek 2001.
69. Buss 2000.
70. Ibid.
71. Stallworthy 1973, p. 282.
72. Sheets et al. 1997; Mathes 1986.
73. Meloy and Gothard 1995.
74. Fremouw et al. 1997.
75. Gugliotta 1997; Meloy 1998.
76. Gugliotta 1997; Meloy 1998; Jason et al. 1984; Hall 1998.
77. Meloy, in press.
78. Dozier 2002.
79. Ibid.
80. Buss 1994; United Nations Development Programme 1995a; Wilson and Daly 1992.
81. E. Goode 2000.
82. Ibid.
83. Wilson and Daly 1992; United Nations Development Programme 1995a.
84. Shakespeare 1936, *Othello,* act III, scene iii, lines 304–7.
85. Wilson and Daly 1992.
86. Daly and Wilson 1988.
87. Wilson and Daly 1992.
88. Dozier 2002.

89. Nadler and Dotan 1992; Shettel-Neuber, Bryson, and Young 1978.
90. Gugliotta 1997.
91. E. Goode 2000.
92. Euripides 1963, p. 17.
93. Ibid.
94. Tiihonen et al. 1997; Panksepp 1998.
95. Ibid.
96. Mace and Mace 1980.
97. Hagen, Watson, and Thomson, in preparation.

### *8. Taking Control of Passion: Making Romance Last*

1. Holmes 1997.
2. Whittier 1988, p. 41.
3. Hamill 1996, p. 13.
4. Yutang 1954, p. 72.
5. Wolkstein 1991, p. 153.
6. Peele 1975, 1988; Carnes 1983; Halpern 1982; Tennov 1979; Hunter et al. 1981; Liebowitz 1983; Mellody et al. 1992; Griffin-Shelley 1991; Schaef 1989; Findling 1999. Because scientists report that many aspects of personality have a genetic basis, I suspect there is a genetic fingerprint to the feelings of romantic love; in short, different people feel this passion to different degrees, with different intensities and durations. In support of this speculation, there are several forms of love disorders. A few people are unable to fall in love (Tennov 1979). They marry and build happy long-term partnerships, but they report they have never felt the passion of romantic love. Others are "love junkies." They are so addicted to this excitement that they are unable to maintain a long-term relationship; as the passion fades, they seek their next romantic "high" (Liebowitz 1983). In fact, psychiatrist Donald Klein named a form of recurrent depression that some of these love junkies suffer: hysteroid dysphoria. As these disastrous love affairs proceed, the lover suffers severe mood swings (Liebowitz 1983). Others suffer what psychologists call Clerambault-Kandinsky syndrome (CKS) or erotomania. In this condition, the obsessed lover does not even know the beloved (often someone who is famous), yet the lover holds the delusion that this person is in love with them (Zona et al. 1993; Rosenthal 2002).
7. Leshner 1997; Rosenthal 2002.
8. Bartels and Zeki 2000.
9. Regis 1995.
10. Alarcon 1992, p. 85.
11. Thayer 1996; Rosenthal 2002.
12. Rosenthal 2002.

13. Kolata 2002.

14. Rosenthal 2002. New data indicate that when mice are kept away from their daily exercise routine of running, brain regions associated with craving for food, sex, or narcotic drugs become active.

15. Rosenthal 2002.

16. Carter 1998.

17. Stallworthy 1973, p. 279.

18. Baumeister, Wotman, and Stillwell 1993.

19. Baumeister and Dhavale 2001.

20. Stallworthy 1973, p. 253.

21. E. Goode, Petersen, and Pollack 2002.

22. E. Goode, Peterson, and Pollack 2002; Stahl 2000.

23. Frohlich and Meston 2000; Rosenthal 2002.

24. Rosenthal 2002.

25. Ashton and Rosen 1998; Labbate et al. 1997; Walker et al. 1993; Clayton et al. 2000; Gitlan et al. 2000; Ascher et al. 1995; Rosenthal 2002.

26. Rosenthal 2002.

27. Brody et al. 2001; Goleman 1996.

28. Brody et al. 2001; Goleman 1996; Rosenthal 2002.

29. Brody et al. 2001.

30. Ibid.

31. For a superb book on how to heal depression, pick up *The Emotional Revolution,* by psychiatrist Norman Rosenthal (Rosenthal 2002).

32. Flexnor 1965, p. 294.

33. Hamill 1996, p. 70.

34. Shakespeare 1936, *All's Well that Ends Well,* act V, scene iii, line 41.

35. Dutton and Aron 1974.

36. Hatfield 1988, p. 204.

37. Dutton and Aron 1974; Berscheid and Walster 1974; Aron and Aron 1986; Reissman et al. 1993; Aron and Aron 1996; Aron et al. 2000.

38. Norman and Aron 1995; Aron and Aron 1996; Aron et al. 2000.

39. Wolkstein 1991, p. 44.

40. Panksepp 1998.

41. Gallup 2003, personal communication.

42. Gallup et al. 2002.

43. Carter 1998.

44. H. Fisher and J. A. Thomson, in preparation.

45. Ibid.

46. M. Fisher, in preparation.

47. Ashton and Rosen 1998; Labbate et al. 1997; Walker et al. 1993; Gitlan et al. 2000.

48. Sternberg 1986; Cancian 1987; Hatfield and Rapson 1996.
49. Helgeson, Shaver, and Dyer 1987.
50. Brod 1987; Fowlkes 1994; Tavris 1992.
51. Tannen 1990.
52. Fisher 1999.
53. Hatfield and Rapson 1996.
54. Brod 1987; Fowlkes 1994; Tavris 1992.
55. Tannen 1994.
56. H. Fisher 1999.
57. Ibid.
58. Rubin et al. 1980; Cancian 1987; Tavris 1992.
59. Tornstam 1992.
60. Fisher 1999.
61. Buss 1988.
62. Cancian 1987; Tavris 1992.
63. Rubin et al. 1980; Tavris 1992.
64. Gottman 1994.
65. Schultz 2000.
66. Hopkins 1994, p. 55.
67. Epstein 2002.
68. Tucker and Aron 1993; Traupmann and Hatfield 1981; Mathes and Wise 1983.
69. Liebowitz 1983.
70. Tucker and Aron 1993; Mathes and Wise 1983; Schnarch 1997.
71. Tucker and Aron 1993.
72. Knox 1970.
73. Ibid.
74. Schultz et al. 2000.
75. Norman and Aron 1995; Aron and Aron 1996.
76. Schultz et al. 2000.
77. LeDoux 1996.
78. Damasio 1994; LeDoux 1996.
79. Damasio 1994.
80. LeDoux 1996.
81. Ibid.
82. Ibid.

## *9. "The Madness of the Gods": The Triumph of Love*

1. Ahearn 2001.
2. Hatfield and Rapson 1996.

3. Buss 1994.
4. Rosenblatt and Anderson 1981; Broude and Green 1983; Prakasa and Rao 1979.
5. Rosenblatt and Anderson 1981; Prakasa and Rao 1979.
6. Mace and Mace 1980.
7. Friedl 1975.
8. H. Fisher 1992; H. Fisher 1999.
9. W. J. Goode 1959; Frayser 1985.
10. H. Fisher 1999, 1992; Stone 1988.
11. Bruce et al. 1995; W. J. Goode 1982.
12. Stone 1988; Stone 1990; W. J. Goode 1982.
13. H. Fisher 1999.
14. United Nations 1995b; United Nations 1995c.
15. Allgeier and Wiederman 1991; Hatfield and Rapson 1996.
16. Hatfield and Rapson 1996.
17. Cancian 1987.
18. Jehl 1997, p. A4.
19. Wattenberg 1997.
20. Rowe 1997.
21. Hatfield and Rapson 1987.
22. Purdy 1995.
23. Wang and Nguyen 1995; Hatfield and Rapson 1987; Butler et al. 1995.
24. Bulcroft and O'Conner-Roden 1986.
25. Cristiani 2003.
26. H. Fisher 1992.
27. Stone 1990; Furstenburg 1996; Posner 1992.
28. Ibid.
29. Holmes 1996; H. Fisher 1999.
30. Espenshade 1984.
31. Lancaster 1994.
32. Arnst 1998.
33. Orr 2003
34. Ibid.
35. Hines 1998.
36. Newberg et al. 2001.

# *Bibliography*

Abbott, A. 2002. Addicted. *Nature* 419(6910):872–74.

Afifi, A. K., and R. A. Bergman. 1998. *Functional Neuroanatomy: Text and Atlas.* New York: McGraw-Hill.

Aharon et al. 2001. Beautiful faces have variable reward value: fMRI and behavioral evidence. *Neuron* 32(3):537–51.

Ahearn, L. M. 1998. "Love keeps afflicting me": Agentive discourse in Nepali love letters. Paper presented at the annual meeting of the American Anthropological Association, Washington, D.C.

———. 2001. *Invitations to Love: Literacy, Love Letters and Social Change in Nepal.* Ann Arbor, Mich.: The University of Michigan Press.

Ainsworth, M. D. S., M. C. Blehar, E. Waters, and S. Wall. 1978. *Patterns of Attachment: A Psychological Study of the Strange Situation.* Hillsdale, N.J.: Erlbaum.

Alarcon, Francisco X. 1992. *Snake Poems: An Aztec Invocation.* San Francisco: Chronicle Books.

Allgeier, E. R., and M. W. Wiederman. 1991. Love and mate selection in the 1990s. *Free Inquiry* 11:25–27.

Allman, J. 1999. *Evolving Brains.* New York: Scientific American Library.

Arnow, B. A., J. E. Desmond, L. L. Banner, G. H. Glover, A. Solomon, M. L. Polan, T. F. Lue, S. W. Atlas. 2002. Brain activation and sexual arousal in healthy, heterosexual males. *Brain* 125 (pt 5):1014–23.

Arnst, C. 1998. Single women in a hostile world. *Business Week* :27+.

Aron, A. 2000. Love: An overview. In *Encyclopedia of Psychology,* ed. A. E. Kazdin. Vol. 5:82–85. Washington, D.C.: American Psychological Association.

Aron, A., and E. Aron. 1991. Love and sexuality. In *Sexuality in Close Relationships,* ed. K. McKinney and S. Sprecher. Hillsdale, N.J.: Lawrence Erlbaum Associates.

Aron, A., and E. Aron. 1986. *Love and the Expansion of Self: Understanding Attraction and Satisfaction.* New York: Hemisphere.

Aron, A., and L. Westbay. 1996. Dimensions of the prototype of love. *Journal of Personality and Social Psychology* 70:535–51.

Aron, A., E. N. Aron, and J. Allen. 1998. Motivations for unreciprocated love. *Personality and Social Psychology Bulletin* 24:787–96.

Aron, A., M. Paris, and E. N. Aron. 1995. Falling in love: Prospective studies of self-concept change. *Journal of Personality and Social Psychology* 69:1102–12.

Aron, A., D. G. Dutton, E. N. Aron, and A. Iverson. 1989. Experiences of falling in love. *Journal of Social and Personal Relationships* 6:243–57.

Aron, A., C. C. Norman, E. N. Aron, C. McKenna, and R. E. Heyman. 2000. Couples' shared participation in novel and arousing activities and experienced relationship quality. *Journal of Personality and Social Psychology* 78(2): 273–84.

Aron, A., H. Fisher, D. Mashek, G. Strong, H. Li, and L. L. Brown. In preparation. Early stage intense romantic love activates cortical-basal-ganglia reward/motivation, emotion and attention systems: An fMRI study of a dynamic network that varies with relationship length, passion intensity and gender.

Aron, E. N., and A. Aron. 1996. Love and expansion of the self: The state of the model. *Personal Relationships* 3:45–58.

Aronson, E. 1998. *The Social Animal,* 7th ed. San Francisco: Freeman.

Arsenijevic, Y., and E. Tribollet. 1998. Region-specific effect of testosterone on oxytocin receptor binding in the brain of the aged rat. *Brain Research* 785(1):167–70.

Ascher, J. A., J. O. Cole, J. N. Colin, J. P. Feighner, R. M. Ferris, H. C. Fibiger, R. N. Golden, P. Martin, W. Z. Potter, E. Richelson, and F. Sulser. 1995. Bupropion: A review of its mechanism of antidepressant activity. *Journal of Clinical Psychiatry* 56(9):396–402.

Ashton, A. D., and R. C. Rosen. 1998. Bupropion as an antidote for serotonin reuptake inhibitor-induced sexual dysfunction. *Journal of Clinical Psychiatry* 59:112–15.

Barash, D. P., and J. E. Lipton. 1997. *Making Sense of Sex: How Genes and Gender Influence Our Relationships.* Washington, D. C.: Island Press.

Barash, D. P., and J. E. Lipton. 2001. *The Myth of Monogamy: Fidelity and Infidelity in Animals and People.* New York: W. H. Freeman and Co.

Baron-Cohen, S. 2003. *The Essential Difference: The Truth about the Male and Female Brain.* New York: Basic Books.

Bartels, A., and S. Zeki. 2000. The neural basis of romantic love. *NeuroReport* 2(17):12–15.

Baumeister, R. F., and D. Dhavale. 2001. Two sides of romantic rejection. In *Interpersonal Rejection,* ed. M. R. Leary. New York: Oxford University Press.

Baumeister, R. F., S. R. Wotman, and A. M. Stillwell. 1993. Unrequited love: on heartbreak, anger, guilt, scriptlessness and humiliation. *Journal of Personality and Social Psychology* 64:377–94.

Beach, F. A. 1976. Sexual attractivity, proceptivity, and receptivity in female mammals. *Hormones and Behavior* 7:105–38.

Beach, S. R. H., and A. Tesser. 1988. Love in marriage; a cognitive account. In *The Psychology of Love,* ed. R. J. Sternberg and M. L. Barnes. New Haven, Conn.: Yale University Press.

Beauregard, M., J. Levesque, and P. Bourgouin. 2001. Neural correlates of conscious self-regulation of emotion. *Journal of Neuroscience* 21(18):RC165.

Beck, A. T. 1996. Depression as an evolutionary strategy. Paper presented at the annual meeting of the Human Behavior and Evolution Society, June 27.

Bell, J. 1995. Notions of love and romance among the Taita of Kenya. In *Romantic Passion: A Universal Experience?,* ed. W. Jankowiak. New York: Columbia University Press.

Berg, S. J., and K. E. Wynne-Edwards. 2001. Changes in testosterone, cortisol, and estradiol levels in men becoming fathers. *Mayo Clinic Proceedings* 76(6):582–92.

Berns, G. S., S. M. McClure, G. Pagnoni, and P. R. Montague. 2001. Predictability modulates human brain response to reward. *Journal of Neuroscience* 21(8):2793–98.

Berscheid, E., and H. T. Reis. 1998. Attraction and close relationships. In *The Handbook of Social Psychology,* ed. D. T. Gilbert and S. T. Fiske. Boston: McGraw-Hill.

Berscheid, E., and E. Walster. 1974. A little bit about love. In *Foundations of Interpersonal Attraction,* ed. T. L. Huston. New York: Academic Press.

Berscheid, E., K. K. Dion, E. Walster, and G. W. Walster. 1971. Physical attractiveness and dating choice: a test of the matching hypothesis. *Journal of Experimental Social Psychology* 7:173–89.

Black, J. M., ed. 1996. *Partnerships in Birds: The Study of Monogamy.* New York: Oxford University Press.

Blum, D. 1997. *Sex on the Brain: The Biological Differences between Men and Women.* New York: Viking.

Booth, A., and J. M. Dabbs. 1993. Testosterone and men's marriages. *Social Forces* 72(2):463–77.

Bowen, M. 1978. *Family Therapy in Clinical Practice.* New York: Jason Aronson.

Bower, B. 2001. Depression therapies converge in brain. *Science News* 160:39.

———. 2002. The DNA divide: chimps, people differ in brain's gene activity. *Science News* 161:227–28.

Bowlby, J. 1960. Grief and mourning in infancy and early childhood. *Psychoanalytic Study of the Child* 15:9–52.

———. 1969. *Attachment and Loss: Attachment* (vol. 1). New York: Basic Books.

———. 1973. *Attachment and Loss: Separation* (vol. 2). New York: Basic Books.

———. 1980. *Attachment and Loss: Loss* (vol. 3). New York: Basic Books.

Breiter, H. C., I. Aharon, D. Kahneman, A. Dale, and P. Shizgal. 2001. Functional imaging of neural responses to expectancy and experience of monetary gains and losses. *Neuron* 30:619–39.

Brod, H. 1987. Who benefits from male involvement in wife's pregnancy? *Marriage and Divorce Today* 12(46):3.

Brodie, F. 1998. *Thomas Jefferson: An Intimate History.* New York: W. W. Norton.

Brody, A. L., et al. 2001. Regional brain metabolic changes in patients with major depression treated with either paroxetine or interpersonal therapy: Preliminary findings. *Archives of General Psychiatry* 58(7):631–40.

Broude, G. J., and S. J. Green. 1983. Cross-cultural codes on husband-wife relationships. *Ethology* 22:273–74.

Brown, L. L. Department of Neurology and Neuroscience, Albert Einstein College of Medicine, personal communication.

Brown, L. L., J. S. Schneider, and T. I. Lidsky. 1997. Sensory and cognitive functions of the basal ganglia. *Current Opinion in Neurobiology* 7:157–63.

Bruce, J., C. B. Lloyd, and A. Leonard with P. L. Engle and N. Duffy. 1995. *Families in Focus: New Perspectives on Mothers, Fathers, and Children.* New York: The Population Council.

Brunet, M., et al. 2002. A new hominid from the upper Miocene of Chad, Central Africa. *Nature* 418:145–55.

Bulcroft, K., and M. O'Conner-Roden. 1986. Never too late. *Psychology Today* 20(6):66–69.

Buss, D. M. 1994. *The Evolution of Desire: Strategies of Human Mating.* New York: Basic Books.

———. 2000. *The Dangerous Passion: Why Jealousy Is as Necessary as Are Love and Sex.* New York: Free Press.

———. 2002. Human mate guarding. *Neuroendocrinology Letters* (special issue, suppl 4) 23:23–29.

———. 2003. *The Evolution of Desire: Strategies of Human Mating.* Rev. and exp. ed. New York: Basic Books.

Buss, D. M., and D. P. Schmitt. 1993. Sexual strategies theory: an evolutionary perspective on human mating. *Psychological Review* 100:204–32.

Buss, D. M., et al. 1990. International preferences in selecting mates: A study of 37 cultures. *Journal of Cross-cultural Psychology* 21:5–47.

Buston, P. M., and S. T. Emlen. 2003. Cognitive processes underlying human mate choice: the relationship between self-perception and mate preference in Western society. *Proceedings of the National Academy of Sciences* 100(15):8805–10.

Butler, R., W. R. Walker, J. J. Skowronski, and L. Shannon. 1995. Age and responses to the love attitudes scale: Consistency in structure, differences in scores. *International Journal of Aging and Human Development* 40(4): 281–96.

Buunk, B. P., and R. B. Hupka. 1987. Cross-cultural differences in the elicitation of sexual jealousy. *Journal of Sex Research* 23:12–22.

Byrne, D., G. L. Clore, and G. Smeaton. 1986. The attraction hypothesis: do similar attitudes affect anything? *Journal of Personality and Social Psychology* 51:1167–70.

Campbell, W. K., C. Sedikides, and J. Bossom. 1994. Romantic involvement, self-discrepancy, and psychological well-being: a preliminary investigation. *Personal Relationships* 1:399–404.

Cancian, Francesca M. 1987. *Love in America: Gender and Self-Development.* Cambridge, Eng.: Cambridge University Press.

Cappella, J. N., and M. T. Palmer. 1990. Attitude similarity, relational history, and attraction: the mediating effects of kinesic and vocal behaviors. *Communication Monographs* 57:161–83.

Cardinali, D. P., C. A. Nagle, E. Gomez, and J. M. Rosner. 1975. Norepinephrine turnover in the rat pineal gland. Acceleration by estradiol and testosterone. *Life Science* 16(11):1717–24.

Carmichael, M. S., R. Humbert, J. Dixen, G. Palmisano, W. Greenleaf, and J. M. Davidson. 1987. Plasma oxytocin increases in the human sexual response. *Journal of Clinical Endocrinology and Metabolism* 64(1):27–31.

Carnes, P. 1983. *Out of the Shadows: Understanding Sexual Addiction.* Minneapolis: CompCare.

Carroll, J. B. 1997. Theoretical and technical issues in identifying a factor of general intelligence. In *Intelligence, Genes, and Success: Scientists Respond to The Bell Curve,* eds. B. Devlin, S. E. Fienberg, D. P. Resnick, and K. Roeder. New York: Springer-Verlag.

Carter, C. S., A. C. DeVries, and L. L. Getz. 1995. Physiological substrates of mammalian monogamy: the prairie vole model. *Neuroscience and Biobehavioral Reviews* 19(2):303–14.

Carter, C. S., A. DeVries, S. E. Taymans, R. L. Roberts, J. R. Williams, and L. L. Getz. 1997. Peptides, Steroids, and Pair Bonding. In *The Integrative Neurobiology of Affiliation,* ed. C. S. Carter, I. I. Lederhendler, and B. Kirkpatrick. Annals of the New York Academy of Sciences, 807:260–72. New York: The New York Academy of Sciences.

Carter, R. 1998. *Mapping the Mind.* Los Angeles, Calif.: University of California Press.

Chase, P. G., and H. L. Dibble. 1987. Middle paleolithic symbolism: a review of current evidence and interpretations. *Journal of Anthropological Archaeology* 6:263–96.

Cherlin, A. J. 1995. Social organization and sexual choices. *Contemporary Sociology* 24(4):293–96.

Chisholm, J. S. 1995. Love's contingencies: the developmental socioecology of romantic passion. In *Romantic Passion: A Universal Experience?*, ed. W. Jankowiak. New York: Columbia University Press.

Churchfield, S. 1991. *The Natural History of Shrews*. Ithaca, N.Y.: Comstock Publishing Associates, a division of Cornell University Press.

Clayton, A. H., E. D. McGarvey, J. Warnock, et al. 2000. Bupropion as an antidote to SSRI-induced sexual dysfunction. Poster presented at the New Clinical Drug Evaluation Unit Program (NCDEU), Boca Raton, Fla.

Coleman, C. C., L. A. Cunningham, V. J. Foster, S. R. Batey, R. M. J. Donahue, T. L. Houser, and J. A. Ascher. 1999. Sexual dysfunction associated with the treatment of depression: a placebo-controlled comparison of bupropion sustained release and sertraline treatment. *Annals of Clinical Psychiatry* 11(4):205–15.

Colle, L. M., and R. A. Wise. 1988. Facilitory and inhibitory effects of nucleus accumbens amphetamine on feeding. In *The Mesocorticolimbic Dopamine System*, ed. P. W. Kalivas and C. B. Nemeroff. New York: The New York Academy of Science, pp. 491–92.

Collins, J., and T. Gregor. 1995. Boundaries of Love. In *Romantic Passion: A Universal Experience?*, ed. W. Jankowiak. New York: Columbia University Press.

Cosmides, L., and J. Tooby. 1992. Cognitive adaptations for social exchange. In *The Adapted Mind: Evolutionary Psychology and the Generation of Culture*, ed. J. H. Barkow, L. Cosmides, and J. Tooby. New York: Oxford University Press.

Cristiani, M. 2003. A life history perspective on dating and courtship among Albuquerque adolescents. Ph.D. dissertation, Dept. of Anthropology, University of New Mexico.

Critelli, J. W., E. J. Myers, and V. E. Loos. 1986. The components of love: romantic attraction and sex role orientation. *Journal of Personality* 54(2): 354–70.

cummings, e. e. 1972. *Complete Poems: 1913–1962*. New York: Harcourt, Brace, Jovanovich.

Dagg, A. I., and J. B. Foster. 1976. *The Giraffe: Its Biology, Behavior, and Ecology*. New York: Van Nostrand Reinhold Co.

Dai, W. J., L. M. Lu, and T. Yao. 1996. Effects of gonadal steroid hormones on hypothalamic vasopressin mRNA level in male and female rats. *Sheng Li Xue Bao* 48(6):557–63.

Daly, M., and M. Wilson. 1988. *Homicide*. New York: Aldine de Gruyter.

Daly, M., M. Wilson, and S. J. Weghorst. 1982. Male sexual jealousy. *Ethology and Sociobiology* 3:11–27.

Damasio, A. R. 1994. *Descartes' Error: Emotion, Reason, and the Human Brain*. New York: G. P. Putnam's Sons.

———. 1999. *The Feeling of What Happens: Body and Emotion in the Making of Consciousness.* New York: Harcourt Brace and Co.

Damsma, G., J. G. Pfaus, D. G. Wenkstern, A. G. Phillips, and H. C. Fibiger. 1992. Sexual behavior increased dopamine transmission in the nucleus accumbens and striatum of male rats: Comparison with novelty and locomotion. *Behavioral Neuroscience* 106:181–91.

Darwin, C. 1859/1978. *The Origins of Species by Means of Natural Selection.* Franklin Center, Pa.: Franklin Library.

———. 1871/n.d. *The Descent of Man and Selection in Relation to Sex.* New York: The Modern Library/Random House.

———. 1872/1965. *The Expression of the Emotions in Man and Animals.* Chicago: The University of Chicago Press.

Davies, D. C., G. Horn, and B. J. McCabe. 1985. Noradrenaline and learning: effects of the noradrenergic neurotoxin DSP4 on imprinting in the domestic chick. *Behavioral Neuroscience* 99(4):652–60.

Deacon, T. W. 1988. Human brain evolution: II. Embryology and brain allometry. In *Intelligence and Evolutionary Biology,* ed. H. J. Jerison and I. Jerison. New York: Springer-Verlag.

DeLamater, J. 1995. The NORC sex survey. *Science* 270:501–03.

Delgado, M. R., L. E. Nystrom, C. Fissel, D. C. Noll, and J. A. Fiez. 2000. Tracking the hemodynamic responses to reward and punishment in the striatum. *Journal of Neurophysiology* 84:3072–77.

Delville, Y., and C. F. Ferris. 1995. Sexual differences in vasopressin receptor binding within the ventrolateral hypothalamus in golden hamsters. *Brain Research* 68(1):91–96.

Delville, Y., K. M. Mansour, and C. F. Ferris. 1996. Testosterone facilitates aggression by modulating vasopressin receptors in the hypothalamus. *Physiology and Behavior* 60(1):25–29.

De Ridder, E., R. Pinxten, and M. Eens. 2000. Experimental evidence of a testosterone-induced shift from paternal to mating behavior in a facultatively polygynous songbird. *Behavioral Ecology and Sociobiology* 49(1):24–30.

De Waal, F. 1996. *Good Natured: The Origins of Right and Wrong in Humans and Other Animals.* Cambridge, Mass.: Harvard University Press.

Dickinson, E. 1955. The brain (#632). In *The Poems of Emily Dickinson,* ed. T. H. Johnson. Cambridge, Mass.: Belknap.

Dion, K. K. 1981. Physical attractiveness, sex roles and heterosexual attraction. In *The Bases of Human Sexual Attraction,* ed. M. Cook. New York: Academic Press.

Dion, K. K., and K. L. Dion. 1985. Personality, gender and the phenomenology of romantic love. In *Review of Personality and Social Psychology,* ed. P. Shaver. Vol 6. Beverly Hills, Calif.: Sage.

Dion K. K., E. Berscheid, and E. Walster. 1972. What is beautiful is good. *Journal of Personality and Social Psychology* 24:285–90.

Dion, K. L., and K. K. Dion. 1988. Romantic love: Individual and cultural perspectives. In *The Psychology of Love,* ed. R. J. Sternberg and M. L. Barnes. New Haven: Yale University Press.

Dluzen, D. E., V. D. Ramirez, C. S. Carter, and L. L. Getz. 1981. Male vole urine changes luteinizing hormone-releasing hormone and norepinephrine in female olfactory bulb. *Science* 212:573–75.

Dozier, R. W. 2002. *Why We Hate: Understanding, Curbing, and Eliminating Hate in Ourselves and Our World.* New York: Contemporary Books.

Duncan, J., R. J. Seitz, J. Kolodny, D. Bor, H. Herzog, A. Ahmed, F. N. Newell, and H. Emslie. 2000. A neural basis of general intelligence. *Science* 289: 457–60.

Dutton, D. G., and A. P. Aron. 1974. Some evidence of heightened sexual attraction under conditions of high anxiety. *Journal of Personality and Social Psychology* 30(4):510–17.

Eblen, F., and A. M. Graybiel. 1995. Highly restricted origin of prefrontal cortical inputs to striosomes in the macaque monkey. *Journal of Neuroscience* 15:5999–6013.

Edwards, J. N., and A. Booth. 1994. Sexuality, Marriage, and Well-Being: The Middle Years. In *Sexuality across the Life Course,* ed. A. S. Rossi. Chicago: University of Chicago Press.

Eibl-Eibesfeldt, I. 1989. *Human Ethology.* New York: Aldine de Gruyter.

Ekman, P. 2003. *Emotions Revealed: Recognizing Faces and Feelings to Improve Communication and Emotional Life.* New York: Henry Holt and Co.

Elliott, R., J. L. Newman, O. A. Longe, and J. F. W. Deakin. 2003. Differential response patterns in the striatum and orbitofrontal cortex to financial reward in humans: a parametric functional magnetic resonance imaging study. *Journal of Neuroscience* 23(1):303–07.

Ellis, B. J. 1992. The Evolution of Sexual Attraction: Evaluative Mechanisms in Women. In *The Adapted Mind: Evolutionary Psychology and the Generation of Culture,* ed. J. H. Barkow, L. Cosmides, and J. Tooby. New York: Oxford University Press.

Ellis, B. J., and N. M. Malamuth. 2000. Love and anger in romantic relationships: A discrete systems model. *Journal of Personality* 68(3):525–56.

Ellis, B. J., and D. Symons. 1990. Sex differences in sexual fantasy: An evolutionary psychological approach. *Journal of Sex Research* 27:527–55.

Enard, W., P. Khaitovich, J. Klose, S. Zollner, F. Heissig, P. Giavalisco, K. Nieselt-Struwe, E. Muchmore, A. Varki, R. Ravid, G. M. Doxiadis, R. E. Bontrop, and S. Paabo. 2002. Intra- and interspecific variation in primate gene expression patterns. *Science* 296:340–43.

Epstein, R. 2002. Editor as guinea pig. *Psychology Today,* June 2.

Erikson, E. H. 1959. Identity and the life cycle. *Psychological Issues* 1(1).

Espenshade, T. J. 1984. *Investing in Children: New Estimates of Parental Expenditures.* Washington, D.C.: Urban Institute Press.

Etgen, A. M., and J. C. Morales. 2002. Somatosensory stimuli evoke norepinephrine release in the anterior ventromedial hypothalamus of sexually receptive female rats. *Journal of Neuroendocrinology* 14(3):213–18.

Etgen, A. M., H. P. Chu, J. M. Fiber, G. B. Karkanias, and J. M. Morales. 1999. Hormonal integration of neurochemical and sensory signals governing female reproductive behavior. *Behavioural Brain Research* 105(1): 93–103.

Euripides. 1963. *Euripides: Medea and Other Plays,* trans. P. Vellacott. New York: Penguin Books.

Evans, D. 2001. *Emotion: The Science of Sentiment.* New York: Oxford University Press.

Fabre-Nys, C. 1998. Steroid control of monoamines in relation to sexual behavior. *Reviews of Reproduction* 3(1):31–41.

Fabre-Nys, C., et al. 1997. Male faces and odors evoke differential patterns of neurochemical release in the mediobasal hypothalamus of the ewe during estrus: An insight into sexual motivation. *European Journal of Neuroscience* 9:1666–77.

Falk, D. 2000. *Primate Diversity.* New York: W. W. Norton.

Farb, P., and G. Armelagos. 1983. *Consuming Passion: The Anthropology of Eating.* New York: Pocket Books.

Fehr, B. 1988. Prototype analysis of the concepts of love and commitment. *Journal of Personality and Social Psychology* 55(4):557–79.

Ferkin, M. H., E. S. Sorokin, M. W. Renfroe, and R. E. Johnston. 1994. Attractiveness of male odors to females varies directly with plasma testosterone concentration in meadow voles. *Physiology and Behavior* 55(2):347–53.

Fernandez, B. E., N. A. Vidal, and A. E. Dominguez. 1975. Action of the sexual hormones on the endogenous norepinephrine of the central nervous system. *Revista Española de Fisiologia* 31(4):305–7.

Ferrari, F., and D. Giuliani. 1995. Sexual attraction and copulation in male rats: Effects of the dopamine agonist SND 919. *Pharmacology, Biochemistry, and Behavior* 50(1):29–34.

Ferris, C. F., and Y. Delville. 1994. Vasopressin and serotonin interactions in the control of agonistic behavior. *Psychoneuroendocrinology* 19(7):593–601.

Finck, H. T. 1891. *Romantic Love and Personal Beauty: Their Development, Causal Relations, Historic and National Peculiarities.* London: Macmillan.

Findling, R. 1999. *Don't Call That Man!: A Survival Guide to Letting Go.* New York: Hyperion.

Finlay, B. L., and R. B. Darlington. 1995. Linked regularities in the development and evolution of mammalian brains. *Science* 268:1578–83.

Fiorillo, C. D., P. N. Tobler, and W. Schultz. 2003. Discrete coding of reward probability and uncertainty by dopamine neurons. *Science* 299:1898–1901.

Fisher, H. 1989. Evolution of serial pairbonding. *American Journal of Physical Anthropology* 78:331–54.

———. 1992. *Anatomy of Love: A Natural History of Mating, Marriage, and Why We Stray.* New York: W. W. Norton.

———. 1998. Lust, attraction, and attachment in mammalian reproduction. *Human Nature* 9(1):23–52.

———. 1999. *The First Sex: The Natural Talents of Women and How They Are Changing the World.* New York: Random House.

Fisher, H., A. Aron, D. Mashek, G. Strong, H. Li, and L. L. Brown. 2003. Early stage intense romantic love activates cortical-basal-ganglia reward/motivation, emotion and attention systems: An fMRI study of a dynamic network that varies with relationship length, passion intensity and gender. Poster presented at the Annual Meeting of the Society for Neuroscience, New Orleans, November 11.

———. 2002a. Defining the brain systems of lust, romantic attraction and attachment. *Archives of Sexual Behavior* 31(5):413–9.

———. 2002b. The neural mechanisms of mate choice: A hypothesis. *Neuroendocrinology Letters* 23 (suppl 4):92–97.

Fisher, H., and J. A. Thomson. In preparation. Do the sexual side effects of antidepressants jeopardize romantic love and marriage?

Fisher, M. In preparation. Female intrasexual competition decreases female facial attractiveness.

Fisher, R. A. 1915. The evolution of sexual preference. *Eugenics Review* 7:184–92.

Flament, M. F., J. L. Rapoport, and C. L. Bert. 1985. Clomipramine treatment of childhood obsessive-compulsive disorder: A double-blind controlled study. *Archives of General Psychiatry* 42:977–86.

Flexnor, J. T. 1965. *George Washington: The Forge of Experience (1732–1775).* Boston: Little, Brown and Co.

Ford, C. S., and F. A. Beach. 1951. *Patterns of Sexual Behavior.* New York: Harper and Row.

Fowler, B. H. 1994. *Love Lyrics of Ancient Egypt.* Chapel Hill: The University of North Carolina Press.

Fowlkes, M. R. 1994. Single worlds and homosexual lifestyles: Patterns of sexuality and intimacy. In *Sexuality across the Life Course,* ed. A. S. Rossi. Chicago: University of Chicago Press.

Fox, R. 1980. *The Red Lamp of Incest.* New York: E. P. Dutton.

Frayser, S. 1985. *Varieties of Sexual Experience: An Anthropological Perspective on Human Sexuality.* New Haven: HRAF Press.

Fremouw, W. J., D. Westrup, and J. Pennypacker. 1997. Stalking on campus:

the prevalence and strategies for coping with stalking. *Journal of Forensic Sciences* 42:664–67.

Freud, S. 1917. Mourning and Melancholia. In *The Freud Reader,* ed. P. Gay. New York: W. W. Norton and Co.

Friedl, E. 1975. *Women and Men: An Anthropologist's View.* New York: Holt, Rinehart and Winston.

Frohlich, P. F., and C. M. Meston. 2000. Evidence that serotonin affects female sexual functioning via peripheral mechanisms. *Physiology and Behavior* 71:383–93.

Furstenberg, F. F., Jr. 1996. The future of marriage. *American Demographics* 6:34+

Galdikas, B. M. F. 1995. *Reflections of Eden: My Years with the Orangutans of Borneo.* Boston: Little, Brown and Co.

Galfi, M., T. Janaky, R. Toth, G. Prohaszka, A. Juhasz, C. Varga, and F. A. Laszlo. 2001. Effects of dopamine and dopamine-active compounds on oxytocin and vasopressin production in rat neurohypophyseal tissue cultures. *Regulatory Peptides* 98(1–2):49–54.

Gallup, G. G., Jr. 2003. Department of Psychology, State University of New York at Albany, personal communication.

Gallup, G. G., Jr., R. L. Burch, and S. M. Platek. 2002. Does semen have antidepressant properties? *Archives of Sexual Behavior* 13(26):289–93.

Galton, F. 1884. The measurement of character. *Fortnightly Review* 36:179–85.

Gangestad, S. W., and R. Thornhill. 1997. The evolutionary psychology of extrapair sex: the role of fluctuating asymmetry. *Evolution and Human Behavior* 18(2):69–88.

Gangestad, S. W., R. Thornhill, and R. A. Yeo. 1994. Facial attractiveness, developmental stability, and fluctuating asymmetry. *Ethology and Sociobiology* 15:73–85.

Gardner, H. 1983. *Frames of Mind: The Theory of Multiple Intelligences.* New York: Basic Books.

Gehring, W. J., and A. R. Willoughby. 2002. The medial frontal cortex and the rapid processing of monetary gains and losses. *Science* 295 (5563):2279.

Gingrich, B., Y. Liu, C. Cascio, Z. Wang, and T. R. Insel. 2000. D2 receptors in the nucleus accumbens are important for social attachment in female prairie voles (*Microtus ochrogaster*). *Behavioral Neuroscience* 114(1):173–83.

Ginsberg, S. D., P. R. Hof, W. G. Young, and J. H. Morrison. 1994. Noradrenergic innervation of vasopressin- and oxytocin-containing neurons in the hypothalamic paraventricular nucleus of the macaque monkey: Quantitative analysis using double-label immunohistochemistry and confocal laser microscopy. *Journal of Comparative Neurology* 341(4):476–91.

Gitlan, M., R. Suri, J. Zuckerbrow-Miller, et al. 2000. Bupropion sustained release as a treatment of SRI-induced sexual side effects. Poster presented at the 153rd annual meeting of the American Psychiatric Association, Chicago, Illinois.

Gold, J. I. 2003. Linking reward expectation to behavior in the basal ganglia. *Trends in Neuroscience* 26(1):12–14.

Goleman, D. 1996. Psychotherapy found to produce changes in brain function similar to drugs. *New York Times,* Feb. 15:B12.

Goleman, D. 1995. *Emotional Intelligence.* New York: Bantam Books.

Gonzalez, M. I., F. Farabollini, E. Albonetti, and C. A. Wilson. 1994. Interactions between 5-hydroxytryptamine (5-HT) and testosterone in the control of sexual and nonsexual behaviour in male and female rats. *Pharmacology Biochemistry and Behavior* 47(3):591–601.

Goodall, J. 1986. *The Chimpanzees of Gombe: Patterns of Behavior.* Cambridge, Mass.: The Belknap Press, Harvard University Press.

Goode, E. 2000. When women find love is fatal. *New York Times,* February 15.

Goode, E., M. Petersen, and A. Pollack. 2002. Antidepressants lift clouds, but lose "miracle drug" label. *New York Times,* June 30, section A, 1,16.

Goode, W. J. 1959. The theoretical importance of love. *American Sociological Review* 24(1):38–47.

———. 1982. *The Family.* Englewood Cliffs, N.J.: Prentice-Hall.

Gottreich, A., I. Zuri, S. Barel, I. Hammer, and J. Terkel. 2000. Urinary testosterone levels in the male blind mole rat (*Spalaz ehrenbergi*) affect female preference. *Physiology and Behavior* 69(3):309–15.

Gottman, J. 1994. *What Predicts Divorce: The Relationship between Marital Processes and Marital Outcomes.* Hillsdale, N.J.: Lawrence Erlbaum Assoc., Inc.

Gregersen, E. 1982. *Sexual Practices: The Story of Human Sexuality.* London: Mitchell Beazley.

Griffin, M. G., and G. T. Taylor. 1995. Norepinephrine modulation of social memory: Evidence for a time-dependent functional recovery of behavior. *Behavioral Neuroscience* 109(3):466–73.

Griffin-Shelley, E. 1991. *Sex and Love: Addiction, Treatment and Recovery.* Westport, Conn.: Praeger.

Gugliotta, G. 1997. The Stalkers Are Out There. *The Washington Post Weekly Edition,* Dec. 8:35.

Guttentag, M., and P. F. Secord. 1983. *Too Many Women: The Sex Ratio Question.* Beverly Hills, Calif.: Sage Publications.

Hagen, E. H., P. J. Watson, and J. A. Thomson. In preparation. Love's Labours Lost: Major depression as an evolutionary adaptation to obtain help from those with whom one is in conflict.

Hall, D. M. 1998. The victims of stalking. In *The Psychology of Stalking: Clinical and Forensic Perspectives,* ed. J. R. Meloy. New York: Academic Press.

Hâllstròm, T., and S. Samuelsson. 1990. Changes in women's sexual desire in middle life: the longitudinal study of women in Gothenburg. *Archives of Sexual Behavior* 19(3):259–68.

Halpern, H. M. 1982. *How to Break Your Addiction to a Person.* New York: McGraw-Hill.

Hamill, S. 1996. *The Erotic Spirit: An Anthology of Poems of Sensuality, Love and Longing.* Boston: Shambhala.

Hamilton, W. D., and M. Zuk. 1982. Heritable true fitness and bright birds: A role for parasites? *Science* 218:384–87.

Harlow, H. F., M. K. Harlow, and S. J. Suomi. 1971. From thought to therapy: Lessons from a primate laboratory. *American Scientist* 59:538–49.

Harrington, F. H., and P. C. Paquet. 1982. *Wolves of the World: Perspectives of Behavior, Ecology and Conservation.* Park Ridge, N.J.: Noyes Publications.

Harris, H. 1995. Rethinking heterosexual relationships in Polynesia: A case study of Mangaia, Cook Island. In *Romantic Passion: A Universal Experience?,* ed. W. Jankowiak. New York: Columbia University Press.

Harrison, A. A., and L. Saeed. 1977. Let's make a deal: An analysis of revelations and stipulations in lonely hearts advertisements. *Journal of Personality and Social Psychology* 35:257–64.

Harrison, S. 1986. Laments for foiled marriages: Love-songs from a Sepik River village. *Oceania* 56:275–88.

Hatfield, E. 1988. Passionate and companionate love. In *The Psychology of Love,* ed. R. J. Sternberg and M. L. Barnes. New Haven: Yale University Press.

Hatfield, E., and R. Rapson. 1987. Passionate love/Sexual desire: Can the same paradigm explain both? *Archives of Sexual Behavior* 16:259–78.

———. 1993. Historical and cross-cultural perspectives on passionate love and sexual desire. *Annual Review of Sex Research* 4:67–98.

———. 1996. *Love and Sex: Cross-Cultural Perspectives.* Needham Heights, Mass.: Allyn and Bacon.

Hatfield, E., and S. Sprecher. 1986a. Measuring passionate love in intimate relationships. *Journal of Adolescence* 9:383–410.

———. 1986b. *Mirror, Mirror: The Importance of Looks in Everyday Life.* Albany, N.Y.: State University of New York Press.

Hatfield, E., and G. W. Walster. 1978. *A New Look at Love.* Lanham, Md.: University Press of America.

Hazan, C., and P. Shaver. 1987. Romantic love conceptualized as an attachment process. *Journal of Personality and Social Psychology* 52:511–24.

Heaton, J. P. 2000. Central neuropharmacological agents and mechanisms in erectile dysfunction: the role of dopamine. *Neuroscience and Biobehavioral Reviews.* 24(5):561–69.

Helgeson, V., P. Shaver, and M. Dyer. 1987. Prototypes of intimacy and distance in same-sex and opposite-sex relationships. *Journal of Social and Personal Relationships* 4:195–233.

Helmuth, L. 2001. New route to big brains. *Science* 293:1746–47.

Henderson, M. 2003. Secret of genius is sexual chemistry. *The New York Times,* July 10.

Hendrick, C., and S. Hendrick. 1986a. Research on love: does it measure up? *Journal of Personality and Social Psychology* 56(3):784–94.

———. 1986b. A theory and method of love. *Journal of Personality and Social Psychology* 50(2):392–402.

Hendrix, H. 1988. *Getting the Love You Want.* New York: Henry Holt.

———. 1992. *Keeping the Love You Find.* New York: Pocket Books.

Henry, J. 1986. *Red Fox: The Catlike Canine.* Washington, D.C.: Smithsonian Institution Press.

Herbert, J. 1996. Sexuality, stress, and the chemical architecture of the brain. *Annual Review of Sex Research* 7:1–44.

Hill, J. E., and J. D. Smith. 1984. *BATS: A Natural History.* Austin, Tex.: University of Texas Press.

Hines, E. 1998. Menage à . . . lot. *Jane* August:119–21.

Hoagland, T. 1998. *Donkey Gospel: Poems.* St. Paul, Minn.: Graywolf Press.

Hollander, E., M. Fay, B. Cohen, R. Campeas, J. M. Gorman, and M. R. Liebowitz. 1988. Serotonergic and noradrenergic sensitivity in obsessive-compulsive disorder: Behavioral findings. *American Journal of Psychiatry* 145:1015–17.

Holmes, R. 1997. *Character Sketches: The Romantic Poets and Their Circle.* London: National Portrait Gallery Publications.

Holmes, S. A. 1996. Traditional family stabilized in the 1990s, study suggests. *New York Times,* Mar. 7:B12.

Holy Bible, King James Version, 2000. San Diego, Calif.: Thunder Bay Press.

Homeida, A. M., and A. E. Khalafalla. 1990. Effects of oxytocin and an oxytocin antagonist on testosterone secretion during the oestrous cycle of the goat (*Capra hircus*). *Journal of Reproduction and Fertility* 89(1):347–50.

Homer. 1990. *Homer: The Iliad,* trans. R. Fagles. New York: Penguin Books.

Hopkins, A. 1994. *The Book of Courtly Love: The Passionate Code of the Troubadours.* San Francisco: HarperSanFrancisco.

Horvitz, J. C., et al. 1997. Burst activity of ventral tegmental dopamine neurons is elicited by sensory stimuli in the awake cat. *Brain Research* 759:251.

Hull, E. M., J. Du, D. S. Lorrain, and L. Matuszewich. 1995. Extracellular dopamine in the medial preoptic area: Implications for sexual motivation and hormonal control of copulation. *Journal of Neuroscience* 15(11):7465–71.

———. 1997. Testosterone, preoptic dopamine, and copulation in male rats. *Brain Research Bulletin* 44(4):327–33.

Hull, E. M., D. S. Lorrain, J. Du, L. Matuszewich, L. A. Lumley, S. K. Putnam, and J. Moses. 1999. Hormone-neurotransmitter interactions in the control of sexual behavior. *Behavioural Brain Research* 105(1):105–16.

Humphrey, N. 2002. *The Inner Eye.* New York: Oxford University Press.

Hunter, M. S., C. Nitschke, and L. Hogan. 1981. A scale to measure love addiction. *Psychological Reports* 48:582.

Insel, T. R. 2000. Lecture to the 6th annual Wisconsin Symposium on Emotion. The neurobiology of positive emotion. HealthEmotions, Research Institute, University of Wisconsin, April 13.

Insel, T. R., and C. S. Carter. 1995. The monogamous brain. *Natural History* 104(8):12–14.

Insel, T. R., and T. J. Hulihan. 1995. A gender-specific mechanism for pair bonding: Oxytocin and partner preference formation in monogamous voles. *Behavioral Neuroscience* 109(4):782–89.

James, W. 1884. What is an emotion? *Mind* 9:188–205.

Jankowiak, W. 1995. Introduction. In *Romantic Passion: A Universal Experience?*, ed. W. Jankowiak. New York: Columbia University Press.

Jankowiak, W. R., and E. F. Fischer. 1992. A cross-cultural perspective on romantic love. *Ethnology* 31(2):149.

Jason, L. A., A. Reichler, J. Easton, A. Neal, and M. Wilson. 1984. Female harassment after ending a relationship: A preliminary study. *Alternative Lifestyles* 6:259–69.

Jehl, D. 1997. One wife is not enough? A film to provoke Iran. *New York Times,* Dec. 24:A4.

Johnson, A. E., H. Coirine, T. R. Insel, and B. S. McEwen. 1991. The regulation of oxytocin receptor binding in the ventromedial hypothalamic nucleus by testosterone and its metabolites. *Endocrinology* 128(2):891–96.

Johnson, T. H. 1960. *The Complete Poems of Emily Dickinson.* Boston: Little, Brown and Co.

Johnston, V. S. 1999. *Why We Feel: The Science of Human Emotions.* Cambridge, Mass.: Perseus Books.

Jones, E., and K. Hill. 1993. Criteria of facial attractiveness in five populations. *Human Nature* 4:271–96.

Jones, T. J., G. Dunphy, A. Milsted, and D. Ely. 1998. Testosterone effects on renal norepinephrine content and release in rats with different Y chromosomes. *Hypertension* 32(5):880–85.

Kanin, E. J., K. R. Davidson, and S. R. Scheck. 1970. A research note on male-female differentials in the experience of heterosexual love. *Journal of Sex Research* 6(1):64–72.

Kano, T. 1992. *The Last Ape: Pygmy Chimpanzee Behavior and Ecology.* Stanford, Calif.: Stanford University Press.

Kapit, W., R. I. Macey, and E. Meisami. 2000. *The Physiology Coloring Book.* New York: Addison Wesley Longman.

Karama, S., A. R. Lecours, J. M. Leroux, P. Bourgouin, G. Beaudoin, S. Joubert, and M. Beauregard. 2002. Areas of brain activation in males and females during viewing of erotic film excerpts. *Human Brain Mapping* 16(1):1–13.

Kawashima, S., and K. Takagi. 1994. Role of sex steroids on the survival, neuritic outgrowth of neurons, and dopamine neurons in cultured preoptic area and hypothalamus. *Hormones and Behavior* 28(4):305–12.

Kenrick, D. T., G. E. Groth, M. R. Trost, and E. K. Sadalla. 1993. Integrating evolutionary and social exchange perspectives on relationships: Effects of gender, self-appraisal, and involvement level on mate selection. *Journal of Personality and Social Psychology* 64:951–69.

Kenrick, D. T., E. K. Sadalla, G. E. Groth, and M. R. Trost. 1990. Evolution, traits and the states of human courtship: Qualifying the parental investment model. *Journal of Personality* 58(1):97–116.

Kernberg, O. 1974. Barriers to falling and remaining in love. *Journal of the American Psychoanalytic Association* 22:486–511.

King, C. 1990. *The Natural History of Weasels and Stoats.* Ithaca, N.Y.: Comstock Publishing Association, a division of Cornell University Press.

Kiyatkin, E. A. 1995. Functional significance of mesolimbic dopamine. *Neuroscience and Biobehavioral Reviews* 19(4):573–98.

Knowlton, B. J., J. A. Mangels, L. R. Squire. 1996. A neostriatal habit learning system in humans. *Science* 273:1399.

Knox, D. H. 1970. Conceptions of love at three developmental levels. 19:151–57.

Kohn, M. 2000. Handaxes and hominid mate choice. Paper presented at the annual meeting of the Human Behavior and Evolution Society, London.

Kolata, G. 2002. Runner's High? Endorphins? Fiction, some scientists say. *The Science Times, New York Times,* May 21, F1 and F6.

Kovacs, G. L., Z. Sarnyai, E. Barbarczi, G. Szabo, and G. Telegdy. 1990. The role of oxytocin-dopamine interactions in cocaine-induced locomotor hyperactivity. *Neuropharmacology* 29(4):365–68.

Kruk, A. L., and C. J. Pycock. 1991. *Neurotransmitters and Drugs.* New York: Chapman and Hall.

Kummer, H. 1995. *In Quest of the Sacred Baboon.* Princeton, N.J.: Princeton University Press.

Labbate, L. A., J. B. Grimes, A. Himes, et al. 1997. Bupropion treatment of serotonin reuptake antidepressant-associated sexual dysfunction. *Annals of Clinical Psychiatry* 9(4):241–45.

Lahr, J., and L. Tabori. 1982. *Love: A Celebration in Art and Literature.* New York: Stewart, Tabori & Chang.

Lampert, A. 1997. *The Evolution of Love.* Westport, Conn.: Praeger.

Lancaster, J. B. 1994. Human sexuality, life histories, and evolutionary ecology. In *Sexuality across the Life Course,* ed. A. S. Rossi. Chicago: University of Chicago Press.

Lancaster, J. B., and C. S. Lancaster. 1983. Parental investment: The hominid adaptation. In *How Humans Adapt: A Biocultural Odyssey,* ed. D. J. Ortner. Washington, D.C.: Smithsonian Institution Press.

Langlois, J. H., and L. A. Roggman. 1990. Attractive faces are only average. *Psychological Science* 1:115–21.

Langlois, J. H., L. A. Roggman, R. J. Casey, J. M. Ritter, L. A. Rieser-Danner, and V. Y. Jenkins. 1987. Infant preferences for attractive faces: Rudiments of a stereotype. *Developmental Psychology* 23:363–69.

Laumann, E. O., J. H. Gagnon, R. T. Michael, and S. Michaels. 1994. *The Social Organization of Sexuality: Sexual Practices in the United States.* Chicago: University of Chicago Press.

Leary, M. R. ed. 2001. *Interpersonal Rejection.* New York: Oxford University Press.

LeDoux, J. 1996. *The Emotional Brain.* New York: Simon & Schuster.

Lee, J. A. 1973. *Colours of Love.* Toronto: New Press.

———. 1988. Love-styles. In *The Psychology of Love,* ed. R. J. Sternberg and M. L. Barnes. New Haven: Yale University Press.

Lerner, R. M., and S. A. Karabenick. 1974. Physical attractiveness, body attitudes, and self-concept in late adolescents. *Journal of Youth and Adolescence* 3:307–16.

Leshner, A. I. 1997. Addiction is a brain disease, and it matters. *Science* 278(5335):45–47.

Lewis, T., F. Amini, and R. Lannon. 2000. *A General Theory of Love.* New York: Random House.

Liebowitz, M. R. 1983. *The Chemistry of Love.* Boston: Little, Brown.

Liu, Y.-C., B. D. Sachs, and J. D. Salamone. 1998. Sexual behavior in male rats after radiofrequency or dopamine-depleting lesions in nucleus accumbens. *Pharmacology Biochemistry and Behavior* 60(1):585–92.

Low, B. S. 1991. Reproductive life in nineteenth-century Sweden: An evolutionary perspective on demographic phenomena. *Ethology and Sociobiology* 12:411–48.

———. 2000. *Why Sex Matters.* Princeton, N.J.: Princeton University Press.

Luciana, M., P. F. Collins, and R. A. Depue. 1998. Opposing roles for dopamine and serotonin in the modulation of human spatial working memory functions. *Cerebral Cortex* 8(3):218–26.

Luu, P., and M. I. Posner. 2003. Anterior cingulate cortex regulation of sympathetic activity. *Brain* 126(10):2119–20.

Mace, D., and V. Mace. 1980. *Marriage East and West.* New York: Dolphin Books.

Manning, J. T., and D. Scutt. 1996. Symmetry and ovulation in women. *Human Reproduction* 11:2477–80.

Manning, J. T., D. Scutt, G. H. Whitehouse, S. J. Leinster, and J. H. Walton.

1996. Asymmetry and menstrual cycle in women. *Ethology and Sociobiology* 17:129–43.

Marazziti, D., H. S. Akiskal, A. Rossi, and G. B. Cassano. 1999. Alteration of the platelet serotonin transporter in romantic love. *Psychological Medicine* 29:741–45.

Martin-Soelch, C., K. L. Leenders, A. F. Chevalley, J. Missimer, G. Kunig, S. Magyar, A. Mino, and W. Schultz. 2001. Reward mechanisms in the brain and their role in dependence: Evidence from neurophysiological and neuroimaging studies. *Brain Research Reviews* 36:139–49.

Mashek, D., A. Aron, and H. Fisher. 2000. Identifying, evoking, and measuring intense feelings of romantic love. *Representative Research in Social Psychology* 24:48–55.

Maslow, A. 1970. *Motivation and Personality.* New York: Harper and Row.

Mathes, E. W. 1986. Jealousy and romantic love: A longitudinal study. *Psychological Reports* 58:885–86.

Mathes, E. W., and P. S. Wise. 1983. Romantic love and the ravages of time. *Psychological Reports* 53:839–46.

Mayerhofer, A., R. W. Steger, G. Gow, and A. Bartke. 1992. Catecholamines stimulate testicular testosterone release of the immature golden hamster via interaction with alpha- and beta-adrenergic receptors. *Acta Endocrinologia* 127(6):526–30.

McCullough, D. 2001. *John Adams.* New York: Simon and Schuster.

McGuire, M. T., and A. Troisi. 1998. Prevalance differences in depression among males and females: Are there evolutionary explanations? *Journal of Medical Psychology* 71:479–91.

McNamee, T. 1984. *The Grizzly Bear.* New York: Alfred A. Knopf.

Mearns, J. 1991. Coping with a breakup: Negative mood regulation expectancies and depression following the end of a romantic relationship. *Journal of Personality and Social Psychology* 60:327–34.

Mech, D. L. 1970. *The Wolf: The Ecology and Behavior of an Endangered Species.* New York: The American Museum of Natural History.

Meikle, A., J. Stringham, D. Bishop, and D. West. 1988. Quantitating genetic and nongenetic factors influencing androgen production and clearance rates in men. *Journal of Clinical Endocrinology Metabolism* 67:104–9.

Melis, M. R., and A. Argiolas. 1995. Dopamine and sexual behavior. *Neuroscience and Biobehavioral Reviews* 19(1):19–38.

Mellody, P., A. W. Miller, and J. K. Miller. 1992. *Facing Love Addiction.* New York: HarperCollins Publishers.

Meloy, J. R. 1996. Stalking (obsessional following): A review of some preliminary studies. *Aggression and Violent Behavior* 1:147–62.

———. 1999. Stalking: An old behavior, a new crime. *Forensic Psychiatry* 22(1):85–99.

———., ed. 1998. *The Psychology of Stalking: Clinical and Forensic Perspective.* New York: Academic Press.
———. In press. When stalkers become violent: the threat to public figures and private lives. *Psychiatric Annals* 33(10):658–65.
Meloy, J. R., and S. Gothard. 1995. A demographic and clinical comparison of obsessional followers and offenders with mental disorders. *American Journal of Psychiatry* 152:258–63.
Millay, E. St. V. 1988. *Collected Sonnets.* New York: Harper & Row.
Miller, G. F. 2000. *The Mating Mind: How Sexual Choice Shaped the Evolution of Human Nature.* New York: Doubleday.
Milton, J. 1949. *Paradise Lost.* IX:906–907. In *The Portable Milton,* ed. D. Bush. New York: Penguin Books.
Mock, D. W., and M. Fujioka. 1990. Monogamy and long-term pair bonding in vertebrates. *Trends in Ecology and Evolution* 5(2):39–43.
Morell, V. 1998. A new look at monogamy. *Science* 281:1982–83.
Moss, C. 1988. *Elephant Memories: Thirteen Years in the Life of an Elephant Family.* New York: William Morrow.
Murray, S. L., and J. G. Holmes. 1997. A leap of faith? Positive illusions in romantic relationships. *Personality and Social Psychology Bulletin* 23:586–604.
Murstein, B. I. 1972. Physical attractiveness and marital choice. *Journal of Personality and Social Psychology* 22:8–12.
Nadler, A., and I. Dotan. 1992. Commitment and rival attractiveness: Their effects on male and female reactions to jealousy arousing situations. *Sex Roles* 26:293–310.
Nemeroff, C. B. 1998. The neurobiology of depression. *Scientific American* 278(6):42–49.
Nesse, R. 1990. Evolutionary explanations of emotions. *Human Nature* 1:261–89.
———. 1991. What good is feeling bad—the evolutionary benefits of psychic pain. *The Sciences: Journal of the New York Academy of Sciences* 31:30–37.
Netter, P., J. Hennig, B. Meier, and S. Rohrmann. 1998. Testosterone as an indicator of altered 5-HT responsivity in aggressive subjects. *European Psychiatry* 13(4):181s.
Newberg, A., E. D'Aquili, and V. Rause. 2001. *Why God Won't Go Away: Brain Science and The Biology of Belief.* New York: Ballantine Books.
Niculescu, A. B., and H. S. Akiskal. 2001. Sex hormones, Darwinism and depression. *Archives of General Psychiatry* 58:1083–84.
Norman, C., and A. Aron. 1995. The effect of exciting activities on relationship satisfaction: A laboratory experiment. Paper presented at the International Network Conference on Personal Relationships, Williamsburg, Virginia.
Nyborg, H. 1994. *Hormones, Sex and Society.* Westport, Conn.: Praeger.
Oates, J. C. 1970. *Love and Its Derangements.* Baton Rouge: Louisiana State University.

Olds, J. 1956. Pleasure centers in the brain. *Scientific American* 195:105–16.
Olds, J., and P. M. Milner. 1954. Positive reinforcement produced by electrical stimulation of septal area and other regions of rat brain. *Journal of Comparative and Physiological Psychology* 47:419–27.
Öngür, D., and J. L. Price. 2000. The organization of networks within the orbital and medial prefrontal cortex of rats, monkeys and humans. *Cerebral Cortex* 10:206–19.
Orr, A. 2003. *Meeting, Mating, and Cheating: How the Internet Is Revolutionizing Romance.* Upper Saddle River, N.J.: FT Prentice Hall.
Ortega y Gasset, J. 1957. *On Love.* New York: Meridian Books.
Panksepp, J. 1998. *Affective Neuroscience: The Foundations of Human and Animal Emotions.* New York: Oxford University Press.
Pedersen, C. A., J. D. Caldwell, G. F. Jirikowsk, and T. R. Insel, eds. 1992. *Oxytocin in Maternal, Sexual and Social Behaviors.* New York: New York Academy of Sciences.
Peele, S. 1975. *Love and Addiction.* New York: Taplinger Publishing Company.
———. 1988. Fools for love: The romantic ideal, psychological theory and addictive love. In *The Psychology of Love,* ed. R. J. Sternberg and M. L. Barnes. New Haven, Conn.: Yale University Press, pp. 159–90.
Penny, M. 1988. *Rhinos: Endangered Species.* New York: Facts on File Publications.
Peplau, L., and S. Gordon. 1985. Women and men in love: Gender differences in close heterosexual relationships. In *Women, Gender and Social Psychology,* ed. V. O'Leary, R. Unger, and B. Wallston. Hillsdale, N.J.: Erlbaum.
Perrett, D. I., et al. 1998. Effects of sexual dimorphism on facial attractiveness. *Nature* 394:884–86.
Pfaff, D. W. 1999. *DRIVE: Neurobiological and Molecular Mechanisms of Sexual Motivation.* Cambridge, Mass.: The MIT Press.
Pines, A. M. 1999. *Falling in Love: Why We Choose the Lovers We Choose.* New York: Routledge.
Pitkow, L. J., C. A. Sharer, X. Ren, T. R. Insel, E. F. Terwilliger, and L. J. Young. 2001. Facilitation of affiliation and pair-bond formation by vasopressin receptor gene transfer into the ventral forebrain of a monogamous vole. *Journal of Neuroscience* 21(18):7392–96.
Plato. 1999. *The Symposium,* trans. C. Gill. London: Penguin Books.
Pleim, E. T., J. A. Matochik, R. J. Barfield, and S. B. Auerbach. 1990. Correlation of dopamine release in the nucleus accumbens with masculine sexual behavior in rats. *Brain Research* 524:160–63.
Posner, R. 1992. *Sex and Reason.* Cambridge, Mass.: Harvard University Press.
Post, R. M., S. R. B. Weiss, and A. Pert. 1988. Cocaine-induced behavioral sensitization and kindling: Implications for the emergence of psychopathology and seizures. In *The Mesocorticolimbic Dopamine System,* ed. P. W. Kalivas

and C. B. Nemeroff. New York: The New York Academy of Sciences, pp. 292–308.

Potts, R. 1988. *Early Hominid Activities at Olduvai.* Hawthorne, N.Y.: Aldine de Gruyter.

Povinellia, D., and T. M. Preussc. 1995. Theory of mind: Evolutionary history of a cognitive specialization. *Trends in Neuroscience* 18(9):418–24.

Prakasa, V. V., and V. N. Rao. 1979. Arranged marriages: an assessment of the attitudes of the college students in India. In *Cross-Cultural Perspectives of Mate-Selection and Marriage,* ed. G. Kurian. Westport, Conn.: Greenwood Press, pp. 11–31.

Price, J. S., L. Sloman, R. Gardner, P. Gilbert, and P. Rohde. 1994. The social competition hypothesis of depression. *British Journal of Psychiatry* 164: 309–15.

Purdy, M. 1995. A sexual revolution for the elderly. *New York Times,* Nov. 6:A16.

Quiller-Couch, Arthur, ed. 1919. *The Oxford Book of English Verse: 1250–1900.* Oxford, Eng.: Oxford University Press.

*Random House Treasury of Favorite Love Poems.* 2000. New York: Random House Inc.

Raouf, S. A., P. G. Parker, E. D. Ketterson, V. Nolan, Jr., and C. Ziegenfus. 1997. Testosterone affects reproductive success by influencing extra-pair fertilizations in male dark-eyed juncos (*Aves: Junco hyemalis*). *Proceedings of the Royal Society of London—Series B, Biological Sciences* 264(1388):1599–1603.

Rebhun, L. A. 1995. Language of love in northeast Brazil. In *Romantic Passion: A Universal Experience?,* ed. W. Jankowiak. New York: Columbia University Press.

Regis, H. A. 1995. The madness of excess: Love among the Fulbe of North Cameroun. In *Romantic Passion: A Universal Experience?,* ed. W. Jankowiak. New York: Columbia University Press.

Reik, T. 1964. *The Need to Be Loved.* New York: Bantam.

Reinisch, J. M., and R. Beasley. 1990. *The Kinsey Institute New Report on Sex.* New York: St. Martin's Press.

Reissman, E., A. Aron, and M. R. Bergen. 1993. Shared activities and marital satisfaction: Causal direction and self-expansion versus boredom. *Journal of Social and Personal Relationships* 10:243–54.

Reno, P. L., R. S. Meindl, M. A. McCollum, and C. O. Lovejoy. 2003. Sexual dimorphism in *Australopithecus afarensis* was similar to that of modern humans. *Proceedings of the National Academy of Sciences* 10:1073.

Richmond, B. J., Z. Liu, and M. Shidara. 2003. Neuroscience: Predicting future rewards. *Science* 301(5630):179–80.

Rilling, J. K., and T. R. Insel. 1999a. Differential expansion of neural projection systems in primate brain evolution. *NeuroReport* 10:1453–59.

———. 1999b. The primate neocortex in comparative perspective using magnetic resonance imaging. *Journal of Human Evolution* 37:191–223.
Robbins, T. W., and B. J. Everitt. 1996. Neurobehavioural mechanisms of reward and motivation. *Current Opinion in Neurobiology* 6:228–68.
Rocamora, C., trans. 1998. *Chekhov: "The Vaudevilles" and Other Short Works.* Lyme, N.H.: Smith and Kraus, Inc.
Roethke, T. 1975. *The Collected Poems of Theodore Roethke.* New York: Anchor.
Rolls, E. T. 2000. The orbitofrontal cortex and reward. *Cerebral Cortex* 10(3):284–94.
Rosenblatt, P. C., and R. M. Anderson. 1981. Human sexuality in cross-cultural perspective. In *The Bases of Human Sexual Attraction,* ed. M. Cook. New York: Academic Press, pp. 215–50.
Rosenthal, N. E. 2002. *The Emotional Revolution: How the New Science of Feelings Can Transform Your Life.* New York: Citadel Press Books.
Rothman, R. B., M. H. Baumann, C. M. Dersch, D. V. Romero, K. C. Rice, F. I. Carroll, and J. S. Partilla. 2001. Amphetamine-type central nervous system stimulants release norepinephrine more potently than they release dopamine and serotonin. *Synapse* 39(1):32–41.
Rowe, J. W. 1997. Editorial: a new gerontology. *Science* 278(5337):367.
Rubin, Z. 1970. Measurement of romantic love. *Journal of Personality and Social Psychology* 16:265–73.
Rubin, Z., L. A. Peplau, and C. T. Hill. 1981. Loving and leaving: Sex differences in romantic attachments. *Sex Roles* 7:821–35.
Rubin, Z., C. T. Hill, L. A. Peplau, and C. Dunke-Schetter. 1980. Self-disclosure in dating couples: Sex roles and the ethic of openness. *Journal of Marriage and the Family* 42:305–17.
Rushton, J. P. 1989. Epigenesis and social preference. *Behavioral and Brain Sciences* 12:31–32.
Ryan, M. J. 1998. Sexual selection, receiver biases, and the evolution of sex differences. *Science* 281:1999–2003.
Ryden, H. 1989. *Lily Pond: Four Years with a Family of Beavers.* New York: William Morrow.
Sadalla, E. K., D. T. Kenrick, and B. Vershure. 1987. Dominance and heterosexual attraction. *Journal of Personality and Social Psychology* 52:730–38.
Saint-Cyr, J. A. 2003. Frontal-striatal circuit functions: Context, sequence, and consequence. *Journal of the International Neuropsychological Society* 9(1):102–27.
Salamone, J. D. 1996. The behavioral neurochemistry of motivation: methodological and conceptual issues in studies of the dynamic activity of nucleus accumbens dopamine. *Journal of Neuroscience Methods* 64(2):137–49.
Sankhala, K. 1977. *Tiger!: The Story of the Indian Tiger.* New York: Simon and Schuster.

Schaef, A. W. 1989. *Escape from Intimacy: The Pseudo-Relationship Addictions.* San Francisco: Harper & Row.

Schaller, G. B. 1973. *Golden Shadows, Flying Hooves.* New York: Alfred A. Knopf.

Schmitt, D. P. 2001. Desire for sexual variety and mate poaching experiences across multiple languages and cultures. Paper presented at the annual meeting of the Human Behavior and Evolution Society, London.

Schmitt, D. P., and D. M. Buss. 2001. Human mate poaching: Tactics and temptations for infiltrating existing relationships. *Journal of Personality and Social Psychology* 80:894–917.

Schnarch, D. 1997. *Passionate Marriage.* New York: Henry Holt and Co.

Schultz, W. 2000. Multiple reward signals in the brain. Nature reviews. *Neuroscience* 1(December):199–207.

Schultz, W., P. Dayan, and P. R. Montague. 1997. A neural substrate of prediction and reward. *Science* 275:1593–98.

Schultz, W., L. Tremblay, and J. R. Hollerman. 2000. Reward processing in primate orbitofrontal cortex and basal ganglia. In *The Mysterious Orbitofrontal Cortex,* ed. C. Cavada and W. Schultz. New York: Oxford University Press.

Schwarzberg, H., G. L. Kovacs, G. Szabo, and G. Telegdy. 1981. Intraventricular administration of vasopressin and oxytocin affects the steady-state levels of serotonin, dopamine and norepinephrine in rat brain. *Endocrinologia Experimentalis* 15(2):75–80.

Semendeferi, K., H. Damasio, R. Frank, and G. W. Van Hoesen. 1997. The evolution of the frontal lobes: A volumetric analysis based on three-dimensional reconstructions of magnetic resonance scans of human and ape brains. *Journal of Human Evolution* 32:375–88.

Seybold, V. S., J. W. Miller, and P. R. Lewis. 1978. Investigation of a dopaminergic mechanism for regulating oxytocin release. *The Journal of Pharmacology and Experimental Therapeutics* 207(2):605–10.

Shakespeare, W. 1936. *The Complete Works of William Shakespeare: The Cambridge Edition Text,* ed. W. A. Wright. New York: Doubleday.

Shaver, P. R., and C. Hazan. 1993. Adult romantic attachment: Theory and empirical evidence. In *Advances in Personal Relationships,* ed. D. Perlman and W. Jones. Greenwich, Conn.: JAI Press.

Shaver, P. R., C. Hazan, and D. Bradshaw. 1988. Love as attachment: the integration of three behavioral systems. In *The Psychology of Love,* ed. R. J. Sternberg and M. Barnes. New Haven, Conn.: Yale University Press.

Sheets, V. L., L. L. Fredendall, and H. M. Claypool. 1997. Jealousy evocation, partner reassurance and relationship stability: An exploration of the potential benefits of jealousy. *Evolution and Human Behavior* 18:387–402.

Shepher, J. 1971. Mate selection among second-generation kibbutz adolescents and adults: Incest avoidance and negative imprinting. *Archives of Sexual Behavior* 1:293–307.

Shepherd, G. 1983. *Neurobiology.* New York: Oxford University Press.

Sherwin, B. B. 1994. Sex hormones and psychological functioning in postmenopausal women. *Experimental Gerontology* 29(3/4):423–30.

Sherwin, B. B., and M. M. Gelfand. 1987. The role of androgen in the maintenance of sexual functioning in oophorectomized women. *Psychosomatic Medicine* 49:397.

Sherwin, B. B., M. M. Gelfand, and W. Brender. 1985. Androgen enhances sexual motivation in females. *Psychosomatic Medicine* 47:339–51.

Shettel-Neuber, J., J. B. Bryson, and C. E. Young. 1978. Physical attractiveness of the "other person" and jealousy. *Personality and Social Psychology Bulletin* 4:612–15.

Shostak, M. 1981. *Nisa: The Life and Words of a !Kung Woman.* Cambridge, Mass.: Harvard University Press.

Sill, G. 2002. *The Cure of the Passions and the Origins of the English Novel.* New York: Cambridge University Press.

Simpkins, J. W., S. P. Kalra, and P. S. Kalra. 1983. Variable effects of testosterone on dopamine activity in several microdissected regions in the preoptic area and medial basal hypothalamus. *Endocrinology* 112(2):665–69.

Singh, D. 1993. Adaptive significance of waist-to-hip ratio and female physical attractiveness. *Journal of Personality and Social Psychology* 65:293–307.

———. 2002. Female mate value at a glance: Relationship of waist-to-hip ratio to health, fecundity and attractiveness. *Neuroendocrinology Letters* 23(suppl 4):81–91.

Sirotkin, A. V., and J. Nitray. 1992. The influence of oxytocin, vasopressin and their analogues on progesterone and testosterone production by porcine granulosa cells in vitro. *Annales d'endocrinologie* (Paris) 53(1):32–36.

Small, D. M., R. J. Zatorre, A. Dagher, A. C. Evans, and M. Jones-Gotman. 2001. Changes in brain activity related to eating chocolate: from pleasure to aversion. *Brain* 124:1720–33.

Smith, D. E., and M. Hoklund. 1988. Love and salutogenesis in late adolescence: A preliminary investigation. *Psychology: A Journal of Human Behavior* 25:44–49.

Smuts, B. B. 1992. Male aggression against women: An evolutionary perspective. *Human Nature* 3:1–44.

Smuts, B. B. 1985. *Sex and Friendship in Baboons.* New York: Aldine de Gruyter.

Solomon, R. 1990. *Love, Emotion, Myth and Metaphor.* New York: Prometheus Books.

Solomon, Z. 1986. Self-acceptance and the selection of a marital partner: An assessment of the SVR model of Murstein. *Social Behavior and Personality* 14:1–6.

Spearman, C. 1904. General intelligence, objectively determined and measured. *American Journal of Psychology* 15:201–93.

Spitz, R. 1946. Anaclitic depression: An inquiry into the genesis of psychiatric conditions in early childhood. II. *Psychoanalytic Study of the Child* 2:313–42.

Sprecher, S., A. Aron, E. Hatfield, A. Cortese, E. Potapove, and A. Levitskaya. 1994. Love: American style, Russian style, and Japanese style. *Personal Relationships* 1:349–69.

Stahl, S. M. 2000. *Essential Psychopharmacology: Neuroscientific Basis and Practical Applications.* New York: Cambridge University Press.

Stallworthy, J. 1973. *A Book of Love Poetry.* New York: Oxford University Press.

Stephan, H. 1983. Evolutionary trends in limbic structures. *Neuroscience and Biobehavioral Reviews* 7:367–74.

Stephan, H., and O. J. Andy. 1969. Quantitative comparative neuroanatomy of primates: An attempt at phylogenetic interpretation. *Annals of the New York Academy of Science* 167:370–87.

Stephan, H., G. Baron, and H. D. Frahm. 1988. Comparative size of brain and brain components. *Comparative Primate Biology* 4:1–38.

Stephan, H., H. D. Frahm, and G. Baron. 1981. New and revised data on volumes of brain structures in insectivores and primates. *Folia Primatologica* 35:1–29.

Sternberg, R. J. 1985. *Beyond IQ: A Triarchic Theory of Human Intelligence.* New York: Cambridge University Press.

———. 1986. A triangular theory of love. *Psychological Review* 91(2):119–35.

Stone, L. 1988. Passionate attachments in the West in historical perspective. In *Passionate Attachments: Thinking about Love,* ed. W. Gaylin and E. Person. New York: The Free Press.

———. 1990. *Road to Divorce: England 1530–1987.* New York: Oxford University Press.

Sundblad, C., and E. Eriksson. 1997. Reduced extracellular levels of serotonin in the amygdala of androgenized female rats. *European Neuropsychopharmacology* 7(4):253–59.

Szezypka, M. S., Q. Y. Zhou, and R. D. Palmiter. 1998. Dopamine-stimulated sexual behavior is testosterone dependent in mice. *Behavioral Neuroscience* 112(5):1229–35.

Taffel, R. 1990. The politics of mood. *The Family Therapy Networker* September/October:49–53.

Tan, G. J., and T. K. Kwan. 1987. Effect of oxytocin on plasma testosterone levels in the male macaques (*Macaca fascicularis*). *Contraception* 36(3):359–67.

Tannen, D. 1990. *You Just Don't Understand: Women and Men in Conversation.* New York: Ballantine Books.

———. 1994. *Talking from 9 to 5.* New York: William Morrow.

Tavris, C. 1992. *The Mismeasure of Woman.* New York: Simon and Schuster, pp. 15–25.

Tavris, C., and S. Sadd. 1977. *The Redbook Report on Female Sexuality.* New York: Delacorte.

Teasdale, J. D., R. J. Howard, S. G. Cox, Y. Ha, M. J. Brammer, S. C. Williams, and S. A. Checkley. 1999. Functional MRI study of the cognitive generation of affect. *American Journal of Psychiatry* 156(2):203–15.

Tennov, D. 1979. *Love and Limerence: The Experience of Being in Love.* New York: Stein and Day.

Tesser, A., and R. Reardon. 1981. Perceptual and cognitive mechanisms in human sexual attraction. In *The Bases of Human Sexual Attraction,* ed. M. Cook. New York: Academic Press.

Thayer, R. E. 1996. *The Origin of Everyday Moods: Managing Energy, Tension and Stress.* New York: Oxford University Press.

Thomas, A., N. B. Kim, and J. A. Amico. 1996a. Differential regulation of oxytocin and vasopressin messenger ribonucleic acid levels by gonadal steroids in postpartum rats. *Brain Research* 738(1):48–52.

———. 1996b. Sequential exposure to estrogen and testosterone (T) and subsequent withdrawal of T increases the level of arginine vasopressin messenger ribonucleic acid in the hypothalamic paraventricular nucleus of the female rat. *Journal of Neuroendocrinology* 8(10):793–800.

Thomas, E. M. 1993. *The Hidden Life of Dogs.* New York: Houghton Mifflin.

Thoren, P., Asberg, M., and L. Bertilsson. 1980. Clomipramine treatment of obsessive disorder: biochemical and clinical aspects. *Archives of General Psychiatry* 37:1289–1294.

Thornhill, R. 1994. Is there psychological adaptation to rape? *Analyse und Kritik* 16:68–85.

Thornhill, R., and S. W. Gangestad. 1993. Human facial beauty. *Human Nature* 4(3):237–69.

Thornhill, R., S. W. Gangestad, and R. Comer. 1995. Human female orgasm and mate fluctuating asymmetry. *Animal Behavior* 50:1601–15.

Tiihonen, J., J. T. Kuikka, K. A. Bergstrom, J. Karhu, H. Viinamiki, J. Lehtonen, T. Hallikainen, J. Yang, and P. Hakola. 1997. Single-photon emission tomography imaging of monoamine transporters in impulsive violent behaviour. *European Journal of Nuclear Medicine* 24(10):1253–60.

Tiihonen, J., J. Kuikka, J. Kupila, K. Partanen, P. Vainio, J. Airaksinen, M. Eronen, T. Hallikainen, J. Paanila, I. Kinnunen, and J. Huttunen. 1994. Increase in cerebral blood flow of right prefrontal cortex in men during orgasm. *Neuroscience Letters* 170:241–43.

Tinbergen, N. 1959. *Social Behaviour in Animals.* London: Methuen and Co. Ltd.

Tornstam, L. 1992. Loneliness in marriage. *Journal of Social and Personal Relationships* 9:197–217.

Traupmann, J., and E. Hatfield. 1981. Love and its effect on mental and physical health. In *Aging: Stability and Change in the Family,* ed. J. March, S. Kiesler, R. Fogel, E. Hatfield, and E. Shana. New York: Academic Press, pp. 253–74.

Troisi, A., and M. Mcguire. 2002. Darwinian psychiatry and the concept of mental disorder. *Neuroendocrinology Letters* 23(suppl 4)23:31–38.

Tucker, P., and A. Aron. 1993. Passionate love and marital satisfaction at key transition points in the family life cycle. *Journal of Social and Clinical Psychology* 12(2):135–47.

Turner, J. H. 2000. *On the Origins of Human Emotions: A Sociological Inquiry into the Evolution of Human Affect.* Stanford, Calif.: Stanford University Press.

United Nations Development Programme. 1995a. *Human Development Report: 1995.* New York: Oxford University Press.

United Nations. 1995b. *Women in a Changing Global Economy: 1994 World Survey on the Role of Women in Development.* New York: United Nations.

United Nations. 1995c. *Women: Looking beyond 2000.* New York: United Nations.

United Nations. 1995d. *The World's Women 1995: Trends and Statistics.* New York: United Nations.

Ustun, T. B., and N. Sartorius. 1995. *Mental Illness in General Health Care: An International Study.* New York: John Wiley on behalf of the World Health Organization.

Van de Kar, L. D., A. D. Levy, Q. Li, and M. S. Brownfield. 1998. A comparison of the oxytocin and vasopressin responses to the 5-HT1A agonist and potential anxiolytic drug alnespirone (S-20499). *Pharmacology, Biochemistry, and Behavior* 60(3):677–83.

Van Goozen, S., V. M. Wiegant, E. Endert, F. A. Helmond, and N. E. Van de Poll. 1997. Psychoendocrinological assessment of the menstrual cycle: The relationship between hormones, sexuality, and mood. *Archives of Sexual Behavior* 26(4):359–82.

Viederman, M. 1988. The nature of passionate love. In *Passionate Attachments: Thinking about Love,* ed. W. Gaylin and E. Person. New York: The Free Press.

Villalba D., C. J. Auger, and G. J. De Vries. 1999. Antrostenedione effects on the vasopressin innervation of the rat brain. *Endocrinology* 140(7):3383–86.

Vizi, E. S., and V. Volbekas. 1980. Inhibition of dopamine of oxytocin release from isolated posterior lobe of the hypophysis of the rat; disinhibitory effect of beta-endorphin/enkephalin. *Neuroendocrinology* 31(1):46–52.

Volkow, N. D., et al. 1997. Relationship between subjective effects of cocaine and dopamine transporter occupancy. *Nature* 386:827.

Voracek, M. 2001. Marital status as a candidate moderator variable of male-female differences in sexual jealousy: The need for representative population samples. *Psychological Reports* 88:553–66.

Wade, N. 2001. Study finds genetic link between intelligence and size of some regions of the brain. *New York Times,* Nov. 5, A15.

———. 2003. Prime numbers: What science and crime have in common. *New York Times,* July 27, Week in Review, p. 3.

Walker, A., and R. Leakey. 1993. *The Nariokotome* Homo erectus *Skeleton.* Cambridge, Mass.: Harvard University Press.

Walker, L. E., and J. R. Meloy. 1998. Stalking and domestic violence. In *The Psychology of Stalking: Clinical and Forensic Perspectives,* ed. J. R. Meloy. New York: Academic Press.

Walker, P. W., J. O. Cole, E. A. Gardner, et al. 1993. Improvement in fluoxetine-associated sexual dysfunction in patients switched to bupropion. *Journal of Clinical Psychiatry* 54:459–65.

Waller, N., and P. Shaver. 1994. The importance of nongenetic influences on romantic love styles: a twin-family study. *Psychological Science* 5(5):268–74.

Walster, E., and E. Berscheid. 1971. Adrenaline makes the heart grow fonder. *Psychology Today,* June, 47–62.

Walster, E., V. Aronson, D. Abrahams, and L. Rottman. 1966. The importance of physical attractiveness in dating behavior. *Journal of Personality and Social Psychology* 4:508–16.

Wang, A. Y., and H. T. Nguyen. 1995. Passionate love and anxiety: a cross-generational study. *The Journal of Social Psychology* 135(4):459–70.

Wang, Z., and G. J. De Vries. 1995. Androgen and estrogen effects on vasopressin messenger RNA expression in the medial amygdaloid nucleus in male and female rats. *Journal of Neuroendocrinology* 7(1):827–31.

Wang, Z. Z., C. F. Ferris, and G. J. De Vries. 1994. The role of septal vasopressin innervation in paternal behavior in prairie voles (*Microtus ochrogaster*). *Proceedings of the National Academy of Sciences (USA)* 91:400–404.

Wang, Z., W. Smith, D. E. Major, and G. J. De Vries. 1994. Sex and species differences in the effects of cohabitation on vasopressin messenger RNA expression in the bed nucleus of the stria terminalis in prairie voles (*Microtus ochrogaster*) and meadow voles (*Microtus pennsylvanicus*). *Brain Research* 650(2):212–18.

Wang, Z., G. Yu, C. Cascio, Y. Liu, B. Gingrich, and T. R. Insel. 1999. Dopamine D2 receptor-mediated regulation of partner preferences in female prairie voles (*Microtus ochrogaster*): A mechanism for pair bonding? *Behavioral Neuroscience* 113(3):602–11.

Watson, P. J., and P. W. Andrews. 2002. Toward a revised evolutionary adaptationist analysis of depression: The social navigation hypothesis. *Journal of Affective Disorders* 72:1–14.

Wattenberg, B. J. 1997. The population explosion is over. *New York Times Magazine,* Nov. 23:60–62.

Wedekind, C., et al. 1995. MHC-dependent mate preferences in humans. *Proceedings of the Royal Society of London* 260:245–49.

Wenkstern, D., J. G. Pfaus, and H. C. Fibiger. 1993. Dopamine transmission increases in the nucleus accumbens of male rats during their first exposure to sexually receptive female rats. *Brain Research* 618:41–46.

Wersinger, S. R., and E. F. Rissman. 2000. Dopamine activates masculine sexual behavior independent of the estrogen receptor alpha. *Journal of Neuroscience* 20(11):4248–54.

West, C. H. K., A. N. Clancy, and R. P. Michael. 1992. Enhanced responses of nucleus accumbens neurons in male rats to novel odors associated with sexually receptive females. *Brain Research* 585:49–55.

Whittier, S. L. 1988. *One Hundred and One Classic Love Poems.* Chicago: Contemporary Books.

Wickelgren, I. 1997. Getting the brain's attention. *Science* 278:35–37.

Williams, J. R., T. R. Insel, C. R. Harbaugh, and C. S. Carter. 1994. Oxytocin administered centrally facilitates formation of a partner preference in female prairie voles (*Microtus orchrogaster*). *Journal of Neuroendocrinology* 6(3): 247–50.

Wilson, C. A., I. Gonzalez, and F. Farabollini. 1992. Behavioural effects in adulthood of neonatal manipulation of brain serotonin levels in normal and androgenized females. *Pharmacology, Biochemistry, and Behavior* 41(1):91–98.

Wilson, G. D., and R. J. Land. 1981. Sex differences in sexual fantasy patterns. *Personality and Individual Differences* 2:343–46.

Wilson, M., and M. Daly. 1992. The man who mistook his wife for a chattel. In *The Adapted Mind: Evolutionary Psychology and the Generation of Culture,* ed. J. H. Barkow, L. Cosmides, and J. Tooby. New York: Oxford University Press.

Winch, R. 1958. *Mate Selection: A Study of Complementary Needs.* New York: Harper and Row.

Wingfield, J. C. 1994. Hormone-behavior interactions and mating systems in male and female birds. In *The Differences Between the Sexes,* ed. R. V. Short and E. Balaban. New York: Cambridge University Press.

Winslow, J. T., and T. R. Insel. 1991a. Social status in pairs of male squirrel monkeys determines the behavioral response to central oxytocin administration. *The Journal of Neuroscience* 11(7):203–8.

———. 1991b. Vasopressin modulates male squirrel monkeys' behavior during social separation. *European Journal of Pharmacology* 200(1):95–101.

Wise, R. A. 1988. Psychomotor stimulant properties of addictive drugs. In *The*

*Mesocorticolimbic Dopamine System,* ed. P. W. Kalivas and C. B. Nemeroff. New York: The New York Academy of Science, pp. 228–34.

———. 1989. Brain dopamine and reward. *Annual Review of Psychology* 40:191–225.

———. 1996. Neurobiology of addiction. *Current Opinion in Neurobiology* 6:243–51.

Wolkstein, D. 1991. *The First Love Stories.* New York: HarperPerennial.

Woolf, V. 1996. *Night and Day.* New York: Penguin.

World Health Organization. 2001. *The World Health Report 2001—Health Systems: Improving Performance.* Geneva: World Health Organization.

Yang, S. P., K. Y. F. Pau, D. L. Hess, and H. G. Spies. 1996. Sexual dimorphism in secretion of hypothalamic gonadotropin-releasing hormone and norepinephrine after coitus in rabbits. *Endocrinology* 137(7):2683–93.

Young, L. J., Z. Wang, and T. R. Insel. 1998. Neuroendocrine bases of monogamy. *Trends in Neurosciences* 21(2):71–75.

Young, L. J., R. Nilsen, K. G. Waymire, G. R. MacGregor, and T. R. Insel. 1999. Increased affiliative response to vasopressin in mice expressing the V1a receptor from a monogamous vole. *Nature* 400:766–68.

Yutang, L. 1954. *Famous Chinese Short Stories.* New York: Pocket Books.

Zahavi, A. 1975. Mate selection: A selection for a handicap. *Journal of Theoretical Biology* 53:205–14.

Zick, R. 1970. Measurement of romantic love. *Journal of Personality and Social Psychology* 16(2):265–73.

Zona, M. A., K. K. Sharma, and J. A. Lane. 1993. Comparative study of erotomanic and obsessional subjects in a forensic sample. *Journal of Forensic Sciences* 38(4):896.

# *Acknowledgments*

Thank you, Ray Carroll, for your wisdom, humor, and genuine support. Thank you, Amanda Urban, my literary agent, for your dedication to this project. Thank you very much, Deb Brody and Jennifer Barth, my editors, for your astute guidance, Daniel Reid for your valuable assistance, John Sterling, and everyone else at Henry Holt for their enthusiasm for this book. I am particularly grateful to my collaborators Lucy Brown, Art Aron, Deb Mashek, Greg Strong, and Haifang Li for the enormous amount of time, intelligence, and dedication they gave to our fMRI brain scanning project, as well as the women and men who volunteered for our experiments. I thank Michelle Cristiani, Mariko Hasegawa, and Toshikazu Hasegawa for helping me collect questionnaire data on romantic love in the United States and Japan, and MacGregor Suzuki and Tony Oliva for their statistical analysis of this material. I thank Jennifer LeClair and Jonathan Stieglitz for assisting me with some of the research. I am indebted to many colleagues and friends for their good counsel or comments on sections of the manuscript, including Judy Andrews, Sydney Barrows, Laura Betzig, Michael Breton, Arnold Brown, Ray Carroll, Hillary DelPrete, Perry Faithorn, Fletcher Hodges, Brendan Perreault, Don Pfaff, Michelle Press, Carolyn Reynolds, Brenda Sexton,

Greg Simpson, Edward E. Smith, Barb Smuts, Fred Suffet, Lionel Tiger, Andy Thomson, Janel Tortorice, Edie Weiner, and Jeff Zeig. I thank Jack Harris and the rest of my colleagues at Rutgers University for their support and I give a special thank-you to F.H. for his insight, wit, support, and companionship. All errors in this manuscript are mine.

# *Index*

# Index